MARRIED PRIESTS and the REFORMING PAPACY: The Eleventh - Century Debates

MARRIED PRIESTS and the REFORMING PAPACY: The Eleventh - Century Debates

ANNE LLEWELLYN BARSTOW

Texts and Studies in Religion
Volume 12

The Edwin Mellen Press
New York and Toronto

Library of Congress Cataloging in Publication Data

Barstow, Anne Llewellyn.
    Married priests and the reforming papacy.

    (Texts and studies in religion ; v. 11)
    Bibliography: p.
    Includes index.
    1. Celibacy--History. 2. Catholic
Church--clergy. 3. Church history--11th
century. I. Title. II. Series.
BV4390.B33 1982   262'.142   82-7914
ISBN 0-88946-987-3   AACR2

    The Edwin Mellen Press
    P.O. Box 450
    Lewiston, NY   14092

Texts and Studies in Religion ISBN 0-88946-976-8

Grateful acknowledgement is made to the University of
Chicago Press for permission to reprint exerpts from
Christianity, Social Tolerance, and Homosexuality by John
Boswell, 1980.

        Printed in the United States of America

CONTENTS

ABBREVIATIONS

CC   Corpus Christianorum, Series Latina
(Turnholt, 1954-)

CCO   Les canons des conciles oecuméniques,
ed. P. P. Joannu. (Rome, 1962)

CH   Church History (Chicago, 1932-)

CHJ   Cambridge Historical Journal (Cambridge,
1945-)

COD   Conciliorum Oecumenicorum Decreta, eds. J.
Alberigo, et al., 3rd edn. (Bologna, 1972)

CSEL   Corpus Scriptorum Ecclesiasticorum Latinorum
(Vienna, 1866-)

DDC   Dictionnaire de Droit Canonique, ed. R. Naz
(1935)

DNB   Dictionary of National Biography, ed. L. G.
Wickham Legg (1959)

DTC   Dictionnaire de Théologie Catholique,
ed. A. Vacant, E. Mangenot, E. Amann (1903-50)

EHR   English Historical Review (London, 1886-)

H-L   Histoire des conciles d'après les
documents originaux, C. J. Hefele, trans. H.
Leclercq (1907-)

Jaffé   Regesta Pontificum Romanorum, ed. P.
Jaffé; 2nd edn. corrected by W. Wattenbach, et
al. (Leipzig, 1885)

Mansi   Sacrorum Conciliorum Collectio, J. D. Mansi
(Florence, 1759-98; Paris, 1901-)

MGH   Monumenta Germaniae Historica

    Const.
           Constitutiones et acta publica imperatorum

    Ep. select.
           Epistolae Selectae

    LdL   Libelli de lite Imperatorum et
           Pontificum.

    LL   Legum sectio

    Register
           Registrum Gregorii VII, ed. E. Caspar.

    SS   Scriptorum tomus

MS   Medaeval Studies (Toronto, 1939-)

NCE   New Catholic Encyclopedia (New York, 1967)

ODCC   Oxford Dictionary of the Christian
           Church, 2nd edn., ed. F. L. Cross (London, 1974)

PG   Patrologia Graeca, ed. J. P. Migne (Paris,
           1857-66)

PL   Patrologia Latina, ed. J. P. Migne (Paris,
           1844-64)

PREFACE

The heated debate over whether priests can marry, which has emerged yet again in the Roman Church since Vatican II, coincided with research interests of mine centered in the eleventh and twelfth centuries. I had been working on the theological concepts of the Norman Anonymous, and was impressed by his impassioned defense of the right of priests to marry. Reading the arguments against compulsory celibacy made by my contemporarires, I saw that little in the debate had changed. Wanting to explore the history of this long debate in more depth than had been done, I enlarged the scope of my research to the wider celibacy struggle of the eleventh century, in order to document the battle fought by Western clergy when celibacy was for the first time successfully imposed on them.

It has not ceased to surprise me that most persons today, including historically knowledgeable laity and clergy, do not know that until the twelfth century many of the secular clergy in the West were married. So completely has the Roman Church's indentification of priesthood with celibacy succeeded that it is in our time largely taken for granted.

I offer this study as a corrective to that misapprehension, with the hope that the reader will see that the papacy's decision against priestly marriage has made a fundamental difference in the life of the church and, indeed, in the Christian faith, since that time.

This book began as a dissertation, and the dissertation began as a study of the Norman Anonymous. My first thanks are thus due to Prof. John H. Mundy for suggesting that I study the Anonymous, and to Mrs. Ruth Nineham for generously sharing her own careful work on the Anonymous manuscript.

I owe further thanks to Prof. Mundy for his help while I shaped a large amount of material into a dissertation, and to Prof. Robert Somerville for essential guidance through the canonical sources. I am grateful to Hilah Thomas, Beatrice Gottlieb, Suzanne Wemple, Wim Smit, and especially to Betty Fuller, for encouragement and sound advice when they were most needed. Carolyn Heilbrun tactfully but relentlessly reminded me that dissertations must be finished, and Susannah Driver helped out with timely library research. My colleagues in the Comparative History, Ideas, and Cultures Program at the SUNY College at Old Westbury granted me release from Program duties in 1973-74 while I extended my research to the Anonymous' compatriots in the

celibacy struggle. Staley Hitchcock and Sharon Abner
provided beautiful typing, with narry a complaint about the
pages of Latin.

I offer special thanks to Fr. Robert Schmidt for encour-
aging me to publish this material, and to Tom F. Driver,
both for asking indispensable questions about the eleventh
century and for working through with me the challenges of a
two-career, twentieth-century clerical marriage.

INTRODUCTION

It is now generally agreed that the majority of clergy in the early church were married, a condition that remained unchanged until the Western Church began to debate the issue of clerical marriage in the fourth century. Even after that, married clerics were not forbidden by universal canon law to perform the ministry of the altar until 1139. They were prohibited from the fifth century onwards from enjoying sexual relations with their wives (a prohibition always difficult to enforce), but not from remaining married. There is thus a long history, indeed a millenium, of clerical marriage to be considered in the traditions of the Western Church. This study examines three questions: why, despite the early prohibition, many clerics continued to take wives and to raise families, even after ordination to the diaconate and priesthood; why the church, after tolerating this condition for centuries, began to demand around 1050 that married clerics be prohibited from serving the altar, a demand made universal by the law of the Second Lateran Council in 1139 destroying these marriages; and what effects this new celibacy law may have had on the

1

course of religion in the twelfth century. And considering
the present debate on celibacy within the Roman Church, the
question may well be extended to ask what consequences that
twelfth-century decision may have on the Church of Rome
today.

Although the initial, fourth-century actions produced
an immediate defense of clerical marriage, that of
Jovinian, Vigilantius and their followers around 400, the
primary evidence for this struggle is lost to us; we know
of their arguments only through the writings of their
enemies Jerome and Augustine. Some sources for the next
concentrated resistance to the imposition of celibacy, that
of the eleventh century, are available, however, thanks
mainly to works published in the <u>Monumenta Germaniae
Historica</u>.

The eleventh-century decrees against married clerics
caused a widespread defense of clerical marriage, in which
married clergy left an eloquent vindication of their way of
life. Little has been written in English about this polemical literature since Henry C. Lea's research of over a hundred years ago, research which did not include a number of
important documents. My study draws on chronicles, papal
correspondence, and conciliar decrees, but centers on the
tractates and letters written by married clerics and their

supporters: Bishop Ulric, Sigebert of Gembloux, clergy of Cambrai and Noyon, Wenric of Trier, Alboin and several anonymous authors. I will utilize examples from Germany, France and Italy but will concentrate on the Anglo-Norman kingdom, because, as Christopher Brooke has pointed out, much of the best of this literature came from Normandy. Accordingly, I will devote a chapter to the boldest arguments of that group, the Norman Anonymous' defense of priestly marriage and of the rights of priests' sons. As late as 1100, possibly as late as 1120, the Anonymous still insisted on the rights of clergy to legal connubium.

Before the documents can be discussed, however, basic terms and problems need to be defined, and the available literature must be surveyed. In working on these documents I found that two terms were difficult to define, "clerical marriage" and "priestly marriage." They are not identical in meaning: "priestly" refers only to those ordained to perform the sacrament of the altar, whose right to cohabit with their wives was challenged as early as the fourth century; the more general term "clerical" includes also deacons and subdeacons, some of whom were allowed to marry until the eleventh-century decrees, and those in minor orders as well, lectors, exorcists, and doorkeepers, whose marriages were never challenged.[1] These clear legal

distinctions break down, however, in light of the Gregorian
goal of purifying the service of the altar. Since deacons
and subdeacons may assist at the Eucharist, the Gregorian
decrees forbade to both ranks marriage or sexual union with
wives previously espoused, thus imposing celibacy on both
of the major and one of the minor orders. Lacking a
phrase such as "the sacramental orders" to describe those
who serve the altar, it is awkward to discuss the changing
prohibitions against marriage for the several orders.

The term "marriage" itself is also a problem.
Medieval marriage law was chaotic and vague even for laity,
and this loose legal structure was even more confusing when
clerics attempted to apply it to themselves. James
Brundage offers this formulation as the church's working
definition of marriage during the medieval period:
marriage consisted of the consent of the two partners,
ratified by intercourse. As for the question of its
sacramental nature, Brundage observed:

> ...the notion of the sacramentality of mar-
> riage was slow to develop and did not begin
> to bear the meanings that modern theolo-
> gians assign to it until late in the medi-
> eval period.... In contrast to all other
> sacraments, marriage required no special
> form for validity.[2]

Concubinage was not condemned by the medieval church
but rather was considered a secondary form of marriage and

was tolerated, enabling a concubine to receive, and keep as her own, gifts and legacies from her consort.

Given these ill-defined norms, the clergy who took wives before 1139 considered themselves fully married and their children legitimate, while other clergy contracting concubinous liaisons, before and after 1139, expected that their consorts would benefit from the general acceptance of concubinage. But matters changed with the Gregorians, to whom any sexual relationship between a cleric and a woman was _fornicatio,_ while all clerical wives were concubines or worse and the offspring of these unions were illegitimate. I will, therefore, refer to the same union as a marriage or as concubinage, depending on which point of view I am presenting.

Among the larger problems that need clarifying is the question of the relationship between feudalism and clerical marriage. Despite the acknowledgement today by virtually all scholars that clerical marriage was widespread from the beginning of the church, still when historians discuss the feudalization of society in the ninth, tenth, and eleventh centuries many of them speak as if feudalism caused or even created clerical marriage. Although it is outside the purview of this study to correct this view, I assume that priestly marriage had a long history before the feudal period and was not dependent on it.

Other problems relate to the need to evaluate and separate the various factors working aginast clerical marriage after the fourth century. One set of factors centered around the church's increasing emphasis on the cultic purity, that is to say the sexual purity, of those who served the altar. There was a tendency in the late Roman world to equate sexuality with impurity, a belief brought on by the seemingly insupportable burdens of citizenship which required marriage, parenthood, military and civil service, and payment of sometimes crushing tax levies. Increasing numbers of Roman citizens despaired of fulfilling these demands and retired from worldly life altogether.[3] As asceticism became highly valued throughout late antique society, the church's ministers were challenged to become more ascetic than the laity. The resulting rejection of family ties contributed to the growing emphasis on the special nature of the priesthood, to the church's increasing hostility towards sexuality and admiration of virginity, and to the increasing power of monks in the church.

Forces arose in the eleventh-century church which, combining with this ancient ascetic tradition, worked further against clerical marriage. The struggle for institutional power in Europe, that is, the Gregorian determination to reduce lay interference in ecclesiastical affairs, to tighten control over the priesthood and to heighten the difference between priesthood and laity, allied well with

the idea of a celibate priesthood. All of these factors
are important to this history, and yet it is difficult to
determine which were causes, which were effects.

Within the eleventh-century struggle itself the motives and goals of both parties are sometimes conflicting.
In general, but not always, within the party defending clerical marriage, the secular priests spoke up for legal recognition of such marriage, whereas the monks deplored these
marriages but defended them in order to preserve order in
the church. As for the papal group, some based their attack against priestly unchastity on ideals of asceticism,
that is, on the need for cultic purity, while others empha-
sized the necessity to discipline and control the priesthood. The attack on simony was closely related to, but
separate from, this struggle. And behind all of the motives
and ideals lay the desperate political struggle between the
papacy and the monarchies for control of Europe. In the
furor over this issue, the wives and families of priests became pawns in a contest for empire.

Because these events have been studied primarily
through the records of the papal party, the fact that there
was strong opposition to the enforcement of celibacy from
priesthood and in some cases from laity has received little
comment. Yet the defenders of clerical marriage have left

us eloquent proof of their belief in the tradition of a married priesthood, material which I believe we must use in order to see this eleventh-century struggle accurately.

This material is indeed extensive, for the church has
been debating for a very long time whether priests can marry. When de Roskovany completed his bibliography on celibacy in 1888, his work filled seventeen volumes.[4] The question I faced in drawing up a working bibliography for the
defense of clerical marriage in the late eleventh century
was to determine how far back into this vast literature I
need go. The date 1897 became my cutoff point, for in that
year the third and final volume of the Libelli de Lite
was published, furnishing not only critical editions of
many works but offering the first publication of a number
of writings, especially from Anglo-Norman authors. Works
written on eleventh-century celibacy without access to the
material in these three volumes are therefore incomplete.

General works on the Gregorian movement present a
major problem in that they make almost no mention of the
celibacy-marriage issue. Historians of this period, if
they refer to the celibacy struggle, do so in passing, and
without exception they do not reflect on it as an integral
part of the Gregorian plan. Walter Ullman, for example,
devotes a chapter in The Growth of Papal

Government in the Middle Ages to the opposition
to the Gregorian program, a chapter appropriately called
"Defense of the Lay Thesis," but neither there nor
elsewhere does he mention clerical marriage. Apparently he
did not consider the struggle to impose celibacy on the
clergy as part of the growth of papal power.[5].

Since the enforcement of celibacy clearly was one of
the essential goals of the movement, one of the first to be
taken up and one which was worked on relentlessly, and
since in fact it was pursued with more success[6] than some
other issues, I am surprised that it is largely ignored by
historians of the period. An exception to this
generalization is found in the works of Augustin Fliche,
who maintained that the abolition of simony and nicolaitism
were Gregory's chief goals and provided lengthy analyses of
the celibacy problem. Fliche tended to be uncritical of
Gregory and to find fault with all of his opponents, and
failed to separate clearly the political from the ascetic
goals, a recurring problem among scholars working on the
history of celibacy. Although for these reasons he does
not explore the celibacy struggle adequately, still the
third volume of La Réforme Grégorienne gives a
useful discussion of much of the source material for the
eleventh-century defense of clerical marriage.[7]

And there are other useful works. By studying the
growth of clerical marriage and simony in tenth- and
eleventh-century imperial Italy, Albert Dresdner analyzed
the effects of feudalism and secularization on the priesthood. He offered arguments of both married and reforming
clergy, but again one finds that the lack of knowledge of
key documents defending the clergy inevitably weights the
historian's judgments in favor of the papal party.[8]

Norman Cantor's study of the English investiture struggle provides a basis for interpreting the celibacy issue,
for it includes numerous examples of the attempts to force
English clerics to give up their wives.[9] In summing up,
however, he does not mention the enforcement of celibacy at
all, even though it was largely successful among the
English clergy in major orders by 1150. In fact, along
with access to legal appeal to Rome, it was the only part
of the Gregorian platform to be established permanently in
England at that time. Cantor presumably knew this because
he quotes Christopher Brooke's articles proving that
celibacy was effectively enforced upon English ministers of
the altar during the twelfth century.[10] But Cantor
concludes that the entire Gregorian movement in England
failed. Apparently he did not consider clerical marriage a
factor in the Gregorian reforms and did not utilize its

destruction in evaluating the success of the papal platform there.

In taking seriously the celibacy issue Fliche, Dresdner and Brooke are exceptions to the rule, and I conclude that the questions of whether or not clergy were married, of what the church thought of marriage in general, and what its doctrine of priesthood was, are not matters that have interested historians of the Gregorian period. To them it was principally an "Investiture Struggle."

A further example of the historian's preference for political ideology can be found in G. H. Williams' study of the Norman Anonymous, where he gave but little attention to the Anonymous' three tracts on priestly marriage, concentrating instead on his views of sacred kingship. However, Williams saw the unusual nature of the Norman theologian's thinking about sexuality, affirming as he did the goodness of procreation and marriage for all Christians, and denying that there is a major distinction between laity and clergy. Thus, Williams asserted, the Anonymous challenged part of the ideology on which the medieval church's power over the clergy was based, namely the idea that chastity and the ordained state are superior.[11]

It is not surprising that Williams found a nascent affirmation of creation and of sexuality in a late eleventh-century writer's thoughts, because a newly revived admiration for ascetic purity had begun to appear in western society, a trend which eventually would challenge the ethical position of married clerics. A theological debate over priests' sexual conduct had begun in 1049 when Peter Damian sent his views on priestly sexuality to Leo IX, and the defenders of clerical marriage were impelled eventually to respond. It was not sufficient for them to argue for marriage on ecclesio-political grounds alone when the papal party used the goal of sexual purity as its strongest point.

Another phenomenon emerging at the same time as the new asceticism was the rise of heretical sects, and the two movements must be looked at together.[12] The most convincing account of the interaction between heresy and papal reform is that of Arno Borst.[13] Reflecting on the temporary disappearance of heresy from the records of the last half of the eleventh century, Borst concludes that the Gregorian movement and the monastic reforms took over from the sects their passion for purity and asceticism, putting them temporarily out of business. When the impetus of the Gregorian reform lessened after the 1130's, slowed down by imperial, monarchical and ecclesiastical opposition, new sects arose to press for a further spiritualizing and purifying of religion.

Even Borst's thesis does not do justice to all the complexities of the issue, however, for some of the twelfth- and thirteenth-century groups (at Le Mans and Cologne, and some of the Waldensians) were not ascetic; they permitted marriage for both clergy and laity and affirmed procreation.[14] And conversely, the papacy, whenever it was blocked in its attempt to assert domination over secular rulers, continued to pour its energies into enforcement of celibacy and into backing further monastic reforms.

From my reading of the connections between heretical and papal asceticism, I conclude that it is very difficult for the historian to deal satisfactorily with a category such as asceticism, which has a strong psychological component. It will be well to keep this warning in mind while considering two other categories with extensive moral-psychological implications, celibacy and marriage. It became clear to me early in studying clerical marriage that more elements must be considered than the obvious institutional and theological issues, that the attack on priestly marriage contained a psycho-sexual dimension that renders it an unusually complex issue to analyze. I will evaluate

the writings specifically on clerical marriage with these
points in mind.

A work which places clerical marriage in a social context, thereby shedding light on some of the psychological
dimensions of the subject, is Henry C. Lea's History of
Sacerdotal Celibacy, first published in 1867.[15]   It
is, in fact, the basic work on clerical marriage. Lea's extensive research posed many questions that challenged the
then-current Catholic interpretation that celibacy was apostolic doctrine,[16] but his work left much to be done. He
does not mention the "Epistolae" of the clerics of Cambrai
and of Noyon, or the opinions of Manegold of Lautenbach,
Honorious of Autun, Benzo of Alba, Serlo of Bayeux, Cardinal Beno, Sigebert of Gembloux, Bonizo of Sutri, or any
of the anonymous Norman tracts. But because there has not
been another extensive scholarly study of the entire history of sacerdotal marriage since Lea's, we must continue
to refer to it.

In fact, no substantial new work appeared on celibacy
until Christopher Brooke's articles on the English church
in 1956.[18]   Brooke's detailed research made it possible
for the first time to see the effect of the Gregorian decrees on the lives of English clergy, to trace the steady
retreat of married clergy in major orders, until by 1200

marriage among ministers of the altar was virtually elimi-
nated.[19] Similar regional studies for the rest of Europe
would be most helpful.

In works on celibacy in the early church, Jean-Paul
Audet is at pains to stress the prevalence of married clergy in the early church and produces some new and plausible
explanations for that fact. He then allows himself to advo-
cate that the practice of celibacy instituted in the following period should now end. Reasoning that the rule of celibacy was supported by a view of sexuality no longer believed in, he argues that, since we no longer hold that sex
is evil, we can no longer define purity as abstinence.
Roger Gryson concurs, concluding from detailed research of
conciliar actions that ritual purity was the main goal of
the ascetic trend in the early church. He believes that
this goal was based on a negative view of sexuality, indeed
a view that considered sex as "bestial."[20]

As for studies of the canons on celibacy, Martin
Boelens has launched a multi-volume work surveying the entire history of legislation against clerical marriage.[21]
He makes a number of observations about the preponderance
and the harshness of punitive legislation, the invasion of
privacy created by the necessity for reporting on a
cleric's sexual activity, the frequent mention of women,

who are otherwise not often referred to in the canons, and
the increasingly hostile attitude towards women and marriage.   Boelens concludes that the increasing attack on
clerical marriage was caused by an excessive idealization
of virginity and sexual purity.

Among examinations of individual synods, Samuel
Laeuchli's study of the fourth-century synod of Elvira concludes that the church of Spain was strongly committed to
exercising power by controlling the sexuality of both its
clergy and laity, and that in fact sexual discipline was
its chief concern.[22]

A number of recent articles provide competent, up-to-
date historical studies,[23] but as they do not offer particularly new points of view, I conclude that the state of
scholarly research into the eleventh-century celibacy struggle has not advanced far since Lea's third edition of 1907.
The work of Fliche and Brooke stands out, and recent
studies inspired by the latest series of debates about celibacy have made available more canonical information.   The
following problems, however, run through much of the material: a failure to connect the prevalence of married clergy
in the early church with the continuing practice of clerical marriage, a want of distinction between the pressures
for political restructuring of the church and pressures to

establish cultic purity, and a lack of familiarity with the viewpoint of married clergy, which causes an overemphasis on the papal point of view.

I will, therefore, investigate the defense, and will conclude by asking what effect the suppression of clerical marriage may have had on the church and society of the high middle ages. Several remarkable changes that appear in European society from the twelfth century on may have been produced by the further "setting aside" of all the clergy: the growth of anti-clericalism, for example, the astonishing proliferation of lay reform sects, and the opposition of reform groups such as the Waldensians and Wycliffites to compulsory celibacy. Likewise, the attempt to monasticize the secular clergy may have stimulated the flourishing of the Marian cult, the increase of the erotic element in devotional literature, and the increasing polarization of the images of woman between Mary and Eve. Possible connections between this new view of the clergy and the transformation of the Eucharist alone, into a sacrament attended chiefly by and intended chiefly for the priesthood, indicates the importance of studying the celibacy struggle, for it becomes clear that nothing less than two differing concepts of the church are at war and are brought into focus by this issue. And finally, whatever conclusions may be reached on

these questions, the fact remains that the increasingly
sharp division of Christian society into two classes, the
priestly above the laity, set the stage for deeper
struggles in the late middle ages.

CHAPTER ONE

CLERICAL MARRIAGE IN THE WESTERN CHURCH BEFORE 1050

> "... if you find bishops, priests, or
> deacons who are violating canons or the
> rules of the fathers -- that is, living in
> adultery or having more than one
> wife ... -- you shall on no account permit
> them to perform the duties of priests by
> apostolic authority." [Emphasis mine]
>   -- Pope Zachary in 742

Because the Roman priesthood has been celibate formal-
ly for about eight centuries, one might assume that celibacy had always been the norm. It is evident, however, that
clerical marriage was widespread in the early church.[1]
Where the marital status of the clergy is known, the indications are clear that until at least the fifth century the
majority was married. For four hundred years married and
single clerics had served together in the church, and marriage was the norm. On surveying clerical marriage in the
first millenium of the church, one finds that the period di-
vides roughly in half: the four centuries of a mixed ministry followed by a period of growing ascetic influence.

Given the silence of the early church concerning the
sexuality of Jesus, it is not surprising that the church
did not recommend celibacy for its ministers. There are no

known references to Jesus' marital state before the third
century, except for some Gnostic material.[2] Not until after 250 did numbers of clergy begin to live out the ideals
of singleness and virginity. The customs of the new cult
make it clear why celibacy was not an obvious choice for
its ministers: the congregation was an "extended family",
which worshipped in homes and carried out its social services on a one-to-one basis. From these conditions
Jean-Paul Audet concludes that pastoral care was more important than sacramental service.[3] As for the sacrament,
the Eucharist was still close to the sacred feast of the
Jewish passover out of which it had been born, and did not
yet require a priesthood endowed with the charisma to perform miracles.

The minister, who was not consecrated to office but
merely ordained, earned his living in the community along-
side the other congregants, sharing their economic and social problems. And since Christian attitudes toward sexuality still reflected many of the affirmations of the body
found in Hebrew scriptures, it remained possible for married life to be valued as highly as the virginal state.[4]

In this small, struggling cult there was as yet no need or desire for a priestly class, set aside from the other believers. Instead, the laity wanted and accepted pastors who lived as they did.[5] The young church's attitude was expressed by Clement of Alexandria, writing c. 200, who interpreted that dedicated celibate St. Paul as sanctioning marriage for priests and even bishops.[6]

The fourth and early fifth centuries saw a remarkable change in the way the ministry was described. Utilizing ideas primarily of Origen, Ambrose, and Jerome, and responding to the powerful impact of desert ascetics and of ascetic Spanish bishops who came to Rome in the mid-fourth century, popes Damasus I, Siricius and Innocent I decreed that priests could not have sexual relations with their wives. They did not forbid clerical marriage, but instead sexual union.[7] For one matter, since the majority of clergy were married, the papacy could not afford to disqualify large numbers of the church's personnel. Furthermore the church, devoted to the concept of indissoluble marriage, shrank from breaking up licit unions: it could not yet accept the fact that a celibacy law would destroy valid marriages. Caught between an increasing asceticisim and a commitment to affirm marriage, church leaders had to settle for compromise until the eleventh century.

The model for the new ascetic views was the Hebrew
priesthood, that had abstained from sex for three days before sacrificing at the altar. If the priests of the old
dispensation had thus disciplined themselves, should not
then the servants of the final revelation do more? Once
the church was favored by Constantine, moreover, it needed
new ways to prove its superiority over other cults, and added to its growing adminration for celibacy the powerful
concept of a priesthood set aside, set above others by heroic asceticism.[8] The antisexuality found in many aspects
of the late Roman world became the ally of the new imperial
religion. Commenting on this interaction, E. R. Dodds
proposes

> that contempt for the human condition and
> hatred of the body was a disease endemic in
> the entire culture of the period; that
> while its more extreme manifestations are
> mainly Christian or Gnostic, its symptoms
> show themselves in a milder form in pagans
> of purely Hellenic education; and that
> this disease found expression in a wide va-
> riety of myths and fantasies, some drawn
> from Greek, others from oriental origi-
> nals.... I incline to see the whole develop-
> ment less as an infection from an extrane-
> ous source than as an endogenous neurosis,
> an index of intense and widespread guilt-
> feelings. The material distresses of the
> third century certainly encouraged it, but
> they did not occasion it, since its begin-
> nings[9] as we have seen, lie further
> back.

There was no sudden break with the earlier custom of married clergy, but instead a gradual accumulation of rulings sacralizing the clergy. During the succeeding two hundred years these decrees created the expectation that ministers of the altar would be chaste. Legal evidence for this change of image is found in the earliest collection of canons to survive in the church's history. Around 305, the synod of Elvira, meeting in southern Spain, had approved a canon stating:

> Bishops, presbyters, and deacons and all other clerics having a position in the ministry are ordered to abstain completely from their wives and not to have children. Whoever, in fact, does this, shall be expelled from the dignity of the clerical state.[10]

The eighty-one canons of Elvira seldom mention theological matters, whereas almost half of them deal with sexual problems. Samuel Laeuchli conjectures that the clergy assembled at Elvira must have been concerned with sex _as a problem_, because they dealt with it more extensively and more vehemently than with apostasy, persecution, or idolatry, all of which were still serious threats to the church at that time. Their heaviest penalty, that of forever withholding communion, was meted out to both clergy and laity for even slight sexual offenses. The Spanish bishops were here exerting their control over their congregations not only by limiting the ordinary believers' sexual relations but also by distinguishing themselves from the pagan priesthood, who were obliged by law to marry. They thereby set themselves above both the laity and the pagan priesthood by declaring their lives to be more pure and moral, by defining themselves as men divorced from any contact with women, against whom they had legislated with exceptional harshness. One wonders, indeed, if the bishops at Elvira actually wished to abolish clerical marriage; apparently this was impossible, so they contented themselves with denying the higher clergy and their wives the usual privileges of married life.

Bishop Ossius of Cordoba, who had been present at Elvira, attended the council of Nicaea in 325 and may well have been among those attempting to persuade the council to make sexual continence for clergy the law of the church. His appeal was rejected by Pafnutius, the Egyptian martyr, who convinced the assembled bishops that chastity was too heavy a burden for most men to bear, and that marriage was anyway an honorable state.[11]

Further examples of the anti-ascetic sentiment that won out at Nicaea can be seen in the deliberations of the synod of Ancyra in 314, which required deacons to state their intention whether or not to marry before ordination;

if they chose marriage they might carry out their intention before or after ordination.[12] This sentiment was borne out also by the ruling at Gangra in 345 excommunicating all who refused to partake of the sacrament performed by a married priest.[13]

Pressure continued to mount, however, against clerical marriage. Although there is no canon from this period stating that a priest or deacon could not marry, the intent of all of the papal pronouncements beginning in the 370's, declaring that a minister of the altar could not have sexual relations with a wife, made it clear that marriage after ordination was in fact prohibited and that unmarried candidates were preferred.[14] As a result, defenders of clerical marriage were provoked to a mjajor defense of this practice at the end of the fourth century. The men who spoke out against the increasing asceticism and sacerdotalism of the church claimed that their argument reflected the practice and doctrines of the apostolic church. Bishop Bonosus of Sardica, for example, denied the perpetual virginity of the virgin Mary, a doctrine which had begun to be accepted only towards the end of the fourth century.[15] The celebrated Helvidius built on Bonosus' position, declaring that Mary was the mother of Jesus' brothers, and used this argument to prove that marriage was as acceptable a

state as virginity.[16] Their beliefs were popular as late
as the seventh century. A monk, Jovinian, carried their arguments into the centers of ecclesiastical power, was condemned, and was driven out of both Rome and Milan. Returning to Rome, he convinced some of the holy virgins to break
their vows and marry, whereupon he was scourged and sent
permanently into exile. The struggle was taken up by Vigilantius, who preached aaginst all aspects of the new sacerdotalism, especially celibacy, because it encouraged sinful
ways among the clergy. His ideas spread as far as Rouen
and Spain, but his was the last recorded systematic opposition to clerical celibacy for many centuries.[17]

Meanwhile numerous cases of married clergy, including
bishops, continued to be recorded. Philippe Delhaye reports:

> Gregory Nazianus the Elder (d. 374) was a
> bishop when his son was born. Gregory of
> Nyssa lived with his wife after consecra-
> tion in 372. Gregory the Illuminator (d.
> 332) handed down his title of Catholicus of
> Armenia to three more generations of his
> family.... The Council of Ancyra (314) had
> decreed that deacons could marry after ordi-
> nation, and the Synod of Gangra (c. 345)
> condemned those who refused the services of
> married priests.... Pope Agapitus I (535-
> 36) was the son of a priest.[18]

Synesius, Bishop of Ptolemais and neo-Platonic philosopher,
wrote around 400:

> I cannot hide from my brother what I wish
> everyone to know.... God, the law, and the
> sacred hand of Bishop Theophilus (of Alexan-
> dria) have given me a wife. I declare open-
> ly that I do not intend to separate from
> her, nor to have clandestine relations with
> her.... Separation would be impious, clan-
> destine relations would be contrary to the
> rule of marriage.[19] I wish to have numerous
> children with her.

The Apostolic Constitutions, written at the same time and reflecting Syrian usage, decreed that higher clergy were expected to live with their wives and would be excommuni-cated if they separated from them.[20] Synesius kept his job, but the fact that he had to explain his position indicates that times were changing, that bishops might be expected to put away their wives.

Within the next century two men who were sons of priests became popes, Felix II in 483 and Agapitus I in 535.[21] Leo I, normally a strict reformer, had to bow to the overwhelming acceptance of clerical marriage by allowing ministers of the altar to live with their wives, while observing continence.[22] But the attitude of church councils became more punitive toward offenders. Whereas the council of Carthage in 390, for example, had ruled that all ministers of the altar must avoid intercourse with their wives because ministers touch the sacraments, but mentioned no penalty, when the African fathers met again in 401 they added that those who did not comply would be deprived of their offices.[23]

A vow of chastity at ordination was required for the first time in 401 at Carthage.[24] Subdeacons were included in the prohibitions beginning with the decree of Leo I in 446.[25] The first prohibition against marriage after ordination was enacted at the council of Vannes in 465, although there was no universal canonical affirmation for this step for over two hundred years.[26]

As the campaign increased in the sixth century, a priest's family life was no longer private. His wife might live with him, but must sleep in another room guarded by a maidservant, and his clergy were to sleep in the same room with him. The wives of clergy must be virgins at marriage and could not remarry after their husbands' deaths.[27] At Toledo in 655 clerics' sons were ruled to be held in servitude by the church. It is clear from these canons that until the end of the seventh century the church legislated primarily to enforce continency, not celibacy. A further step in that effort was the ruling that ministers of the altar must separate from their wives at ordination, first decreed at Gerona in 517.[28] The various prohibitions were finally summed up at the Trullan synod in 692, dominated by Eastern bishops and convoked as a General Council although it is not numbered as one; it ruled that there could be marriage before but not after ordination to the diaconate, except for monks and bishops, and that deacons and priests might -- indeed, must -- continue to live with their wives.[29]

Thus it appears that the main impetus for clerical continence came from the West and that the chief motive of these restrictions was the desire for cultic purity. With the growing custom of daily mass, it was essential for the priest to abstain from sex at all times. The concern with sexual abstinence for priests resulted in the use of a new derogatory term, "nicolaitans," first used at the council of Tours in 567 to describe priests who had sexual relations with their wives.[30] The term was taken from a sect called Nicolaitans in Revelation 2:6 and 2:14, although there was no reason to associate it there with unchaste priests.[31]

Thus we see that by around 500 A.D., clerical marriage continued to be widespread but now co-existed in tension with an aggressive ascetic doctrine of the priesthood. The old ideas of a pastoral ministry, of voluntary chastity, of an intermingling of sacred and secular values in the sacraments were challenged in two ways, challenged so strongly that Jean-Paul Audet, commenting on the fourth century, remarks that he "senses a profound transformation taking place in people's minds."[32] One aspect of change centered on the idea of sexual purity: a cult developed around the practice of virginity; chastity was considered superior to marriage; sexuality was discussed in increasingly negative terms. The origins of these new ideals came, ironically, from the East. Prominent Christians at Rome had been inspired by a new model of asceticism when two famous Egyptian monks, Athanasius and Peter of Alexandria, had spent a period of exile in the Western capital in the mid-fourth century. It became the fashion among devout Romans to tour the hermitages in the Egyptian desert, in order to learn further of the mortifications now considered necessary to the spiritual life. This adulation for a rigorous, indeed heroic, discipline grew further during the Roman visits of Jerome and Rufinus,[33] and, by the time Popes Damasus and Siricus decreed abstinence for ministers of the altar in the late fourth century, the new ideal of the priest was established at Rome and among the leading bishops.

The other pressure for change came from a need for the liturgy to provide the basis for great imperial celebrations. The priesthood presiding over these mysteries gradually became a spiritual elite whose role was defined in strongly sacral terms. These changes were indeed profound, and began to dominate the western church at some point in the late fourth century.

The explanation for this major change is not yet entirely clear. Reflecting on the intellectual climate of early medieval Christianity, John Boswell remarks that

> erotic pleasure and romantic passion were deplored by Western fathers of the church, and human relations based on such values found no place in Western theological development after contact with less ascetic Eastern theology ceased.[34]

That may be so, yet Samuel Laeuchli, utilizing the analysis of E. R. Dodds mentioned above, reminds us that we cannot yet know what caused the sexual dilemma apparent everywhere in ancient society, and that much work remains to be done on the patristic age before its anti-sexuality can be understood.[35]

To turn now to the issue of clerical marriage in the post-classical world, one may begin with Friedrich Kempf's speculation that the unsettled conditions of the succeeding centuries, while increasing the flow of men into monasteries, also made family life all the more necessary for parish priests. Life in the villages and towns of Europe became a question of survival; a wife and growing children could help to farm the parish's lands and to organize the

production of clothing and necessities for the priest.
Kempf concludes "that rural life was extremely difficult
without a woman's aid."[36] Imbart de la Tour describes
the difficulties of poor secular priests in a time of anar-
chy and increasing feudalism and allows that these men,
especially in rural areas, turned to marriage as a way of
coping with the problems of daily living. He observes that
these marriages fitted well into the new feudal patterns of
lay patronage and proprietary church ownership and perpetu-
ated themselves by the custom of inheritance of benefices
by priests' sons.[37] Neither author asks whether the ar-
rival of children may have been more of a bane than a blessing in a poor parish, and indeed we do not have enough information about attitudes toward family size in rural areas
during the early medieval centuries to draw conclusions
about this question.

In observing that the Italian laity gained control
over large amounts of chuch property, Albert Dresdner argued that this fact was the basis for the low clerical morality of the tenth and eleventh centuries. This shift in
wealth was begun by the bishops, who gave out large amounts
of church lands and serfs or dependents in feudal tenure.
As this tenure became hereditary, the priests assigned to
these lands became dependent on the barons. Because the la-

ity had neither respect for the clergy nor concern for their own salvation, they were not afraid to seize church property when a bishop, abbot, or pope died. Dresdner concluded that this material dependency so impoverished the clergy that they were forced to acquire wives in order to survive. Marriage brought property and income to clerics and, in the case of unfree clergy, marriage to free women brought a rise in status. But these clergy became tied to family businesses and could no longer serve their churches adequately. Neglect of duty added to the laity's low regard for them, to the point that clergy no longer held rank over laity and lost their consciousness of themselves as superior.[38]

Whatever may be concluded about the ultimate cause, we know that clerical marriage proliferated, and that church legislation had to accommodate to that fact. The council of Agde in 506 ruled that wives of candidates to the diaconate had to consent to their husbands' ordinations and might receive a special blessing on the same day at the ceremony and wear special clothing.[39] They might be called, sometimes scornfully, by the titles "presbyteriae," "diaconissae," and "subdiaconissae."[40] But still the clerical wife did not disappear from the scene. Correspondence between Pope Zachary and St. Boniface confirms that the

church still accepted the fact that many ordinands were married, and that the church was reduced to trying to enforce
abstinence on the priestly couples. Boniface showed no sym-
pathy for any incontinent cleric. That all were fornicators to him becomes clear from his correspondence with
Zachary in 742:

> If I find among these men certain so-
> called deacons who have spent their lives
> since boyhood in debauchery, adultery, and
> every kind of filthiness, who entered the
> diaconate with this reputation, and who
> now, while they have four or five concu-
> bines in their beds, still read the Gospel
> and are not ashamed to call themselves dea-
> cons -- nay rather, entering upon the
> priesthood, they ... advance ... as bishops
> -- may I have your authority ... that they
> may be ... dealt with as sinners?[41]

To this Zachary replied that

> ... if you find bishops, priests, or dea-
> cons who are violating the canons or the
> rules of the fathers -- that is, living in
> adultery or having <u>more</u> <u>than</u> <u>one</u>
> <u>wife</u> ... -- you shall on no account permit
> them to perform the duties of priests by
> apostolic authority.... How can they be-
> lieve themselves to be priests, or what do
> they think of God's word: "Let my priests
> marry once," and the words of the Apostle,
> "husband of one wife," etc. And this is
> lawful only before entering the priesthood;
> for after that they are prohibited from a
> regular marriage.[42] [Emphasis mine]

It is clear that having one wife was still permitted by the
papacy, but Boniface did not take cognizance of that fact
in his condemnation of all clerical arrangements with

women.   Under   Carloman's   patronage   he   held   the   first

Frankish reform synod, which decreed:

> ... any of the servants of God or the maids
> of Christ falling into carnal sin shall do
> penance in prison on bread and water.   If
> it be an ordained priest he shall be impris-
> oned for two years, first flogged to bleed-
> ing and afterward further disciplined at
> the bishop's discretion.   But if a clerk or
> monk fall into this sin, after a third flog-
> ging he shall be imprisoned for a year and
> there do penance.   Likewise a veiled nun
> shall be bound to do the same penanace, and
> all her hair shall be shaved.[43]

Still the clergy would not give up their ancient cus-

toms.   In 745 Bishop Clemens, born a Celt, had declared he

could retain his grade of bishop even though he had fa-

thered two children after he had received this office.[44]

In 895 a Gallic _presbyter_ appealed to the synod of Cha-

lons to accept his public marriage to one Grimma.   He was

only temporarily suspended from communion and presumably

continued to enjoy his wife.   This leniency is not surpris-

ing when one recalls that one of the popes of that era,

Adrian II (867-72), had been married before his elec-

tion.[45]   And there is evidence for the beginnings of in-

herited clerical privileges: at the council of Tours in

925 two priests, father and son, claiming tithes from an-

other priest, were awarded their claim, to be received _for-_

ever.[46]   Since the decision is granted into the time of their successors, the possibility of an hereditary claim is involved.

Some clerics, in spite of the canons, married public-ly. The law, although declaring these marriages illicit, did not render them null. The church held back, allowing them to be valid. The only penalty, that of deposition, was seldom invoked in the ninth, tenth, and early eleventh centuries. Peter Damian tells of a widowed Gallic priest who, deciding to take a second wife (Damian said pellex), gathered his friends, offered a wedding feast, and ex-changed vows.[47]

An aspect of the celibacy issue that is not mentioned in most histories is the conflict between the Eastern and Roman Churches over priestly marriage. A heretofore unno-ticed chapter in that debate was contributed by the monk Ratramnus in response to Pope Nicholas I's arguments with the Patriarch Photius in 867. In process of defending the primacy of the papacy over the entire church Ratramnus com-posed arguments justifying the compulsory celibacy of west-ern higher clergy.[48] To the Greek accusation that the Latins disparaged the institution of marriage by refusing to allow ministers of the altar to marry, Ratramnus replied that Christ, while remaining a virgin, praised marriage and that Peter did not spurn his marriage when he became a disciple of Christ. Nevertheless, Ratramnus concluded, the argument in favor of celibacy was overwhelming, namely that a man cannot serve both God and a wife. To cap his argument, Ratramnus quoted the council of Nicaea, interpreting its ruling against virgines subintroductae as forbidding clerical marriage, and the council of Neocaesaria's decree that a presbyter who marries shall be deposed. Ratramnus wrote as one who, although familiar with married and concubinous clergy, totally disapproved of them. He closed by accusing the Greeks of not following the ecumenical decrees of the church, which he, of course, had misinterpreted.

The tenth century is claimed to be the high point of clerical marriage in the Latin communion. Statistics are of course not available, but it is generally agreed that most rural priests were married, and that many urban clergy and bishops had wives and children.[49] Although the main objection to clerical marriage continued to be that of sexual impurity, the widespread holding of church office by men with families raised the further issue of loss of church income and property to the needs of the clerics' wives and children. This aspect of the celibacy issue was hotly debated among the Anglo-Saxons of Ethelred's reign, from which time comes the following comment:

> It is all the worse when they have it all,
> for they do not dispose of it as they
> ought, but decorate their wives with what
> they should the altars, and turn everything
> to their own worldly pomp.... Let those who
> before this had the evil custom of decorat-
> ing their women as they should the altars,
> refrain from this evil custom, and decorate
> their churches, as they best can; then
> would they command for themselves both di-
> vine counsel and worldly worship. A
> priest's wife is nothing but a snare of the
> devil, and he who is ensnared thereby on to
> his end, he will be seized fast by the
> devil, and he also must afterwards pass in-
> to the hands of fiends and totally
> perish.[50]

As for priests' sons the church had attempted to declare them illegitimate and therefore disqualified for ordination. Despite the impressive number and quality of "clerical families" recorded by the early church, the medieval hierarchy remained hostile to the idea of priests' children inheriting the property of their fathers. In Italy, Rather of Verona complained that priests married off their daughters to other priests and that in order to provide benefices for their sons, they have them ordained and thus perpetuate the evil.[51] But Rather was not able to break up his clergy's marriages; he could not even enforce the rule of continence but had to settle for asking for sexual abstinence during the periods prohibited to lay people, such as Advent and Lent. In desperation he observed that, if he expelled from office all priests who live with women or who marry after receiving sacred orders, there would be no one left to serve the church except young boys.[52] Rather's asceticism finally led him to a show-down with his clergy, and he imprisoned those who refused to leave their wives and threatened them with heavy fines. Protesting that marriage was necessary to protect them from vice and to provide for their wants, they allied themselves with the count of Verona who, as their proprietary lord, ordered them to ignore Rather. The old bishop was defeated and was forced to retire into a monastery.[53]

A further protest came from Atto of Vercelli who complained that his clergy flaunted their "harlots" (no doubt, their wives) in public and willed church property to their wives and offspring, while seeking protection from secular lords and then bribing them to continue their favors. Atto wrote a long letter to his clergy castigating them for stripping the church in order to finance their involvements with women.[54]

The prelates of Germany did more than complain. Libentius of Bremen in 1049 drove his canons' wives out of the city and sent them under custody to scattered villages. At the council of Augsburg in 952 the German bishops had ordered that subdeacons as well as deacons, priests and bishops could not live with wives, that even the lower grades of clergy must be continent (a new ruling) and that women suspected of being priests' concubines have their heads shaved and be marked with stripes.[55]

Whether or not these charges were accurate and whether or not they reflected a condition widespread in the church, reformers in the hierarchy increasingly claimed that hereditary offices meant loss of control over churches and their property. The struggle between bishops and lay lords for control of proprietary churches had, in fact, opened the way for the clergy to build some claim to income and property for themselves. Through the beneficium, the cleric obtained the possessory right to the church, its property and revenues, rights as stable and indivisible as the proprietary right of the lord, granted even for the duration of a number of lives.[56]

This is only to say that ecclesiastical custom began to reflect the feudal world in which offices are tied to service on the land and become hereditary. However one may judge these changes, the fact remains that during the tenth and eleventh centuries the number of hereditary churches increased noticeably, and that the Gregorian party denounced both lay proprietorship and clerical inheritance.

Monasteries were also not immune from corruption. One of the ecclesiastical innovations produced by feudalism was

the installation of lay abbots, some of whom moved into the
monasteries with their wives, children, soldiers, and hunt-
ing dogs, and made no attempt at observing a communal rule.
It is not surprising that many of the inmates followed the
example of their superior by marrying and living with their
families in the cloister.[57] In the Italian abbey of
Farfa, for example, the monks publicly acknowledged their
concubines.[58] The council of Soissons in 909 complained
that at the monastery of Trosly enclosure had been abandoned and that many monks had married.[59] And an example
from Normandy around 1000 illustrates how secular control
of monastic property converted lay lords into quasi-
clerical status. Our case is the family who owned the es-
tate of Bellême, who moved easily in both monastic and
secular worlds. Two Bellême daughters received from
their brother Avesgaud, bishop of Le Mans, the proprietary
rights and dues of churches which he had bought from his
canons. Hildeburg married Aubert le Riche, who became abbot of Jumièges and later of St. Mesimin; their son
Aubert II was abbot of St. Mesimin and father of Arnold,
bishop of Tours. The other daughter took her ecclesiastical dowry and married a secular lord.[60] This family par-
ticipated in secular rule over church property for three

generations, controlling two monasteries and a bishopric
through the means of clerical marriage.

As the Ottonian emperors became more active in ecclesiastical reform, however, ascetic churchmen could be bolder
in their threats and punishments against uxorious clerics.
Emperor Henry II, presiding over the synod of Pavia in
1022, accepted Pope Benedict VIII's numerous celibacy decrees. In sum, Benedict had ruled to depose all clergy of
the Subdiaconate and above who keep wives or concubines
with them and to declare the children of clerks who had
been serfs to be themselves serfs of the Church, even
though their mothers were free women.

The synod provides us with a clue that western defenders of clerical marriage were quoting the eastern practice
of allowing clerics in major orders to raise families. In
order to answer this challenge, Benedict directly quoted
the Justinian novel 123.c14 as proof that priests who married after ordination were not only to be deposed but also
handed over to the local court, with all their goods. On
the subject of canonical proof, Benedict observed of the
married churchmen that they could not provide judicial
proof for their claims whereas he could quote Justinian
(correctly) and Nicaea (incorrectly).[61] This was far

from the last time that married priests would get the worst
of it in a battle of the canons.

Around 1050 Pope Leo IX gave warning of the renewed attack about to be launched against married priests: he ordered that the damnabiles feminae of Roman priests be
seized and made ancillae in the Lateran palace, and he
recommended this policy to other prelates.[62] As the reader may have noticed, the terminology used in decrees to describe the woman of a priest has become harsher: the
change from uxor, diaconissa, even episcopissa to
concubina, meretrix, scortum, pellex, degrades the
woman, implicitly denies the possibility of her being law-
fully married (already a century before the canons decreed
such a change) and increases the immoral connotation.[63]
Bernard Verkamp observes of the hundreds of decrees issued
on clerical chastity during these centuries:

> While none showed any concern for the care
> of the clergyman's wife and children after
> separation, a number dictated what was to
> happen to these latter if they did not sepa-
> rate from the cleric. Both the wives and
> children were made subject to being sold or
> taken into slavery.[64]

None of these changes in any way lessened the number
of married clergy. We learn, for example, that Segenfrid,
bishop of Le Mans for thirty-three years, married Hilde-
berga while serving as bishop and engendered many children

by her. She is referred to as his _Episcopissa_. Bishop
Albert of Marsico had a wife and managed to leave his bishopric to his son.[65] Adalbero II of Metz (d. 1005) readily granted ordination to priests' sons. According to Orderic Vitalis,[66] Archbishop Hugh of Rouen (d. 989) passed on
his see to his son Robert, who was publicly married and had
three sons, and the next archbishop, Mauger, also had a
son.

In Anglo-Saxon England the reform party that gathered
around the monastic bishops in the mid-tenth century aimed
its wrath at the canons who lived with their wives in cathedral centers. Aethelwold at Winchester, Oswald at Worcester, and Dunstan at Glastonbury offered "the debased, degraded and lascivious clerks" the chance of becoming celibate. Most refused, were then driven out, and were replaced by Benedictine monks.[67] Despite these efforts,
the normal condition of the English clergy of the tenth and
first three-quarters of the eleventh centuries was to be
married. Chastity was expected only from monks.[68]

Such was the situation in the western church in 1049
when the first of the so-called Gregorians became pope.
Clerical marriage was so widespread as to be the usual condition of parish clergy; it was frequently found in every
level and branch of the church, even on occasion in monas-

teries. Despite six hundred years of decrees, canons, and increasingly harsh penalties, the Latin clergy still did, more or less illegally, what their Greek counterparts were encouraged to do by law -- they lived with their wives and raised families. In fact, although many celibacy decrees had followed the original one of 465 at Vannes, in practice ordination was still not an impediment to marriage; therefore some priests did marry even after they were ordained. And of course a married man still might, on abstaining from his wife, _legally_ be ordained. But that "concession," as we shall see, was soon to go. The desire for a better-disciplined clergy and for a ministry of the altar that was sexually unpolluted began, in the eleventh century, to grow stronger, as monarchs and urban laity became interested in the ascetic movement and as reformed monasticism influenced the church more profoundly. The married clerics, challenged to repudiate their wives and children and to give up their place in society, fought the rigorist or "reforming" party with every weapon at hand. The rest of this study will consider the questions raised by this struggle: of new definitions of the priesthood and of the sacraments, of the relation between priesthood and laity, and of the Church's attitude toward sexuality.

CHAPTER TWO

THE GREGORIAN ATTACK AGAINST MARRIED PRIESTS

> We forbid absolutely the cohabitation with concubines or wives by priests, deacons, or subdeacons. If any of that kind, however, should be found, they are to be deprived of their offices and benefits.... Indeed, if they will not have corrected their filthy ways, they should be deprived of Christian communion.
>
> -- Pope Calixtus II
> Council of Rheims, 1119

> [For priests, deacons, subdeacons, canons regular, monks, and lay brothers] we sanction that copulation of this kind, which was contracted against ecclesiastical rule, is not matrimony.
>
> -- Pope Innocent II
> Lateran Council II, 1139

When the Council of Bourges in 1031 ruled for the first time that, in order to extirpate clerical families, no one should give his daughter as wife to a priest or a

priest's son and that no one should accept the daughter or
the wife of a priest as his wife, French chuchmen were
attesting to the remarkable legacy of clerical offspring
engendered by the recent increase in clerical marriage.
Bourges was a fair example of the renewed zeal for
enforcing the canons on clerical celibacy. The more
rigorist rulings from earlier councils, most of them long
since lapsed, were revived. Bourges, for example,
reinstated the requirement of a vow of chastity at
ordination to the subdiaconate, insisted that priests not
merely abstain from but separate from their wives, and
stated explicitly that sons born during their fathers'
ministry could not be ordained, on grounds that they were
illegitimate.[1] These rulings were, of course, not
original, but combined with the new canons against marrying
into priestly families, they signify a changing outlook
towards clerical sexuality.

Actions such as these were a beginning, but it is a
long way from the isolated legislation of a provincial
council, meeting without benefit of a papal legate, to the
powerful, European-wide campaign of the Gregorian leaders.
Our question, then, is how and when did the entrenched custom of clerical marriage become the subject of a vigorous

campaign to abolish it? In order to see the moves clearly, it is best to divide the period of struggle treated in this chapter into three sections. After the period beginning with the election of Leo IX had prepared the way by means of the publication of polemical literature and of new papal and conciliar decrees, the attack reached its height in the 1070's during the pontificate of Gregory VII; the ultimate legislation was finally promulgated at the Second Lateran Council of 1139.

This chapter in all three sections will concentrate on papal action, both in the Roman synods and in legatine action in France, Germany, and England, and on the publicist literature which supported the papacy. Mention will also be made of examples of the resistance, often violent, against the Papal reforms. The theoretical defense of priestly marriage, however, will receive two chapters to itself so that it can be analyzed in detail.

I

Pope Leo IX reached Rome from Lorraine in 1049 filled with the new reforming zeal of that province. In Lorraine, Wazo of Liège had already challenged imperial control of the church, and the monks of Gorze had begun preaching

against simony and clerical unchastity. Although not a
monk, Leo shared their militant zeal for cleansing the
church. He was, in fact, a soldier-priest who had led the
military defense of his diocesan city and who would again
take the field as pope.[2] In Rome his vigorous bent for
reform was further encouraged by the presence of three
zealous colleagues, Hildebrand and Peter Damian, both
Italians, and Humbert of Silva Candida, a fellow
Lotharingian.

The influence of northern reform movements on Rome
must not be overlooked. From the monastic schools such as
St. Vannes, Lobbes, and Gorze came many of the clerics who
followed the German emperors on their Italian expeditions,
clerics used by Henry II to strengthen his power in Italy
by systematically filling the episcopal sees with Germans.
Equally important were the appointments by the emperors of
five German or Lotharingian popes, Gregory V, Clement II,
Damasus II, Leo IX, Victor II, and Stephen IX. When the
Burgundian Nicholas II is added to the appointments, one
sees that northern churchmen ruled the papacy for the entire crucial period from 1046-1061.[3] In addition, a con-
tinuity previously lacking to the papal forces was now provided in the form of a stable College of Cardinals, consist-

ing of northerners such as Humbert, Frederick of Lotharing-
ia (later Stephen IX) and Hugh the White, in alliance with
Hildebrand and Damian.   These men, in conjunction with emis-
saries from Cluny, brought both a higher level of discipline than the Italian church could claim and a new spirituality, based on the striking liturgical changes begun in
the north during the Carolingian era.[4]

The first effort towards reform came when Humbert, allied with the radical Florentine Vallombrosan reformers,
urged Leo to attack the practice of simony, convincing him
that ordinations by simoniacal bishops were invalid.   If
they together could have convinced the Roman Council of
1049 of this doctrine, the church would have verged toward
donatism,[5] but the assembled prelates refused to take
this radical step.   The focus on simony, however, could
serve as a warning to those practising clerical marriage,
because the two evils were frequently, although not always,
attacked together.   While simony, meaning the buying or sel-
ling of any spiritual favor, was practised by both laity
and clergy, it was particularly related to the power of the
laity over the church, of lay patrons purchasing church offices for their candidates and investing churchmen with office.   This infringement of ecclesiastical rights was made
worse when clergy married into and became involved with the

affairs of lay families, thereby making it possible for laity to share control of church property. Both issues were
offensive to the Gregorians on grounds of political interference and of moral impurity, points which are woven together in Ronald Knox's observation on the Gregorian
movement:

> It was from the first a question of hands;
> hands that perform a sacramental function
> must be chaste, that is the moral issue.
> Hands that perform a supernatural feat can-
> not receive this power from secular hands;
> that is the issue of legitimacy.[6]

As for Damian, at this time he did not take a radical
position on simoniacal reform but was deeply concerned a-
bout clerical incontinence. In approaching Leo about what
he saw as a scandal in the church, he began playing the
role of conscience of the popes, a role which he continued
until his retirement.[7] Damian wrote for Leo the Liber
Gomorrhianus, describing what he considered to be the endless sexual vices of the clergy, homosexual as well as het-
erosexual. In it he used the word "nicolaitan" to describe
all incontinent clergy, the term's popular usage in the
eleventh century debates dating from this time. Damian
closed with a plea to the pope to use severe penalties and
not to rest until this evil was wiped out.[8]

Leo responded less forcefully to this crusade than to the one against simony, perhaps because he himself was reported to have been unchaste.[9] Unless one counts his attack on the women of the Roman priests, whom he said should become slaves in the Lateran palace,[10] there is no mention of celibacy in the surviving canons of his early councils in Rome or Rheims.[11] He seemed intent then on focusing all his powers on the attack on simony. But in Mainz in late 1049 he anathematized married clergy along with simoniacs, condemning both to perpetual damnation.[12] A contemporary observer claimed that when Leo returned to Rome for the synod of May 1050 he not only continued to attack priestly fornicators but also took the very radical step of directing the laity not to attend their masses,[13] a proposal which would have opened the way for laity to sit in judgment over their pastors. He apparently was unable to secure acceptance of this controversial ruling, however, because there was no recorded response to it; it reappears as a crucial piece of Gregorian legislation in 1059.

In addition to these measures Leo ruled that only a married man could accede to the subdiaconate only after taking a vow of continence and with the permission of his wife.[14] In any case, reflecting on what happened later in Mantua, one doubts that the Italian church was ready for the enforcement of celibacy. On going to Mantua in 1053 to promulgate his celibacy and simony reforms, Leo was confronted with a fierce fight between the bishop's forces and his retainers, during which Leo's life was endangered.[15] Doubtless discouraged by this violent response to his attempted reform, and hard-pressed by the new military aggressions of the Normans to the south, Leo led his army into southern Italy and was not able again to work for the enforcement of celibacy.

Meanwhile, Leo had dispatched Cardinal Humbert to Constantinople to settle several important issues with the Greek church. On the subject of celibacy, Humbert attacked the Greeks for permitting their clergy to marry, compared their church to the brothel of Jezebel, and declared all priestly marriage a heresy. Using the epithet "nicolaitan" for married priests, Humbert made it clear that he considered the practice heretical, the first such claim during the Gregorian period.[16] Humbert delared that there were no grounds for negotiation between the churches about clerical marriage. In any event, his final act, the excommunication of the Greek patriarch, rendered the debate about celibacy irrelevant for the immediate future.

Some Latin clergy, however, continuing to claim the Greek practice as a model, insisted that the clerics married before ordination to the diaconate could enjoy the uses of marriage with their wives. When Leo challenged the archbishop of Spalato to give up his wife, the archbishop publicly defended his marriage on the grounds that the Greek church permitted it. For this insubordination he was degraded.[17] Stephen IX was forced to reaffirm that the Eastern church's custom of priestly marriage was not acceptable to Rome.[18] Damian, debating with priests who argued for marriage on the grounds of the Trullan canons, denied that such rulings had been accepted in the West.[19]

By the end of Leo IX's pontificate in 1054 the outline of a new papal program to promote the chastity of ministers of the altar had been advanced: Leo had revived as papal policy the insistence that subdeacons take a vow of chastity and that unchaste priests be excommunicated, and had attempted to introduce an important innovation, the lay boycott of the masses of married priests. Only the restrictions recently revived at Bourges against priests' sons and the reintroduction of the demand that priests married while in minor orders separate from their wives remained to be incorporated into the papal program. The issue of enforcing actual separation, rather than abstention, on couples mar-

ried before the husband entered major orders was not long
in coming, although at first it was not dealt with in a systematic way. Victor II, for example, instructed his legates at Compostella in 1056[20] and at Lisieux[21] to insist that married priests and deacons separate from their
wives, on pain of excommunication, whereas at Toulouse he
demanded only abstinence, with a penalty of excommunication
as well as removal from office.[22]

When the papal party met in 1059 under the new pope
Nicholas II, they struck boldly, attacking not only clerical marriage but several other practices which hindered
their restructuring of the church. By placing the election
of the pope in the hands of the cardinals, this important
Roman synod lessened the power of secular groups over the
papacy, and in announcing that henceforth simoniacs would
not only be dismissed from office but would also have their
ordinations annulled, they attempted to curb the power of
patronage, especially of the laity. Concerning clerical unchastity, they ruled against subdeacons and above who kept
concubines or _mulieres_ _subintroductae_, without mentioning wives, denying these clerics the right to receive communion or to enter churches, and finally put into law the
bold concept that the laity must boycott the sacraments of

priests who lived with women, thereby placing the laity in
the position of judging their pastors. Although this interference in the authority of parish priests instigated a
kind of social war in the church, the synod did not leave
the matter there. It decreed the excommunication of any
concubinous priest who officiated and of any clerk who assisted at the mass of an unchaste priest, thus making universal law of what had been attempted only locally before.
And to make sure that the priesthood lived continently
henceforth, the council at Hildebrand's urging insisted
that all in major orders must live in a clerical household,
with a communal dormitory and refectory, supporting each
other's "moral purity" and, if necessary, reporting on each
other.[23] While this move was originated by Hildebrand,
the influence of Humbert and Damian is shown in Nicholas'
letter to the bishops of Gaul announcing the synod's decisions, when he refers to married clerics as nicolaitist
heretics.[24]

The reaction to these sterner measures came immediately; an Italian bishop, Ulric of Imola, composed the first
known literary defense of clerical marriage written in six
hundred yers.[25] But most of the initial reaction took
place in the streets rather than in the study. In Milan,
for example, where the city had been divided into factions

for some years by the reforming crusade of the Patarenes,[26] many of the clergy and people rioted against the
pope's legates, Damian and Anselm of Lucca, when they arrived to cleanse the church of simony and unchastity.
Again at Lodi Damian's life was threatened when he tried to
convince priests to leave their wives. In debate married
clergy defended their way of life adamantly: when Damian
met with a group of Italian bishops they firmly defended
their right to have wives, saying that otherwise they
would live in sin, and we learn from Damian that the same
was true of the parish priests of Duke Godfrey of Tuscany
who insisted that their marriages were canonical.[27]

Damian was at this time tireless in his crusade
against what he saw as the clerical vice, and became the
single most virulent foe of married clerics. We may speculate that the traumatic events of his childhood had turned
him against all idea of family or of sexuality; we do know
for certain that Damian, not satisfied by ordinary monasticism, turned to the extreme asceticism of the eremitic
life. Born the last of a large, poor family in Ravenna,
Damian was rejected by his mother, who refused to nurse
him. As the infant Peter lay withering away, an angel of
mercy came from an unexpected and -- as it turned out --

highly ironic source: a neighboring priest's wife took pity on the starving infant and talked his mother into offering him her breast, thereby saving the life of the future scourge of priestly families.[28] From the time of Leo IX's pontificate onwards, Damian did not let up in his campaign. For example, urging Countess Adelaide of Savoy to attack the priest's wives while the bishops were to discipline the husbands, Damian cautioned that, if the episcopal arm would not act, she as temporal ruler should step in against both wives and husbands. Assuring Peter, cardinal archdeacon of the Lateran, that clerical marriage must be wiped out, Damian urged him to accept no excuse from unchaste clergy who refused to break up their marriages.[29]

Immediately after Nicholas' election to the papacy in 1059 Damian had written for him De celibatu sacerdotum, setting out the theoretical reason for the necessity of celibacy: since Christ was born of a virgin he wished to be served by virgin hands. That is, Christ himself, present in the elements of the eucharist, must be touched only by unstained hands. Here Damian described the priests' role in the sacraments in the almost erotic language then becoming popular. On a number of occasions Damian defended priestly chastity on the grounds that "the hands that touch the body and blood of Christ must not have

touched the genitals of a whore," and in a memorable tirade
against married and concubinous bishops he complained that

> I have wanted to place locks on their sa-
> cred thighs. I have attempted to place the
> restraints of continence upon the genitals
> of the priesthood, upon those who have the
> high honor of touching the body and blood
> of Christ.... We extort from them, however,
> a bare promise to observe the ruling, it be-
> ing postponed with trembling backslidings.
> (They do this not secretly but publicly,
> everyone knowing the names of their concu-
> bines, even of their fathers-in-law!) Fin-
> ally, when all doubt is removed, the bel-
> lies are swelling, the children running
> around.[30]

Damian reserved the pinnacle of eloquent anger, however, not for uxorious clerics but for those women whom he
labelled "the seducers of clerics," thereby making plain
what is surely implied in the above passages, that contact
with the female sex is the chief pollutant of clerical purity. The following selection from a rich passage will have
to suffice:

> I speak to you, o charmers of the clergy,
> appetizing flesh of the devil, that cast-
> away from paradise, you, poison of the
> minds, death of souls, venom of wine and of
> eating, companions of the very stuff of
> sin, the cause of our ruin. You, I say, I
> exhort you women of the ancient enemy, you
> bitches, sows, screech-owls, night-owls,
> she-wolves, blood-suckers, [who] cry
> "Give, give! without ceasing" (Proverbs
> 30.15-16). Come now, hear me, harlots,
> prostitutes, with your lascivious kisses,
> you wallowing places for fat pigs, couches

for unclean spirits, demi-goddesses,
sirens, witches, devotees of Diana, if any
portents, if any omens are found thus far,
they should be judged sufficient to your
name. For you are the victims of demons,
destined to be cut off by eternal death.
From you the devil is fattened by the abun-
dance of your lust, is fed by your alluring
feasts.

You vipers full of madness, parading the ar-
dor of your ungovernable lust, through your
lovers you mutilate Christ, who is the head
of the clergy.... You snatch away the unhap-
py men from their ministry of the sacred altar, in which they were engaged, that you
may strangle them in the slimy glue of your
passion.

And just as the Midianites persuaded them
through their prostitutes to worship idols,
thus you compel these others, on whom the
sign of the cross had been in some measure
imprinted, to worship the image of a beast.

Moreover just as Adam desired among all the
fruits of paradise precisely that one which
God had forbidden, thus you from the entire
multitude of human kind have chosen only
those who are utterly prohibited from any
alliance with females.... the ancient foe
pants to invade the summit of the church's
chastity through you.... You suck the blood
of miserable, unwary men, so that you might
inflate into their innermost parts a lethal
poison. They should kill you ... for is
there any hand with sacred chrism that you
shake with fear to touch, or oil that you
do not defile, or even pages of the gospels
and epistles that you do not use familiarly
(in an obscene way)?[31]

We can leave Damian's fulmination at this juncture,
noting further only that he urged the women to repent and
leave their clerical husbands and lovers, offering them the

marriage bed of Christ to replace their beds of iniquity;
for the obdurate, he considered Leo IX's recommendation of
enslavement as a just and equable reply to those who rape
the sacred altars. Such statements may seem somewhat excessive but one must remember the ascetic milieu in which Damian lived, with its daily, indeed hourly, struggles against
the flesh, daily flagellation, etc. Lay women, he explained, were the spiritual daughters of priests; for a
priest to sleep with one is therefore incest. And in the
same document Damian, following Humbert, declared that
clerical marriage was heresy.[32]

Writing again on celibacy a few years later, Damian
composed _Contra intemperantes clericos_. To the argument that wives made it possible for clerics to live more
economically, Damian ironically reminded his oppponents
that along with a wife came many children, expensive to support. He takes more seriously the problem posed by St.
Paul's advice, "Let each man have his own wife." St. Paul
cannot have meant this text to be applied universally, for
if it were, then even monks and sacred virgins, those
Christians closest to Damian's heart, could not live their
lives of consecrated chastity. Besides, every minister of
the altar must remain sexually pure in order to say daily

Mass. Until the pope can restore celibacy, it is better
for an incontinent cleric to leave than to offend the
church.[33]

Damian's position is summed up in his conclusion to
De celibatu clericorum where, reflecting that a
priest cannot serve or please both God and a wife, he
explains that the body, as well as the soul, worships God,
is the temple of God, and must not be defamed therefore by
contact with a courtesan.[34] By this argument he affirms
both that the priest must be without worldly care, as
Damian's hermits were, and that he must be sexually pure,
as all true servants of God are. Given the depth of his
conviction about celibacy, it is not surprising that
Damian's attack on clerical marriage concluded, in his letter on the subject to archbishop Cunibert of Turin, with
his reiteration that nicolaitism was heresy.[35]

In regard to the validity of sacraments performed by
"heretical" priests, Damian took contradictory positions.
He was a moderate as far as simoniacal priests were concerned, claiming that their sin should be forgiven them for
the sake of order in the church. He greatly feared the loss
of priestly dignity if the laity were allowed to judge the
validity of a priest's ordination, and he fought Humbert
and the radicals on this issue until he lost out to them.

But when Damian contemplated married priests he lost his
moderation.   At first, as in his early mission to Milan in
1061, he had been willing to discipline and then forgive
them, but soon he changed and urged that their masses be
boycotted.   He reasoned that, whereas a priest might have
been ordained unknowingly by a simoniac, an unchaste priest
sinned knowingly and publicly; he was a man of unclean
hands whose sin was obvious to all.   He thus argued against
the neo-Donatism of Humbert for all offenses except clerical marriage, a sin so unforgiveable that there could be no
goodness remaining in the priest who had indulged in it.
Even though it meant placing the laity in judgment over the
clergy, Damian preached the liturgical strike against married priests.[36]

It appears from this evidence that Damian had a stronger dislike of clerical marriage than of simony.   And yet
he was himself never certain that he was right not to have
married.   He admitted that he was attracted to women and
asked himself if married priests were not happier than he.
Apparently Damian's passionate nature was not satisfied
even by the ascetic extremes of eremitical life or by his
taxing "marriage" to his cardinal-bishopric which kept him
at work for the curia.[37]

Meanwhile the alarming resistance to celibacy did not deter Pope Nicholas from enforcing his decree. Deposing the bishop of Trani for being publicly married, he ordered his legates at Tours and Vienne to demand separation from wives or deprivation of rank immediately. It appears that similar charges were made at Avignon and Toulouse, under the leadership of Hugh of Cluny.[38]

The next pope, Anselm of Lucca, taking the name Alexander II, pressed on with the papal program by repeating the famous decrees of 1059 at his first Roman synod. But Alexander was handicapped at the start of his pontificate by the existence of a rival, the imperialist pope, Honorius II. Damian tells us that married clerics rallied around Honorius, hoping that he would form a party favoring married clergy and would even declare sacerdotal marriage legal. If such was Honorius' intention it was stillborn, because he spent much of his reign as a prisoner, beseiged in Castel San Angelo. It seems, nevertheless, that the mere threat of such opposition, especially when backed by the imperial party, may have distracted Alexander's pursuit of "reform."[39]

Alexander had already had to compromise on the issue of priests' sons, for in 1070 he allowed the son of a priest to become bishop of Le Mans.[40] His main efforts

had gone into the attempted reconquest of Sicily and Spain
from the Moslems and into the eradication of simony, and he
could claim some success there, having brought about the
deposition of a number of simoniacal abbots and bishops.
At his death, the celibacy reform movement had been at work
for almost twenty-five years. It had absorbed the best
energies of Damian and the persistant efforts of Hildebrand
and the several popes. In spite of this, in practice there
was little change: the majority of parish priests
continued to live with their wives and to raise families,
and some bishops lived openly with women whom they called
their wives.[41] In fact, the aggressive policy of the
papacy had made the married clergy defiant, somewhat more
conscious of themselves as a group within the church. By
the eve of Hildebrand's election as pope some were studying
the canons in order to defend their position better, some
were composing circular letters to alert other married
priests to the new threats, others showed their
determination to resist the papal decrees by force if
necessary. A noticeable change had come over the defenders
of the ancient institution of sacerdotal marriage as they
realized the extent of the papal attack against it.

II

The way in which Gregory VII enforced the decrees on celibacy may be read as a case study of ecclesiastical legal enforcement, for Gregory made far more impact on the institution of clerical marriage than any previous pope.

In doing so he used the ascetic ideals and stricter discipline of the northern churches, turning the reforms against the very areas which had initiated them, creating major upheavals both political and ecclesiastical in areas which would have preferred reform, not revolution. But he who did not hesitate to excommunicate an emperor and bishops by the dozen, was not deterred from attacking the ancient customs of his society, neither by the strong commitment of many priests to their wives and children nor by the society's widespread acceptance of those customs. And yet, the nature of the "vice," involving as it did the deep loyalties of the priests concerned, made it impossible even for Gregory to eradicate it entirely.

At his first synod (1074) Gregory decreed that no one could be admitted to orders without a vow of celibacy and that the laity was forbidden to attend the services of an unchaste priest, deacon, or subdeacon.[42] As we know, these prohibitions were not new. What was different was

the way in which Gregory followed up on them. Sending out
legates to proclaim the decrees at councils across Europe,
he then wrote angry letters to noncompliant prelates. When
that did not have effect he summoned the recalcitrants to
Rome, threatening them with deposition, and, when none of
these measures worked, he excommunicated them. Gregory's
policy was unrelenting; once a prelate showed himself to
be uncooperative, the pope applied escalating punishments.

Already before his first synod, Gregory had written
Gebhardt of Salzburg, admonishing him to discipline his
uxorious clergy.[43] Once every bishop had received the
renewed decrees, Gregory pressed charges against all who
held back. When Otto of Constance actually defended his
married clergy, Gregory released the clergy and people of
Constance from obedience to their bishop and summoned him
to Rome. Ignoring the command, Otto was excommunicated,
but defiantly refused to vacate his see. Gregory, implac-
able, managed shortly before he died (in 1085) to replace
Otto by installing a reform candidate on the episcopal
throne of Constance.[44]

When Gregory's celibacy decrees were read in the
synods of Germany, the German clergy complained angrily
that

> ... the man was clearly a heretic and of un-
> sound mind, who by violent interference

> would force men to live in the manner of an-
> gels, and while denying the ordinary course
> of nature, would release the restraints on
> fornication and filthy behavior; that if he
> should proceed to confirm the decision,
> they would choose rather to desert their
> priesthood than their marriages ...

They finished off their challenge by asking where Gregory would find angels to replace them.[45]

Siegfried, archbishop of Mainz, attempting to take a middle course between the obstinancy of his clergy and the inexorable papal pressure to eradicate their marriages, demonstrates by his difficult career that under Gregory compromise was not possible. When he attempted reform, the clergy of Mainz threatened his life, yet when he did not remove them from their posts, the papal threats against him became unbearable. Finally he joined the imperialist party, denounced Gregory, and was excommunicated by the pope in 1076.[46]

Altmann of Passau, trying to force the new decrees upon his clergy, was attacked by them, and then driven out of his diocese by the imperial army. Returning later as papal legate, he was still unable to enforce the celibacy law.[47] And all the while, Gregory continued to put pressure on the bishops by letter and by a specific canon threatening to suspend any who did not work for reform.[48] Gregory reflected Damian's influence by referring to celi-

bacy in language stressing the idea of cultic purity, a custom becoming increasingly frequent among the Gregorians.
For example, when writing to the archbishop of Cologne in
1075:

> ... I command you to apply yourself with
> more energy to preaching and enforcing the
> celibacy of the clergy ... so that the ser-
> vice of a pure and unspotted family may be
> offered to the bride of Christ who knows no
> spot or wrinkle ...
>
> We urge you to call a council of your
> fellow bishops.... Expound at length ...
> how great is the virtue of chastity, ...
> how fitting for the chamberlains of the vir-
> gin bridegroom and the virgin bride. Then
> declare firmly that it shall no longer be
> permitted to carry on the functions which
> ... they have usurped to their own destruc-
> tion.[49]

He equated clerical marriage with evil and uncleanliness in
his letter to William the Conqueror concerning Judhael,
Bishop of Dol, who

> in the very bishopric he had so destructive-
> ly obtained, was not ashamed to enter open-
> ly into marriage and to take a harlot rath-
> er than a wife, by whom he then also begot
> children, so that he who had already prosti-
> tuted his soul [to simony] might likewise
> dedicate his body in shame to the devil by
> his lewd and foul lust....

To this atrocious deed Judhael had added sacrilege:

> For by a monstrous outrage he married off
> the grown-up daughters of his illicit marr-
> iage, bestowing and alienating church lands
> and revenues by way of their dowries.[50]

In admonishing the bishop of Paris, Gregory wrote

> ... that [all your bishops] are strictly to
> forbid all priests who refuse to give up
> the crime of fornication to perform the of-
> fice of the holy altar.... And if you find
> the bishops lax ... do you prohibit every
> people from receiving their offices ....[51]

Gregory was of course wrong about _fornicatio_, because it
was still licit for a priest, having been married before en-
tering major orders, to retain his wife. Although he usually stressed the need for discipline as the goal of celibacy, he referred also to the ideal of cultic purity in making no distinction between whoredom, fornication, and intercourse of a cleric and his wife. When, in using Humbert's
and Damian's imagery, he wrote to Robert the Frisian that
one cannot touch both the body of Christ and the body of a
whore, one can be sure that he was referring to all clerical incontinency.[52]   Gregory was escalating the conflict
by the vehemence of his language,[53] and was using
language politically to discredit the marital relations of
licit but restricted unions.

Not confining himself to sending out men on specific
missions, Gregory appointed several of his strongest supporters to act as permanent regional legates: Hugh of Die in
France, Amat d'Oleron in southwest France and Spain, Altmann of Passau for Germany and Anselm of Lucca (the canon-

ist) for Lombardy. An idea of their impact can be seen
from Hugh's record: he convoked ten synods in seven years
(1075-82), and deposed or excommunicated fifteen bishops
and four archbishops. Although all of the charges were for
simony or similar infractions and none was for nicolaitism,
still these legates read the celibacy decrees at many councils, and their harsh penalties against other offenses
struck fear in the hearts of men who had offended against
the celibacy law.[54] Married clergy in many areas objected violently to the celibacy decree; in Italy the cities
of Piacenza, Lodi, Florence and Turin remained in turmoil
over the papal attacks on married priests. When the North
Italian schismatic bishops gathered at Pavia in 1076 to condemn the pope, one of their charges against Gregory was
that he separated husbands from wives, showed no respect
for the marriage bond, and thereby forced otherwise moral
clerics to live in sin.[55]

Meanwhile Gregory continued his purge at the Roman synods. 1076 was a particularly effective year: the synod
suspended four French bishops and excommunicated the archbishop of Mainz for tolerating married clerics. All the
Lombard bishops and Cardinal Hugh Candidus, who had claimed
that Gregory had no right to the papacy, were excommunicat-

ed and the archbishops of Ravenna and Narbonne were suspended from all priestly functions.[56]

Considering the number of prelates whom he disciplined, it is not surprising that in some cases Gregory
turned away from the episcopate and went over their heads
to the secular power. In Germany he tried at first to es
tablish common ground with Henry IV by praising the emper-
or's stand against incontinent clergy.[57] When political
tensions made it impossible to continue an alliance with
Henry, Gregory turned to the dukes of Swabia and Carinthia,
complaining that since the bishops would not act,

> ... we now turn to you and to all in whose
> loyalty and devotion we have confidence,
> begging you and directing you by apostolic
> authority, no matter what bishops
> may say or not say, not to recog-
> nize those whom you shall prove to have
> been promoted or ordained simoniacally or
> to be under the charge of fornication.[58]
> [Italics mine]

In similar vein he excused Count Robert of Flanders from
obedience to bishops who did not pursue reform.[59] Having
already rendered the priesthood open to the judgment of the
laity by commanding them to shun the sacraments of unworthy
priests, he now challenged the authority of bishops over
princes, or rather, in both cases Gregory declared that the
unworthy priest or bishop is not in fact a priest or
bishop. The radical nature of these moves distressed many

in the papal party [60] and infuriated the opposition. It was in part because of this attack on priestly power that Gregory was condemned by the imperial party at the assemblies of Utrecht and of Worms.

In the midst of the growing uproar over the enforcement of celibacy, a Gregorian partisan, the monk Bernold of Constance, wrote a defense of the pope's actions, "Apologeticus super decreta contra simoniacos et incontinentes altaris ministros."[61] Bernold gave a thorough enumeration of the scriptural and canonical bases of Gregory's actions and became the first person we have record of to dispute the authenticity of Sozomen's account of the Council of Nicaea. While Sozomen had reported that Pafnutius successfully defended marriage for the priesthood, Bernold declared that it is impossible to believe that a saint and martyr like Pafnutius could have taken such a position, hence Sozomen must have been wrong. Bernold's arguments will be discussed more fully in the next chapter.

The pope delivered his final attack against clerical marriage at the Lenten Synod of 1079. Condemning the Rescript of Ulric, which in its twenty years of circulation had had far too much influence on Gregory's enemies, he declared that the story of Pafnutius' defense of priestly marriage at Nicaea, one of the Rescript's main points, had been false.[62]

After 1079, Gregory's struggle with the Empire became so fierce that he was unable to continue his attack on clerical incontinence. He annulled several episcopal excommunications in France in hope of securing French cooperation while he struggled with the Germans. Their initial excommunication of the pope, at Worms, had been in part a response to the papal claims of the "Dictatus Papae,"[63] but the German bishops were also angry about the enforcement of celibacy. When the imperial party met at Brixen in 1080, they listed the enforcement of celibacy among many grievances, complaining that the pope in granting the laity the right to judge clergy had undermined their authority.[64] The second excommunication against Gregory and the election of a rival pope, Clement III, caused a final break; there was no reconciliation at Canossa this time. Soon a number of Gregory's Roman colleagues deserted to the imperial side, Emperor Henry's army marched on Rome, and Gregory ended his life in exile at Norman-held Salerno.

However ambiguous and weakened may have been Gregory's position at his death, two facts can be stated about his contribution to the imposition of celibacy on the wsetern priesthood: 1) Gregory, in winning over the German princes

who saw that their advantage lay in opposition to Henry IV,
also won them over to his views on clerical reform. We
have seen that Gregory had placed in their hands a novel
power to judge clergy. Some used it zealously to remove
married priests, acting in some cases to make political capital of the priest's plight, in others to seize benefices
for their own appointees.[65] Married priests in pro-papal
regions suffered heavily.

2) Gregory established the ideal of clerical celibacy as the norm for all discussions of the matter among the
prelates of the church. Therefore by the end of his reign
even his staunchest episcopal enemies agreed with him
about celibacy reform. From the emperor's pope on down,
the imperial prelates condemned clerical unchastity. In
their desire to prevent turmoil in the churches the
imperialists may have treated married clergy better, but
they condemned the custom all the same. Opinion among the
laity also had begun to shift. Although at the start of
the reform the laity, with the exception of the Patarenes,
had supported their married clergy, that support could no
longer be counted on. A report, written much later, states
that when the imperialist pope and cardinals were driven
out of Rome in 1084 by the Normans, they were ridiculed not for

their defeat "but for their shaven chins and the wives and concubines whom they publicly carried with them."[66]

It thus appears that Gregory, while not attaining his goal of a celibate priesthood, did succeed in disrupting the ministry of married clergy by moving public opinion toward an acceptance of celibacy.

III

The period from 1080 until the early 1090's, dominated by the schism and by warfare, was a difficult period for the enforcement of celibacy. The papal party did not become silent about priestly marriage or other "evils," however, and this period was a productive one for the theoretical and polemical sides of the struggle.

The most impressive tractate to come from these efforts was Manegold of Lautenbach's _Liber ad Geberhardum_, composed in 1086 to counter Wenric of Trier's attack on Gregory. Writing mainly to refute the imperialist claim that a subject's oath to a king was inviolable, Manegold argued that papal, not monarchical, sovereignty was unlimited. He produced the "contract" theory of political power, arguing that, because the people elect the king and delegate his power to him, they can depose him. These statements have been interpreted as a radical "people's rights" theory, but to do so is to read Manegold out of context. In fact, Manegold reserved the ultimate word for the church, declaring that when the church judges that the prince acts against the faith, then the people are absolved from their oath; Manegold implies that they may then revolt in good conscience. Thus Manegold shifted the basis of power from the king to the church.[67]

Manegold spoke directly about the enforcement of celibacy in the sections defending Gregory's legislation. He maintained that the pope, the entire patristic tradition on his side, had not punished offenders harshly enough.[68]

Quoting Peter Damian's view from 1064 that the offices of incontinent priests should be shunned, Manegold declared that the pope had been right to forbid married priests to perform the sacraments, not only because the canons said so, but because unclean hands must not touch holy objects. The laity must be protected from such sinners, who are to be utterly damned. Priests' sons must not be allowed ordination and should be made chattels of the church.[69] The same punishment should be applied to women who consort with

priests, as Leo IX had recommended, for they are the ruin
of the church.[70]

Making good use of Damian's judgment that married
priests were heretics, Manegold added further that they are
infidels, dangerous imposters who might lead the faithful
away from the teachings of the papacy.[71] In using the
neo-Donatist ideas of another Gregorian apologist, Manegold
reinforced further his support of Gregory's condemnation
of "impure" sacraments: Bernold of Constance had criticised
the Council of Gangra for pronouncing anathema against any-
one who shunned the sacraments of a married priest; Manegold agreed with Bernold that it should be the other way
around.[72] But Manegold went further than his sources,
writing with both originality and boldness. He paid heavily for his curialist views, being imprisoned by Henry IV in
1098.

The other polemicist who treated the celibacy issue,
Bonizo of Sutri, was not, however, Manegold's equal. Driv-
en out of his original diocese by the imperial army and
then named bishop of Piacenza c. 1088, Bonizo was met on ar-
rival with fierce resistance from clergy and people who
knew him as an intransigent Gregorian. Attacked and blind-
ed, and indeed, so severely mutilated that he never fully

recovered, he added an embittered sense of wrong to his already highly emotional and partisan nature.

This attitude pervades the _De_ _vita_ _Christiana_
and may well account for his vituperative language against
married clerics, who are always "fornicatores" or "concubin-
ati," and for his rigid judgment of irregular ordinations
as both null and heretical. For Bonizo all types of sexual
relations for priests were sinful and therefore heretical.
It followed that he condemned any leniency toward married
priests, especially their reordination, and that he was
critical of Urban II's early policy of reconciliation
toward priests who had erred.[73] Even the impassioned
Bonizo, however, saw that there must be a way, a loophole,
whereby the crowds of excommunicated priests, the legacy of
Gregory's unbending zeal and of years of war and partisan
politics, could be brought back into the service of the
church. Although Bonizo did not relent in the slightest
toward unchaste priests, he did allow that a man who _in_
good _faith_ had been ordained by a schismatic or simoniac, not knowing of his bishop's condemnation, could have a
valid ministry. This important distinction, although difficult to establish and to interpret, was made into law by
Urban II at the Council of Piacenza, 1095.[74]

The remaining polemicists of this period did not mention the enforcement of celibacy, being more concerned with
the problem of the reordination of priests loyal to the
antipope. These writers took a hard line against the excommunicated, whom they considered to be heretics. The first
to compose an attack, Gebhardt of Salzburg, in 1081, declared there should be no contact with the excommunicated.
Bernard of Constance agreed, saying that if a member of the
body of Christ breaks off from that body, he should be
shunned. Bernold of Constance furthered that opinion, as
did Anselm of Lucca.[75] This extreme stand against excommunicated priests worked equally against the simoniacal,
the married, and those ordained by bishops loyal to the
antipope, and inevitably caused great hardship for such
clerics. Evidence of their suffering and of the social revolution initiated in the parishes by this attack on priestly authority will be considered in the next chapter.

The papal theoreticians were not the only zealots.
Many secular lords, for example, encouraged by the papacy
to judge their clergy, had become persecutors of married
clerics. Around 1090 Count Robert of Flanders had begun
reaping a profit from deceased clergy, seizing their goods
and turning out their wives and children. He justified his
action more or less on Gregorian lines by asserting that in-

continent priests were not to be obeyed or even acknowledged as clergy. The Flemish churchmen appealed to Urban
II who tried to help them but could not, and finally the
archbishop of Rheims forced the count to stop his harrass-
ment.[76] When lay magnates acted with such independence,
as, for example in England, Henry I's seizing property of
married clerics and collecting _cullagium_ on a wide
scale,[77] they created a difficult legacy for succeeding
popes and contributed strongly to the tensions of the
investiture struggle.

Examples of papal or episcopal leniency did exist. Apparently the necessity to hold the church together, to les-
sen the schism, and to control the increasingly independent
laity, made some concessions necessary. For example, Aldebert, archdeacon of Le Mans, was reported to have several
mistresses and many children, and yet was made bishop of
that diocese.[78]

The first legislation of Urban II, however, would not
have indicated a lenient policy. At the Synod of Melfi,
while reaffirming the now-familiar deposition of married
priests and suspension of bishops who tolerated them, he also applied to the subdiaconate the old plan of Leo IX which
declared clerical wives to be slaves of the church: Urban

intended to offer them to nobles who cooperated in the reform.[79] While he did not repeat this canon in later celibacy decrees, still its existence indicates an attitude
toward the wives. It is not surprising that at this period
one hears of desperate reactions on the part of the wives.
When separated from their husbands some commited suicide,
while others physically attacked the bishops who tried to
separate them. One, maddened by the destruction of her marriage, was said to have poisoned the wife of the lord who
had forced her from her husband.[80]

Even more threatening to clerical marriages than Urban's stricture against the wives was the possible interpretation of his ruling against subdeacon's marriages. It has
been taken as a step toward declaring the institution of
clerical marriage void. This must be seen as a sign that
the church's long toleration of married clerics was at an
end, that the church was ready to move to void those lia-
sons which for centuries it had censured without actually
destroying.[81] And at the same time Urban struck against
one of the powerful weapons of married priests, namely
their ability to hand down their benefices to their sons,
to establish clerical lineages. His weapon against them,
the ruling that priests' sons could not be admitted to orders except as canons regular or as monks, assured that the

sons could function ecclesiastically only in the most closely controlled segments of the church.[82]

As long as Henry IV's allies and armies were strong in
Italy, Urban could not take control of the church effectively.   Finally in 1093, Urban succeeded in backing Henry's
son Conrad to revolt against his father and to drive him
out of Northern Italy. A triumph for the papacy in more
than military or political terms, Henry's defeat was the
signal to launch the reform movement again. The schism led
by Clement III had no chance after Henry's defeat of 1094.
Neither did clerical marriage.

Urban acted immediately by calling a large council at
Piacenza in February, 1095, at which time many imperial sym-
pathizers switched parties and came back to the papal fold.
Ruling that penitence was denied to clerks of major orders
who would not give up their women, Urban returned to the
harsher language of Gregory VII towards married clergy:

> Likewise the heresy of the Nicolaitans,
> that is, the unchastity of subdeacons, dea-
> cons, and especially priests, is condemned
> byond any debate, that those who do not
> fear to remain in that heresy should not be
> allowed to enter into successive offices;
> lest the people should receive their offi-
> ces in any way, if the Nicolaitans should
> presume to minister against this prohibi-
> tion.[83]

Convening a major council at Clermont in November of that
year, Urban decreed that subdeacons, deacons, priests and
canons are deposed if found living with a woman.[84] and repeated the injunction from Melfi that priests' sons will
not be admitted to orders unless as canons regular or as
monks. This last proviso was a powerful blow against the
hereditary character of the priesthood. Hundreds of the
clergy and laity who with enthusiasm heard Urban give the
call to the first Crusade may have listened to these stricter celibacy decrees with the same approval, for at this
time general opinion both within the episcopate and among
the public begins to turn strongly against priestly marriage.

Before documenting the ultimate papal campaigns
against that institution, however, it will be well to take
a closer look at how the Gregorian decrees were carried
out. I will use the Anglo-Norman area as a case study, creating at the same time a detailed background for the majority of the documents to be studied in Chapters III and IV.

Normandy had first heard the new papal celibacy decrees at the council of Lisieux in 1055. The legislation
at Lisieux degraded priests, deacons, and subdeacons who
had women (feminae) living with them, and forbade archdeacons and canons absolutely to have women in their house-

holds, on pain of excommunication.[85] But demotion was
not a harsh penalty, nor did other actions of the council
reveal a strong stand on celibacy. For example, the archbishop of Rouen, Mauger, who had never know monastic discipline and "was unbecomingly addicted to the desires of the
flesh, and involved in worldly pursuits," was deposed. But
since he was disciplined for treason against Duke William,
rather than for living with a woman, his punishment was not
proof of commitment to reform. Nor were the Normans yet
ready to persecute priests' sons: Mauger's son Michael, "a
brave and honest knight," lived to an old age in England,
honoured and beloved by Henry I.[86] A Norman priest in
the 1050's and 1060's might therefore have concluded that
clerical marriage would still be tolerated.

A true omen of the seriousness of "reform" was re-
vealed, however, in 1072 when archbishop John, repeating
the celibacy decrees of Lisieux, added that a priest who
has fallen into mortal sin will be excommunicated and may
not be reconciled easily or quickly. These canons caused a
tumult in which the archbishop was stoned and barely
escaped with his life. John, known for his arrogance and for
taking severe measures to separate priests from their
women, dared to repeat these decrees in 1074.[87] Another

sign of the increasing polarization of the issue was provided by the preaching mission undertaken c. 1100 by abbots
Robert d'Arbrissel of Fontevrault and Bernard of Tiron, who
traveled through Normandy urging the moral reform of the
church. In Coutances the married clergy, refusing to lis-
ten, were ready to attack Bernard, who defended himself so
eloquently that he converted a married archdeacon who dis-
persed the crowd. Robert became famous for his miraculous
asceticism, which he tested regularly by sleeping among the
nuns in his double monastery at Fontevrault.[88]

In the Anglo-Saxon church, although efforts had been
made to impose chastity, especially in cathedral chapters,
the turmoil of the conquest had slowed the change.[89] It
was not until 1076 under a Norman archbishop of Canterbury,
that the Anglo-Norman bishops and abbots issued decrees forbidding clerics to marry after taking orders and ordering
canons immediately to give up their wives. Lanfranc's decree was mild indeed, allowing parish clergy already married to keep their wives while forbidding them further promotion.

The Anglo-Saxon bishop of Worcester, Wulfstan, would
have none of this Norman moderation, insisting instead that
his clergy choose their wives or their churches.[90] Both
Lanfranc and Wulfstan might well have worried over the

state of English clerical morals, since Orderic reported
that not only were most of the parochial clergy married but
in the monasteries "both sexes were inclined to every species of license...."[91] Among the higher clergy we learn
that Albert of Lorraine founded a dynasty at St. Paul's in
the 1060's, that there were married bishops and archdeacons
at St. David's and Llandaff for the next hundred years, and
that at Durham at the turn of the century the dean and the
treasurer were married and the bishop married his daughter
into the local nobility. There were many famous and powerful clerical families, such as Anskar, who became a canon
of St. Paul's, as did his two sons Thurstin, who became
archbishop of York, 1114-40, and Audoen, who was promoted
to the bishopric of Evreux. Anskar's grandson Osbert was
forced out of orders when he murdered St. William of York;
he then continued to raise the large family he had begun as
a cleric.[92] As records are very scanty for this type of
information, we must assume from what we know that the in-
cidence of clerical marriage and hereditary succession was
high.

In Normandy in 1080 Duke William, presiding over the
council of Lillebonne, criticized his bishops for not enforcing celibacy and warned that they must cease collecting

cullagium, the "tax" married priests were forced to pay in order to live with their wives. Since the bishops had failed to purify the priesthood William turned to the laity, setting up mixed courts of both clerical and lay jurors, to try clerics accused of concubinage.[93] William, however, was scarcely a scourge of the episcopate. In his dependency of Brittany he defended Judhael, archbishop of Dol, against papal excommunication, even though Judhael was publicly married and had grown children on whom he bestowed church property. Likewise, the bishopric of Quimper was handed down from father to son for three generations, and the bishops of Rennes, Vannes and Nantes were known to be married. And yet these practices brought no complaint from their Norman overlord.[94]

It is easy to see why William despaired of reforming his own duchy through its bishops, for during that period at least a dozen Norman prelates were married. Clerical dynasties were especially powerful in the Norman church and state, where the ducal family produced seven bishops and three archbishops within a century. Oftentimes these men like Odo, bishop of Bayeux, earl of Kent, and papal aspirant, were counts as well as prelates.[95] The chapter of Bayeux was especially well provided with father-son combinations; a witness list of 1092 confirms four sets (including

two families who were canons for three generations) and six
more possible father-son relationships, several of whom became bishops or archbishops.[96]

The campaign to drive priests' sons out of ecclesiastical office was, however, gaining momentum. We know of penalties in the duchy against priests' sons, such as the local resistance to the appointment of Guitmond of Aversa as
archbishop of Rouen. Accused of being the son of a priest,
Guitmond withdrew and left Normandy.[97] While the same
charge did not prevent William Bona Anima from becoming
archbishop in Guitmond's place, William was later suspended
by the pope for that reason. Serlo of Bayeux lost his benefice on the same accusation. In England a trial occuring
shortly after the Conquest indicates the indignation of
priestly families against the new papal claims. In Shrews-
bury the new Norman lord presented a parish church to the
monks of a new monastic foundation, to be effective at the
deaths of the incumbent cathedral canons who held the living. The children of the canons sued, on the grounds that
the church was theirs by hereditary right. The case was
settled (in the monks' favor, of course) only in the reign
of Henry I.[98]

After the 1090's the main Anglo-Norman efforts toward
the enforcement of celibacy took place in England, where Anselm and Henry I, no doubt for different motives, held two
major councils devoted to stamping out clerical unchastity.
In London in 1102 Anselm ruled that married clergy, including the subdeacons who had professed chastity, must give up
their wives. If they refused but continued to say mass,
they were to be shunned and deprived of all legal privileges. The council concluded by requiring the vow of chastity
at ordination and forbidding priests' sons to inherit their
father's churches.[99] Delegates to the synod complained
that priests were not strong enough to endure this unnatural discipline and that forcing celibacy upon them would
drive them to vice. Archdeacon Henry of Huntingdon, son of
a priest and father of sons with clerical ambitions, reported in his Historia Anglorum that Anselm, in forbidding
wives to the English clergy, was imposing a discipline not
formerly known. Since Henry must have known of Lanfranc's
decree of 1076, as well as of more ancient decrees from
Anglo-Saxon times, he was apparently remembering what he
wanted to remember. Another example of Henry's selective
writing of history was that he did not even mention the second reform council of 1108.[100]

At this second council, Anselm, adamant, instituted new, stricter methods to force priests from their wives. Knowing that centuries of compromise with the living arrangements of these couples had failed, he put in a new proviso to insure chastity. Those who repudiated their wives and wished to continue to serve the altar must send their wives far away out of their district; they might then visit their spouses only in the open air and in the presence of two witnesses. As if these complex arrangements were not enough of a burden, clerics who were still accused of illicit behavior must clear themselves by compurgation, with six witnesses if they were priests, four if deacons, two if subdeacons. If men hesitated to abandon their wives and tried to remain in office by paying cullagium or by hiring substitutes, they were allowed eight days in which to regularize their affairs.[101] Recalcitrant priests were to be excommunicated, driven out by the laity and replaced by monks, their personal property confiscated by the bishop and their wives made chattels of the church.[102]

Anselm apparently was able to enforce these stringent rules only in the neighborhood of his archdiocesan seat. Even there, relatives of the women forced from their husbands raised such violent objections that they had to be

threatened with excommunication. And some married clergy,
even in the shadow of Canterbury, kept their wives and
their benefices, continuing to serve their parishes after
being excommunicated.[103]

Evidence of the hardship and confusion that this legislation caused clergy and laity alike is found in Anselm's
correspondence with Pascal II about pastoral questions. Anselm asks if an unchaste priest can administer the last
rites, and what to do if he refuses to administer on
grounds that he has been refused the right of saying mass.
Pascal replied that the sacrament of an unchaste priest is
better than no sacrament, but Anselm's horror of cultic pollution was so great that he could not accept Pascal's compromise. Throughout Anselm's letters and legislation runs
the sense of urgency, the demand that the purity of the altar be established now.[104]

It was impossible for the English church to change as
quickly as Anselm wished. Most married clerics held out
against his edicts, reuniting with their wives after he was
exiled by the king.[105] Henry I thereupon took up the
task of reform and turned it to his own profit: if a married priest refused to part from his wife he was seized,
put on trial, and his church's lands were confiscated by
the crown. Anselm, outraged when he learned of this

attack upon church property, ordered Henry to cease. Between the feuding monarch and archbishop the reform attempts cancelled each other out -- and England's clergy remained as uxorious as ever.[106]

Meanwhile Anselm disagreed again with the pope, this
time over the ordination of priest's sons. When Anselm refused their ordinations Pascal II reminded him that, given
the overwhelming number of married clergy, the church had
best admit to orders those priests' sons who were well-
educated and of pure life, lest the ranks of the priesthood
should shrink. Since the sons of priests did not bear the
sins of their fathers they should be allowed into orders,
even though they were not to receive promotion, a stipula-
tion guaranteed to keep them out of the hierarchy.[107]

All of these endeavors, in Normandy and England alike,
had no noticeable effect. Ivo of Chartres loudly complains
that a canon publicly took a mistress and even entered into
matrimony, that bishops had children, and that a convent
served as a brothel.[108] It is not until the legislation
of Calixtus II at Rheims in 1119 that ultimately successful
enforcement began. The archbishop of Rouen, Geoffrey, upon
returning from Calixtus' great council, immediately called
together his clergy to announce that they must give up co-

habitation with their women in order to keep their office, and also separate from wife and children in any case, or face excommunication. The Norman clergy, outraged by this judgment, complained as they had in 1072, showing that they still did not accept the papal definition of clerical chastity. This time, however, it was the archbishop, not his priests, who turned the scene into violence. The most outspoken rebel, a cleric named Albert the Eloquent, was seized and thrown into prison. The other priests were utterly confounded that, without being charged with any crime or undergoing any legal examination, a priest was dragged like a thief from a church to a dungeon. The archbishop then turned his soldiers on the unarmed priests, who defended themselves as best they could. At this point the onlookers, joining the archbishop's side, assisted the soldiers in beating up the clergy, and the synod ended in bloodshed and confusion. The embittered clergy carried the sorrowful tidings to their parishioners and concubines, exhibiting their wounds, and many who heard the news were shocked.[109]

In England, however, the clergy responded to this new papal attack on their ancestral privilege not by violence but by invective and slander. Calixtus' decrees, announced at three successive London councils in 1125, 1127, and

1129,[110] were first introduced there by his legate John
of Crema. Henry of Huntingdon, bitter opponent of celibacy
to the end, reported the event thus:

> For in the council (John) dealt with wives
> of priests very severely, saying it was the
> greatest sin to rise from the side of a
> whore and go to create the body of Christ.
> Yet having created the body of Christ that
> same day[111] he was caught after Vespers with
> a whore.

Henry is perhaps more understanding in his observation that
Archbishop William, who accepted _cullagium_ from the married clergy and let them keep their wives, did so because
he was duped by Henry I.[112]

   Whether by bribery, passive resistance, or violent re-
belling, the Anglo-Norman clergy did continue to live with
their wives. The proof is to be found in bishops' regis-
ters and in the large number of papal dispensations for ordination of priests' sons in the last half of the twelfth
century. But these statistics apply mainly to parish clergy,[113] for the time when married men were no longer promoted to the upper clergy was near at hand.

   Brooke has documented the fate of several important
clerical families, showing the effectiveness of papal reform among both seculars and regulars. Whereas in 1100 the
treasurer of Durham could claim a large patrimony in church

lands, his son Eilaf, in order to save one parish of that patrimony, had to struggle against the monks who were taking over the Durham chapter; and Eilaf's son Ailred, converted by the Cistercians, became the famous monk of Rievaulx. Of the canons of St. Paul's at the turn of the twelfth century, at least one-fourth were married and at least eight of these passed their benefices to their sons. Since they were clearly listed as married in the prebendal catalogue, no stigma was associated with their domestic arrangements, and yet, after 1150, there is only one hereditary appointment. Bishop Roger of Salisbury, chancellor and chief justiciar to Henry I, married Matilda of Ramsbury, from an influential Wiltshire family; their son became King Stephen's chancellor and two of their nephews became bishops, one of whom had a son, Richard Fitz Neal, who was royal treasurer and bishop of London, 1189-99. But even this unsurpassed record of a century of power ended when the family's clerical members ceased to marry: William of Ely, royal treasurer after Richard, was the last of the family to achieve power, and the last clerical member to become a father; he died in 1222.[114] Thus we see from Anglo-Norman records how <u>papal</u> actions began to change the established life-patterns of the majority of European higher clergy.

Pope Urban's legislation at Melfi and later at Piacenza in 1095 had been the turning point. While the battle to
save the marital customs of the clergy was not over, as we
shall see in more detail in the next chapters, from now on
the initiative belonged to the papacy. The next pope, Pascal II, was not able to use this initiative because of his
diastrous struggle with the leading monarchs over lay investiture, a struggle which brought him as many critics within
the church as without. But even during this tumultuous period the basic changes which the Gregorians had wrought in
the church persisted and slowly changed the accepted image
of the priest. Gradually the clergy were being more closely controlled by their bishops who were, in turn, more
tightly supervised by Rome. The priesthood was being set
further apart from the laity, who had begun to insist on a
celibate ministry. And, as this happened, the priesthood's
power through the sacraments, especially of confession and
penance, began to increase.

The concrete political results of these far-reaching
changes can best be seen in Germany. By the early years of
the twelfth century the appointment of bishops of the Gregorian party had swung influential opinion in the local
church to a strict policy of enforcement of celibacy. Even

though the emperor continued to name the bishops, he now had far fewer anti-papalists to choose from. New ideas dominating education in the monastic and cathedral schools over the past two or three generations made a difference there. In the period beginning around 1115 the archbishops of Cologne and Salzburg, and many bishops such as those of Utrecht, Strasburg, Constance, Würzburg, Speyer, and Worms, all appointed by Henry V, abandoned him for the papal political cause, and they also espoused the papal ideal for the priesthood. Even Adalbert, chancellor of the empire, when he became archbishop of Mainz, turned against his imperial master and became the leader of the Gregorian party in Germany.[115] Church-state relations in the Empire developed a pattern which foreshadowed the later struggle between Thomas à Becket and the English king Henry II.

It was to be expected, therefore, when the investiture problem began to be resolved, that the papacy would return to the issues of moral reform of the clergy, and under Calixtus II that is exactly what happened. Within a few months of his election (1119), at the Council of Rheims in his native France, he ruled that married clergy are not only to be expelled from office but are to be excommunicated if they continue to live with their wives:

> We forbid absolutely the cohabitation with
> concubines or wives by priests, deacons,
> and subdeacons. If any of that kind howev-
> er should be found,they are to be deprived
> of their offices and benefits.... Indeed,
> if they will not have corrected their fil-
> thy ways, they should be deprived of Chris-
> tian communion.[116]

The sanction of excommunication was not new; it had been
promulgated as early as 1056 at Toulouse, and had been giv-
en an especially harsh interpretation in 1099 by Archbishop
Manasses of Rheims, when he wrote that married priests who
had been excommunicated must still give up their
wives.[117] The decree at Rheims was significant not because it was original but because it was issued in the presence of a pope who, as soon as he established himself in
Rome, would convoke the First Lateran Council. In a disput-
ed canon of this council it appears that he removed the
harsh penalty from the celibacy decree, but still insisted
that "priests, deacons, subdeacons, and monks are forbidden
utterly to contract matrimony or to have concubines, and
those who have contracted marriage ought to be separated
from any such persons and led back to penitence...."[118]

Although this statement does not appear to invalidate
marriages contracted before a man became ordained, still it
pushed the sense of the legislation in that direction.[119]
It implies that the clergy now had no choice: once a

priest, always a priest. Gone was the option to return to
the lay state, or to accept deposition to minor orders.
Once a man is ordained that ordination takes precedence over any other vow. While the enforcement of celibacy thus
contributed to a new ideal of priesthood, Calixtus and his
colleagues seem not to have asked what that decree said
about the church's doctrine of marriage, itself a sacrament
of the church. As Martin Boelens observes of the trend of
the church's decrees during this time,

> marital intercourse [for priests] was esti-
> mated as unclean, just as extramarital,
> both were punished the same. But that was
> not new, but was rather a heritage from the
> Gregorian reform. As a consequence
> of that prohibition, however, priestly mar-
> riage was also forbidden....[120] [Italics
> mine]

Whatever may have been the case "einschlussweise," the
church appears somewhat ambivalent, legislating more forcefully and backing down, but essentially moving toward the
momentous step of declaring that the sacrament of ordination invalidates the sacrament of marriage. Of the first
Lateran Council's anti-cohabitation decree, Boelens comments:

> This rule of separation was not made good;
> so it remains unclear whether this was only
> a disciplinary decree, in order to guaran-
> tee continence, or whether a principle was
> decided therein, that such marriages must
> be seen as invalid.[121]

In any case, Boelens concludes that by the decisions at Melfi, Troyes, and Rheims, the nullity of priestly marriage was gradually decided.

The scant record of legislation on celibacy during Honorius II's reign (1124-30) provides no new formulations and indeed repeats few of the familiar formulas of the past seventy years. Chiefly concerned with claiming the church's full share of the settlement of the Concordat of Worms, Honorious did little to advance clerical reform. The only known reference to chastity from a council presided over by the pope is the brief canon of 1129, "Concubinae clericorum manifeste ejiciantur."[122] Even Leo IX had gone further than that.

Innocent II, however, resumed the celibacy struggle in his first two councils by reiterating the punishment for those in the subdiaconate and above who take wives, namely, the loss of office and benefice.[123] At the council of Pisa in 1135, however, he issued a very different type of statement. Adding canons regular and monks to the list of subdeacons and above, Innocent decreed that if they marry they must be separated, because

> we sanction that copulation of this kind,
> which was contracted against ecclesiastical

rule, *is* *not* *matrimony*.[124]

[Italics mine]

By this ruling, repeated at the tenth ecumenical council, Lateran II of 1139,[125] the papacy established that the vow of ordination takes precedence over the marriage vow. Sacred orders became what is now known as a diriment impediment to marriage.[126]

One may well ask what influences had convinced Innocent to render void marriages which heretofore had been illicit but valid. One can speculate about the effect of Gerhoh of Reichersberg's letter to Innocent in 1131, concluding that all married and concubinous priests, whether or not they defend their position, are heretics. Gerhoh granted that in most cases an accusation of sin is determined more by intention that act, but with two types of behavior, simony and nicolaitism, the deed itself is sufficient to make it heretical.[127] And one can surmise that when Bernard of Clairvaux joined the pope at the synod of Pisa, in 1135, Innocent received strong prodding on the celibacy issue.

There is no need to speculate about the future of sacerdotal marriage after this legislation. Any hope for the legal recognition of clerical marriage, pressed for so firmly in the 1060's and 1070's, was now lost. The repercussions in the lives of priests were immediate, as we shall see. There could be no question from now on in the minds of a priest or deacon (the subdiaconate remained unclear until 1207) and a woman who were married or who contemplated marriage: they could not have a marriage and their children would be illegitimate. Concubinage and illegitimacy -- and possible persecution and excommunication -- were their only prospects. No doubt the inexorable judgment spelled out in this decree did more than any other legislation to destroy priestly _marriage_; the ways then found by some priests to express their sexuality can be traced in the legislation of the following centuries against clerical concubinage.

In this discussion of the Gregorian movement against the marriages of the ministers of the altar, little mention has been made of the resistance of married clergy to this century-long attack on their ancient customs. The next two chapters will consider in detail their struggle, first through the treatises produced in Italy, France, and Germany, and finally in the Anglo-Norman kingdom.

CHAPTER THREE

THE DEFENSE OF CLERICAL MARRIAGE

Since the apostle permits and indulges others to have wives on account of fornication, why are we, who are made from the
same matter and assume the same sin of the
flesh from Adam's sin, why are we not
permitted by the same indulgence to have
wives, but instead must suffer to send them
away?
                -- A Norman priest, anonymous,
                   c. 1075

We have no knowledge of a literary defense of priestly
marriage between the fifth and eleventh centuries, nothing
after the witness of Vigilantius, Jovinian, and Synesius.
Considering the numerous canonical and narrative references
to married priests during that period, this silence is difficult to understand. Works probably existed, but were destroyed. We have seen that documents supporting clerical
marriage were condemned at the Roman synod of 1079,[1] and
it is not hard to imagine that others were rejected and
have been lost to us. In fact, we shall see that one of
the chief documents defending marriage in the Gregorian per-

105

iod was unknown in its era and came to light only in the 1570's.

The absence of documents for so long a period, however, raises the possibility that there was no need for a written defense of married clergy during this long hiatus. Despite the fact that clerics were forbidden to have sexual relations with their wives, or to marry after ordination to the higher grades, they must not have been effectively punished when they did so. On the contrary, it appears that they were not interfered with and had no necessity to argue for their position. This long silence explains why married clerics, when they at last spoke out, could use as their basic argument the claim that marriage always had been allowed to priests.

Other arguments with which they supported their claim -- that marriage was preferable to concubinage or to other sexual arrangements and that they who lived in public marriage were more honorable than their opponents who practiced vice in secret -- reflected the older view of the priesthood as pastors who worked beside their congregations, not the new definition of the priest as one set aside from and above his parishoners in every way. The supporters of marriage were themslves of two minds, the

earlier spokesmen insisting on full recognition of marriage, the second group asking only for toleration, and for
political reasons.

I.

The Demand for Legal Recognition ot Clerical
Marriage

Around the year 1060, a churchman, indeed a bishop,
broke the long silence and took up his pen to defend the
marriage of priests. In an epistle, hereafter referred to
as the Rescript, addressed to Pope Nicholas II, the Italian bishop Ulric of Imola responded to Nicholas' celibacy
decree of 1059.[2] Arguing that the clergy had always been
permitted marriage and that the pope had no right to forbid
them wives, Ulric urged the pope to use scripture as his
primary authority:

> Can't you see, as the common judgment of all
> sensible people holds, that this is vio-
> lence, when one is compelled to enforce the
> special decrees of an individual against the
> evangelical customs and the dictate of the
> Holy Spirit? Since indeed many examples
> from the old and new testaments are avail-
> able, I entreat holy discretion, that your
> teaching and ours not be burdened with the
> Fathers but rather that a little of their
> doctrine be added from their vast writings.
> The Lord, after all, in the old law institut-
> ed the marriage of priests....[3]

Ulric here introduces several sources returned to often by
his continuators, the long Pauline debate on marriage and
celibacy from the seventh chapter of I Corinthians, the ad-
monition in Timothy 3:2, 12 that bishops and deacons should
marry but one woman in the course of their lives, and Jesus' words about becoming a eunuch in Matthew 19:11-12.
Turning to the canonical tradition, he quotes the sixth apostolic canon, that early injunction to bishops and priests
not to leave their wives.[4]

Ulric is so far on solid ground, but in deploring the
popular assumption that Gregory the Great was the founder
of celibacy, he tells an incredible tale in order to prove
that, in fact, Gregory did not insist on celibacy: after
Gregory had decreed that priests separate from their wives,
the pope was shocked to find in his fishpond the heads of
six thousand babies, so shocked, in fact, that he withdrew
his decree.[5]

Claiming that the pope has far over-stepped his bound
in prohibiting priests to have wives, Ulric insists that
the canons must now make it clear that clerical marriage is
not only tolerated but is legal. Every married cleric who
has not taken the vow of chastity should regularize his marital affairs, and the church must rcognize these unions as

legitimate. Rather than forcing (cogere) celibacy on priests unable or unwilling to carry it out, the pope should instruct (monere) them, guide them gently into the higher discipline of chastity. Angered by the radical step which Nicholas had taken, Ulric saw that prohibiting married priests to hold parishes would create endless confusion in the church. He neither wrote intemperately nor envisaged formal revolt, but gave stern warning that the papacy was pursuing a dangerous course.

Ulric used very few canonical references, but he argued well from scripture and the Fathers. Interpreting the passage on becoming a eunuch for the kingdom (Matthew 19:11-12) as intended for a chosen few, he accused the pope of twisting its meaning in order to apply it to all clergy. Nicholas had said that he who cannot make himself a eunuch for the kingdom of heaven will be excommunicated, whereas Christ had explained that "not all men can receive this precept, but only those to whom it is given." Ulric thus believed that Christ did not make celibacy a requirement for all of his disciples. He reminded Nicholas that Paul, receiving no command from God in favor of virginity (I Corinthians 7: 25-28), had declared that marriage is not a sin, and had only recommended virginity as the better way and, indeed, as his own commitment. I Timothy 3: 1-12 is a crucial text for Ulric, supporting, as it does, marriage for deacons and even for bishops. The picture of clerical life which emerges from this passage would have encouraged any defender of priestly marriage, for Paul describes a cleric who is the husband of one wife, dignified, hospitable, managing his children and his household well. "For," asks Paul, "if a man does not know how to manage his own household, how can he care for God's church?"

Quoting from the Fathers, Ulric ingeniously gathers points for his side from those dedicated celibates Jerome and, as we will see, Augustine. Quoting Jerome, "For what use is a chaste body in a debauched mind ...?" Ulric concludes that when married priests are virtuous and live faithfully with their wives, they are therefore "chaste" in the eyes of the Lord.[6]

Another reason that may have prompted Ulric to speak out was the appearance of Peter Damian's recent broadsides against the married priests, or, as Damian called them, "servi libidinis." In discussing St. Paul's concession, "But because of the temptation to immorality, each man should have his own wife and each woman her own husband" (I Corinthians 7:2) Damian had asserted that it applied only to laity,[7] whereas Ulric, by pointing out that marriage for the laity is _assumed_, claimed that St. Paul must have had the clergy in mind when he made this point, and argued

further that these churchmen commit evils when they

themselves do not marry:

> Those hypocrites lie when they say that
> this [scripture] pertains particularly to
> laity; they who are constituted into the
> highest order allowed anywhere, do not hesi-
> tate to make use of other men's wives (we
> weep to tell it), and rage in unspeakable
> evils.

Ulric may have known that the word laicus had been inser-

ted into I Corinthians 7:2 at the Council of Chelsea in 787

and that this narrow interpretation of St. Paul's verse was

therefore not scriptural. At any rate, Ulric concluded

this warning with a remarkable image:

> These, no doubt, have not rightly under-
> stood scripture, since they have pressed
> its breast so hard that they have drunk
> blood in place of milk.[8]

Differing again from Damian over I Corinthians 7: 25-40,

where Damian had claimed that a man cannot please both God

and a wife, Ulric insisted on the goodness of marriage for

everyone, countering with Augustine's stricture that one

may enjoy worldly goods, but not with pride.[9] Although

interpreting "worldly goods" to include a wife may be a

questionable judgment, nevertheless it allowed him to use

Augustine's text as permission to enjoy the pleasures of

marriage.

Ulric's letter further points to Damian's tracts because of its serious concern about homosexuality among the
clergy. Arguing that when celibacy is imposed priests will
commit sins far worse than fornication, Ulric explained
that since _some_ men _cannot_ live by the council of perfect chastity, they will seek sexual release wherever they
can find it,

> forcing themselves on their fathers' wives,
> not abhorring the embraces of other men or
> even of animals.[10]

Ulric is almost sympathetic to these desperate men,
whom he believes are driven to evil behavior out of a desire to please men by "a false continence." A sample from
Damian's _Liber Gomorrhianus_ expresses his dislike of
homosexuality:

> Oh unheard-of-evil! Oh deed to be lamented
> by a fountain of tears! If those who con-
> sent to doing [lesser evils] are to be pun-
> ished by death, what else could have been
> thought a worthy punishment for those who
> commit with their spiritual sons this ex-
> treme evil except to be punished by damna-
> tion?[11]

But these two authors drew opposite conclusions from the
threat of homosexuality among the clergy. Whereas Damian
blamed homosexuality on the general lasciviousness of immoral clergy and sought the remedy in closer discipline and
control of priests, Ulric believed that homosexuality was

encouraged by enforced celibacy. He and many of those who defended marriage for the priesthood advocated marriage as a preventive against what they considered unnatural vice.

Whatever agreement these defenders and opponents of clerical marriage may have found in attacking homosexuality among the clergy, their views do not reflect the _actions_ of the Gregorian church towards homosexuals. The church in the century 1050-1150 created no legislation against gay clergy. Indeed, it has been argued that this was a period in which homosexuality flourished amongst clerics, especially in monasteries, and that since monks gained the ascendency in the church at this time, the legislative centers of the church had little choice but to go light on the question of men who loved men. John Boswell claims that St. Anselm and several of his pupils, Pope Alexander II and Archbishop Lanfranc, Archbishop Ralph of Tours and his beloved "Flora", Bishop John of Orléans, Bishop William Longchamp of Ely, and most notably Ailred of Rievaulx and his Simon all represent influential churchmen whose actions and/or writings helped make this century notable for clerical homosexuality. Boswell goes so far as to claim that

> there was more than a coincidental relation
> between gay sexuality and some of the [celi-
> bacy] reforms. Contemporaries, at least,
> were quick to note that gay priests would
> be more willing than heterosexual ones to

enforce prohibitions against clerical marriage. A satire against a reforming bishop
specifically accuses him of hostility to
clerical marriage because of his own homosexual disposition:

> The man who occupies this (episco-
>   pal) seat is Ganymedier than
>   Ganymede.
> Consider why he excludes the mar-
>   ried from the clergy.
> He does not care for the pleas-
>   ures of a wife.

There is some evidence of a power struggle between gay and
married clergy over whose predilections would be stigma-
tized.[12] Indeed, we will see that several married clerical authors will express themselves vehemently on just that
point.

Ulric closes by recounting the story of Pafnutius' vic-
tory for clerical marriage at Nicaea, based on Sozomen's account, thus introducing into the debate another text which
will be cited by many authors.[13] The bishops at Nicaea,
influenced by the growing ascetic movement in the church
and particularly by Bishop Ossius from Cordoba, had debated
making into law the proposition that clergy of the subdiaconate and above might not sleep with their wives. To this
the Egyptian martyr Pafnutius replied that marriage was an
honorable state, that cohabiting with one's wife was
chaste, and that furthermore, to forbid marriage would en-

courage fornication. The council, swayed by his speech, left the matter of celibacy to each cleric's decision.

Fliche, the scholar who identified Bishop Ulric, criticizes the Rescript's arguments, claiming that Ulric has merely played with the texts and that he does not come up with any new ideas. Surely it was not Ulric's intention to be original, for, like most medieval writers, he wanted to convince by quoting from tradition. Fliche's attitude reveals his own bias: he assumes that the tradition of the early church merely tolerated married clergy and therefore he judges all defenders of clerical marriage as going against tradition. But I would argue that toleration of clerical marriage implies its existence, whereas the many canons and decrees about celibacy express only the clerical ideal. The question raised by the Gregorian enforcement is why the papacy at this time began to insist that the ideal become the norm, that what had been the accomplishment of a spiritual elite must now become the way of life for all who had a religious calling.

Ulric's epistle had no known effect on papal policy in the 1060's. By 1079, however, it was deemed important enough by the Gregorians to be condemned at a Roman synod,[14] its arguments having reappeared in the protestations of some German clergy,[15] in letters written by clerics in the archdioceses of Rheims, and in two versions of the _Rescript_ written in Normandy. By 1079, however, its authorship already was obscured: the Gregorians, attempting, I assume, to distance it in both space and time, ascribed it to a German, Ulrich of Augsburg, the tenth-century bishop, despite the fact that this Ulrich had been the first recipient of papal canonization.[16]

Regardless of the _Rescript's_ fate at the hands of Gregory VII, its ideas had already become part of the defense of clerical marriage. Fliche has traced the influence of the _Rescript_ to Normandy, whence it was taken by a northern Italian cleric who wrote a new version of it, the _Tractatus_ _pro_ _clericorum_ _connubio_, around 1065. The author's Italian origin is indicated by his discussion of the Milanese Patarenes, whose attack on married priests was part of a working-class rebellion against imperial control of church and city. His Norman residence is suggested by his familiarity with the canons of the Council of Lisieux of 1064.[17]

The author of the _Tractatus_ utilized most of Ulric's arguments, stating that sacerdotal marriage had always been permitted, that it is a remedy for fornication, and that because marriage is good, it should be allowed to all churchmen who have not taken a vow of chastity. Mentioning Pafnutius, he agreed with Ulric that the witness of the early church was favorable to priestly marriage and that the Gregorians' decrees went directly against tradition.

In regard to canonical sources, however, this author goes well beyond Ulric. The _Tractatus_' conciliar references added greatly to the _Rescript_'s, arguing chiefly fron Ancyra in 314 that marriage was permitted to clergy who had not taken a vow of continence and observing that such marriages had remained legal up to the author's time.[18]

He is mainly concerned, however, with contemporary legislation enacted against married clergy. The Council of Lisieux in 1064, while prohibiting all future clerical unions, allowed churchmen married before 1063 to keep their wives and to consider themselves legitimately wed. The council excluded only one group from this remarkably lenient compromise, namely cathedral canons, whom it singled out again in ruling specifically that they could not keep _mulieres subintroductae_ in their homes. The author of the _Tractatus_ explained that, in the first place the term _mulier subintroducta_ does not apply to the _uxor_ of a cleric, for the one woman of a cleric is a legitimate wife. He was particularly exercised over the attack on canons, showing that the Nicaean ruling on _mulier subintroducta_ applied to <u>all</u> clergy, and then insisting that all men in clerical orders have the right to take one woman in marriage anyway. Did not the councils of Carthage, Toledo, and Chalcedon and the decrees of popes Siricius, Leo I, and Gregory I permit this? Did not Augustine declare that marriage is good, and that there are not two evils, marriage and fornication, but rather two goods, marriage and continence?[19] He declares that the decision at Lisieux to separate henceforth all clerical couples was done "through the iniquity of hypocrites" and was the work of "authors of novel dogma."[20]

He goes beyond Ulric's basic argument by adding the crucial issue of married priests' sacraments, quoting the council of Gangra's decree of c. 345 that all should participate in the masses of married priests and Nicholas I's reminder that since Christ did not remove Judas from among the disciples, therefore, we should not reject the services of an unchaste priest.[21] Not only does the argument go substantially beyond Ulric's but also the tone has lost is conciliatory air. Calling the papal party adulterers and demolishers of the canons, disturbers of the peace, and authors of new dogma, this author gives the defense of clerical marriage a bolder tone. He also gives it what neither the married churchmen at Pavia in 1022, nor those who debated with Damian at Lodi, nor Ulric himself had been able to provide, namely, numerous proofs from conciliar texts.

After the _Tractatus_ was written[22] there does not seem to have been further use of the _Rescript_ material in Normandy until a second version, _A Treatise on Grace,_ appeared around 1075. Judging from its strident tone, it may well be the first of several treatises to be considered here that was written against Gregory's reissuance of rigorous celibacy legislation at the Roman synod of 1074.[23] It insisted as firmly as the other works that the church needed to declare clerical marriage fully legal, but it used new and better arguments. One, based on the way in which free will depends on grace, uses terminology from Anselm's _De concordia III: de gratia et libero arbitrio._[24] The author argues that celibacy is a gift of grace, incapable of being practiced without divine aid, no matter how much a priest may will to do so. The pope is therefore wrong and is in fact contravening nature when he tries to enforce celibacy on the clergy:

> Since therefore the good of continence, indeed every good, is the gift of divine grace alone, capable of being embraced neither through mandate, nor through one's own free will, they not only err but indeed they labor in vain, who attempt to force chastity on these men.[25]

Comparing Simon of Cyrene carrying Christ's cross to the
priest who bears the "cross" of celibacy, he describes the
suffering caused when those in authority impose this impossible command on men who have no love for the continent
life, on men who may commit worse sins if they are denied
wives.[26] Like our other authors, he worries about those
who undertake celibacy without the strength to carry it
out. He claims that clerics are forced to commit not only
fornication and sodomy but even the abomination of incest,
and fears that these sins are scandalizing the church.[27]
The example of Lot, who wanted to stay in the valley (equated with matrimony) but was forced by an over-zealous angel
to the mountain heights (symbolizing celibacy) where,
pushed beyond endurance, he committed incest, illustrates
the author's point particularly well.[28]

Arguing that marriage is good, just as virginity is,
the author uses Atto of Vercelli's statement, based on
Augustine,[29] that marriage is pure and holy, provided it
is undertaken in order to have children. However, his argument diverges from Atto's at several points. Agreeing that
continence is the better way, he yet insists this is so only for those who have the gift of grace to endure it.
Whereas Atto spoke of marriage as less pernicious than incontinence, our author, emphasizing many positive state-

ments of Paul, insists that marriage needs no apology. He appeals specifically to I Corinthians 7: 26-28a --

> I think that in view of the impending dis-
> tress it is well for a person to remain as
> he is. Are you bound to a wife? Do not
> seek to be free. Are you free from a wife?
> Do not seek marriage. But if you marry
> you do not sin, and if a girl (virgo) mar-
> ries, she does not sin --

using this passage to support the continuation of clerical marriage, even though Atto had interpreted the same passage to reach the conclusion that clergy should be celibate. Here the two authors have given us a clear example of special pleading in biblical interpretation, the Norman author seeming to have the better of the argument.

A new theme which runs throughout this recasting of familiar arguments is the similarity of laity and clergy in terms of their physical natures. This idea, antithetical to the papal program, is examined by the author from several perspectives. Commenting on I Corinthians 7:28, he states that priests have the same sexual needs as other men and asks:

> Since the apostle permits and indulges oth-
> ers to have wives on account of fornica-
> tion, why are we, who are made from the
> same matter and assume the sin of the flesh
> from Adam's sin, why are we not permitted
> by the same indulgences to have wives, but
> instead must suffer to send them away?[30]

Believing that Paul gave the same counsel to both the laity and the clergy, including permission to marry, our author argued from this that priests should be required to observe only the periods of continence required of laymen and no more. In declaring that all Christians should abstain from marital embraces on Sundays and solemn vigils, he appeals to the customs of the Greek church, where, after all, St. Paul preached and gave instruction.[31]

Attacking the papal reformers, the author accuses them of demanding that other men live up to standards they themselves do not attain.[32] What is more, these prelates are not primarily concerned with moral reform, as they claim, but with asserting authority,[33] caring more about wielding power over (praeesse) than serving (prodesse). In short, the papal party attempts to force men to give up their wives in order to gain greater control over their lives.

The Gregorian prelates also are putting themselves above their brothers, increasing the hierarchical power of the papal group. Opposing concepts of the church begin to emerge from this tractate's criticisms of the papacy; the author wants leaders who set a moral example themselves and are merciful towards others' failures, who see all priests as equal (pares), whereas he observes the Gregorians to be obsessed with asserting superiority and with compelling obedience. The tone here is sharper and angrier than in Ulric's _Rescript_; in fifteen years the defenders of clerical marriage, hard pressed by the conciliar decrees, have become more aggressive in attacking the papacy.

At the close of the treatise the tone also becomes personal. The author, declaring that he cannot be chaste because he falls away, a fragile, all-too-human man, alternately chastizes the papacy and implores it to lighten the priesthood's burden, particularly the requirement of saying daily mass.[34]

Calling on the witness of Pafnutius and of Dionysius the Areopagite, who had written that compulsory celibacy should not be imposed on those unable to carry it out,[35] the author asks the papacy to pray with and for married priests. One cannot avoid hearing the urgent and heartfelt quality in this request.

In the importance it gives to the doctrine of grace and in its introduction of the _praeesse_--_prodesse_ argument, this second Norman version anticipates the third and final continuation of Ulric's epistle, the treatise of the Anonymous of Rouen, to be discussed in the next chapter. Meanwhile, a group of married clergy of Cambrai, alarmed by the local pressures against them, used some of the material

from Ulric's <u>Rescript</u> and its continuations in a letter
circulated to their brothers of the archdiocese of Rheims
in 1078, attempting to arouse them to the threat to their
treasured customs.[36] Pafnutius again appeared prominent-
ly, and citations from Augustine and St. Isidore, as well
as an anxious reference to the Patarenes, indicate the epistle's relationship to the <u>Tractatus</u>, as its editor Heinrich Böhmer pointed out. Since, as I have observed, one
passage shows familiarity also with the letter of Dionysius
the Areopagite to which the <u>Treatise</u> <u>on</u> <u>Grace</u> referred,[37] I believe that the authors may have had both
Norman works before them. The churchmen of Cambrai
described their injuries in a manner that becomes all too
familiar in reports such as theirs. The laity no longer
respect them or their sacraments, indeed they hold the
entire catholic religion to be nothing, their enemies (the
Patarenes) detest marriage and its fruits and, in short,
they have been severely injured by the Roman celibacy
legislation of 1074.[38] The prohibition against ordaining
priests' sons seems especially to offend them, and, in
language that exactly follows the 1074 decrees, they blame
their bishop Gerald II (1076-92) for slavishly introducing
this intolerable legislation.[39] The clergy of Cambrai

close with a call to their brothers to act like men and to
resist the calumnious attack on their honored customs.

After receiving this short but strongly-worded statement a group of priests in Noyon composed one of the clever-
est arguments in the polemical literature. Especially outraged over the recent legislation against priests' sons,
they utilized the Council of Ancyra's ruling that deacons
can marry, in order to claim that clerical marriage is legal _and_ _its_ _offspring_ _legitimate_. But even those
clerics who are concubinous rather than married can expect
full acceptance of their children into the church, for a
son does not bear the iniquity of his father (Ezekiel
18:20). In an impertinent use of scripture they ask, did
not our Saviour Jesus himself choose to be born of a line
marked by adulteries? Did not he descend from Judah's issue, born of his concubine Tamar?[40]

Another immediate reaction to the Roman synod of 1074
was the sharp debate between the Gregorian apologist Bernold of Constance and a priest named Alboin.[41] The six
letters they exchanged indicate how tenaciously the publi-
cists fought over the interpretation of historical records,
how each side bent the evidence of tradition to fit its
cause.

Alboin and Bernold debated the validity of Sozomen's report of Pafanutius' actions at the Council of Nicaea. Although heretofore the references to Pafnutius, all made by writers favoring clerical marriage, have been to Cassiodorus' Latin version of the story, now for the first time Alboin argues for the authenticity of the story because the Greek historian Sozomen wrote it, and it was later translated. One might assume that Bernold would be hard-pressed to deny this statement, but he counters, with more opinion than evidence, by insisting that since neither the martyr Pafnutius nor the good Latin father Cassiodorus could have erred, the Greek Sozomen must have fabricated the story.[42] The need at this time to refute certain arguments at their Greek source was pressing, as the imperialists quoted Cassiodorus both to defend clerical marriage and to prove that the emperor had the right to appoint bishops.[43] Bernold's anti-Greek bias no doubt also fitted into the pattern of hostility towards the Greek church prevalent in Rome at that time.

Alboin claimed that Nicaea's refusal to condemn clerical marriage indicated that the fathers had accepted this institution. Bernold, on the other hand, could not believe that the council, much less Pafnutius himself, could have approved such a damnable doctrine. Concluding that Sozomen must have reported the story falsely, he rails at the present-day _Sozomenistae_ who mislead simple clergy into thinking they are permitted to marry. This debate may have precipitated the condemnation of Sozomen's account by the Roman synod of 1079. At any rate, that the condemnation was necessary is evidence of the popularity of the story about Pafnutius. Alboin also introduced a piece of evidence not mentioned elsewhere in the polemics, the assertion that Gregory I had permitted Sicilian subdeacons to marry, but it appears that Alboin was mistaken in this matter,[44] that he attempted to argue a general point from an isolated case. In the end Bernold, denying every point that Alboin raised, was not convinced that Sozomen's account was acceptable evidence. His manner indicates that his mind was made up at the beginning, as if he already had decided that Sozomen's account must be condemned. And indeed, when Bernold reported its condemnation four years later at Rome, he gave no reasons for its rejection.

As an interpretation of historical sources Alboin's defense of Sozomen's account stands up. He reminds Bernold that Sozomen has not been attacked before and implies that Bernold is pleading a special case in attacking him now. But Bernold sweeps in with the last word on the question of sources, claiming that since the story of Pafnutius is not

canonical but merely historical, it does not command our
obedience at any rate.   There could scarcely be a more em-
phatic endorsement of the Gregorian emphasis on the power
of canons.

But Alboin pushes his defense of clerical marriage beyond this debate over sources.   He maintains that heretofore the church has allowed priestly marriage to exist:
while it has not approved it, it has not condemned it.   But
now the Gregorians, in the decrees of 1074, condemn it,
overriding by their new innovations the traditional law of
the church.[45]   Furthermore, if penance is now demanded,
where is it to come from?   Jesus had welcomed sinners, but
the Gregorian party shows no mercy.   In a question that
foreshadows the coming irrevocable judgment against married
priests, Alboin asks

> But you, I believe, oppose that they should
> be penitent.   But I ask where you get off
> believing that you should kill their im-
> pulse to remorse.?[46]

By way of illustration, Alboin reminds his correspondent
that Jesus singled out Zacchaeus, although he was a rich
and hated tax collector, to be his host in Jericho, and
when Zacchaeus announced that he would share his wealth
with the poor, Jesus rejoiced, saying that he had come to
save the lost (Luke 19: 1-10).   Having made the point that

Jesus sought out and forgave sinners, Alboin lists others
who have shown sinners mercy and understanding -- Siricius,
Pafnutius, Gregory the Great, Paul -- and repeats that the
present pope violates the tradition of the church by subjecting priests to lay persecution.

As more letters are exchanged and the argument heats
up, Alboin moves the attack onto personal grounds. Accusing Bernold of being the son of a priest, Alboin asks

> Are you not ashamed to lay bare the shames
> of father Noah? Since it is certain that
> you yourself are involved in the sin of
> your father, do you wish to damn this sin
> in others?[47]

Charging that Bernold is like Ham, who uncovered his father
Noah's nakedness and was cursed, Alboin asks if Bernold is
wise to attack other clerics for fathering children when
his own father had done so. The thrust of Alboin's argument is that for clergy the act of fathering a child is not
a sin, not, that is, until the Gregorians legislate that it
is, and expose (denudare) the sin (pudibunda) by their
harsh disciplines. Furthermore, the Gregorians do not real-
ize the difficulty of renouncing a good which one has, of
sending away one's wife and children.

Bernold does not deny that he is the son of a priest,
but he explains that when these fathers and sons are peni-
tent it is heresy to deny them acceptance and forgiveness.

Just as it was heretical for the third century schismatic
Novatian to disapprove of concessions to those who had compromised with paganism, so Bernold claims that it is not
Christian to refuse to accept the penance of unchaste
priests.[48] By using the very argument of the opposition,
namely that the unchaste should be forgiven, but drawing an
opposite conclusion, that one must stop sinning, repent,
and accept the law of celibacy, Bernold shows how deep was
the division on this issue within the clergy. He broke
with the old pattern, and by doing so, he rose to become a
major Gregorian apologist. Since his father did penance
and he himself was baptized, therefore he lives in full communion with the chruch.

A particularly painful argument between the two corres-
pondents developed over Gregory VII's use of the laity to
attack married priests. Bernold defended Gregory's radical
measure, insisting that Rome had been forced to call on the
laity. Had not those priests who believe in marriage, the
sect of Sozomenistae, corrupted both the laity and fellow
priests?[49] To which Alboin replied that Gregory himself
is the violator of law, that by subjecting priests to the
disdain of and persecution by laity and to non-canonical removal from office, Gregory goes against the decrees of many
previous popes who had protected the priesthood from lay

abuse. Alboin argues that, anyway, penance comes from the heart -- God puts it there! Penance and other virtues cannot be legislated. And since perfection is not possible, the church would do well to settle for a lesser evil. This persecution of priests is thus both inhumane and unconstitutional, and the papacy would do well to emulate the mildness of other reforming popes, such as Siricius and Gregory the Great.

Alboin's final answer, written in 1076, is brief: he offers no more arguments and urges that they become friends again. He appears not to have changed his mind but to have found it expedient to drop his defense. Had he been intimidated by Bernold's approval of the use of force? Had the pressures against married priests in his diocese become heavier? We have seen that the period of the mid-1070s was the turning point in papal efforts to enforce celibacy; in these letters, so richly reflecting the varied intellectual currents of the times, we find an example of how that enforcement affected one priest. And we find an illuminating definition of what the Gregorians held to be canonical: namely, what agrees with the papal position.

The Roman celibacy decree of 1074 evoked violent response in many parts of the chuch. For example, when it was read at the Synod of Paris in that same year it was

overwhelmingly rejected by the delegates as being an insupportable law. When the ascetic abbot of Pontoise, Gautier,
objected that the pope's demands must be accepted, whether
right or wrong, he was attacked by the delegates at the Synod, maltreated, and turned over to the king to be imprisoned.[50]

The initial reaction in Germany was equally violent.
As we have seen, the case of Archbishop Siegfried of Mainz
stands as typical of the uproar being caused all over Europe by Gregory's insistence on _immediate_ _enforcement_ of
the long-standing celibacy decrees. Siegfried might have
remained loyal to Gregory if the pope had compromised on
the celibacy issue, but, caught between a pope who would
not give an inch and clergy who had tried to assassinate
him, Siegfried gave in to this and other political issues
and joined the imperial party. That was by no means the
end of trouble in the archdiocese of Mainz. When in 1077
the rival emperor Rudolph of Swabia arrived there, he
showed his adherence to the reforms of Gregory (to whom he
owed his election) by refusing the ministrations of a simoniacal deacon at his coronation. The clergy and people, re-
jecting both Rudolph's politics and his piety, rioted
against him and drove him out of the city.[51]

A final example of violent reaction should suffice to prove the widespread outrage and fear which greeted Gregory's crusade of purification. In 1077 in Cambrai a man named Ramihrd insisted that the masses of married or simoniacal priests be shunned. He was condemned as a heretic and burned -- and for asserting no more than the papacy had declared canonical for almost twenty years![52] Clearly the anger of married priests and their supporters ran very deep, many believing firmly in the rightness, indeed, the legality of their mariages.

Married priests were forced to defend not only the custom of marriage but also the legitimacy of their children. The promulgation, therefore, of the decree against the ordination of priests' sons at the Synod of Poitiers in 1078 and again at Clermont in 1095 provoked angry responses and a number of polemical writings in their defense. In addition to the letters from Cambrai and Noyon discussed above and the essay by the Norman Anonymous, two other noteworthy pieces of literature dedicated to the subject were written in Normandy around 1100, the earlier being the _Defensio pro filiis presbyterorum_, a verse composition by Serlo of Bayeux.[53] Serlo, the son of a priest and himself a canon of Bayeux, was discharged from the benefice he had inherited from his father when

Bayeux was conquered by Henry I in 1105. Serlo sees the
attack on priests' sons as an innovation and a damnable one
at that.   The essence of his argument is that, because
baptism cleanses from original sin, all baptized persons
are equally holy, no matter who their parents were, and
that the papacy, therefore, insults the power of the
sacrament by calling baptized priests' sons unclean.[54]

In his anger against the Gregorian party Serlo did not
shrink from accusimg them of homosexuality, complaining
that they commit this sin in secret while persecuting men
who, although born illegitimate, lead good lives:

Now men who live the shameful, obscene
lives of sodomites,

And who perform these evils furtively, rant
at us in opprobrium,

And despise those illegitimately born,

Even though we have good morals;

The law oppresses these good men but
supports those inclined to evil.

Why should a man bring shame upon those
whom the supreme king honors?

Therefore why should such men deprive, by
rule of law, the illegitimately born, when
they lead good lives?

Yet you persist in troubling yourself to
attend to the law,

You who enact new laws and prepare harsh
statutes;

And thus you wound us;

But first destroy the evil which damages
more gravely and retreats further from the
law!

Why do you avoid pressing a serious
penality on the sodomites?

Their kind of sickness, which might cause a
grievous end to the human race,

Ought by right to be rooted out first.[55]

Again, like The Treatise on Grace, Serlo offers a
contrasting ideal of the church. With a passion reminis-
cent of Alboin, Serlo condemns the inhumane legalism of the
Gregorian party, and what he sees as its obsessive commit-
tment to controlling the church through the law. Opposing
this narrow practice with the virtues of moral life, openly
led, he then offers his strongest argument, the cleansing
power of baptism, thereby introducing into this debate the
conflict between sacrament (power of the spirit) and the
law (power of papal, man-made decree).

But Serlo's deepest hostility is toward the hypocrisy
of men who practice sex secretly and non-procreatively, the
sodomites. An anonymous poem expressing similar feelings
uses language remarkably like Serlo's:

"Married Clergy"

We married clergy were born to be made fun of,
To be ridiculed, to be criticized by everyone.
If a guiltless man points out the crimes of others,
Those censured can bear the rebuke with patience;

But I bear with ill will the rods wielded by the
    debauched
Who vilify us while failing to cleanse their own
    contamination.
(But) you who attack our sins, have a look at your own.
Leave us alone and chastise yourself, sodomite!
You draw up harsh laws, enact bitter statutes,
And make things generally impossible for us.
You deny that it is right to touch a woman's bed
And to consummate the marriage rite in the bridal
    chamber.
But it is the natural right of a man to enjoy his wife.
This is how we were all born, how we multiply,
How each generation follows the preceding one.
Thus survives the human race in its quest for
    perpetuity.
This response rightly takes account of the laws of
    nature:
If no one propagated, if no man procreated,
Everything would come to an end; the world would be
    finished.
Coitus precedes birth, as the pregnant woman the child
    she bears.
No woman would conceive if no man impregnated.
In my judgment the correct opinion
Holds the natural sin of the (bridal) bed
To be more venial than that contrary to nature.
I applaud what prostitutes do when it leads to birth,
And whatever nourishes the fruit born of its seed.
Let that seed be damned from which no offspring will
    follow,
Which flows vainly and produces nothing useful.
Vilely and dangerously you sin and plot to destroy
In vain what, rightly expended, would produce life.
Do not waste the material for creating offspring.
A half man, a debauchee, you steal the prostitute's
    joys:
Truly, I say, you have the makings of a murderer.
No dumb animal is drawn to this evil;
No creature's lust is accustomed to abusing its like.
The doe submits to the stag; subdued, the she-goat weds
    the ram;
The bear lies down with the mate appropriate to it.
The rest of the animals mate according to nature's law,
(But) you are driven by a lust which all of nature
    abhors.[56]

Perceiving that monks, who are fast gaining control over the church, are the ultimate enemy of the secular married clergy, Serlo asks if putting on a monk's robe counts more towards sanctity than being baptized.[57]

In arguing for the sanctity of baptism Serlo uses a key argument of the later polemical materials, where we find it maintained that the power of the grace conferred by baptism supercedes that of ordination or all other sacraments, as well as the power of law.

Concluding that sons are not responsible for the sins of their fathers, Serlo pleads that the church should begin fighting the great scandals of the time -- immorality and simony -- and leave priests' sons alone. Don't bring in damnable innovations; the old customs are good ones.

The other Norman spokesman for priests' sons, Theobald of Étampes, a secular clerk who had studied as an outsider in the Abbaye-aux-Hommes at Caen, remained a lifelong partisan of the secular clergy against monks, writing c. 1130 an attack on monks who claimed the right to a parish ministry. Theobald was the son of a priest, as were both his master and the abbot at Caen, Arnoul and William Bona Anima. Both of these men suffered under the attacks on priests' sons -- William was at first excommunicated by the papacy as archbishop of Rouen on grounds of illegitimacy,

and Arnoul was for a while denied the patriarchate of Jerusalem on the same grounds. Although Theobald seems to have
escaped penalty himself (perhaps because he did not seek
the episcopal grade) he may well have wanted to defend his
superiors. He wrote two letters to friends, Roscelin and
Philippe, defending the marriage of secular priests,[58]
the earlier epistle to Roscelin being more pertinent to us
because it discusses priests' sons as well as clerical marriage. Theobald, who shared with Serlo the championing of
seculars against regulars and the belief that the efficacy
of baptism overcame all spiritual blemishes, was inspired
by Serlo's Defensio pro filiis presbyterorum, whose
argument about baptism he uses, and by the letter of the
priests of Noyon who had defended men of illegitimate
birth. The epistle to Roscelin, written after Theobald
moved to Oxford (1100) to be a master of theology and liber-
al arts in the new school there, mentions the celibacy legislation decreed by Calixtus II at Rheims in 1119.

Theobald, defending priests who had lapsed from their
vow of celibacy, declared that they should be reinstated
and that their sons should be permitted full rights in the
church, including the privileges of ordination and promotion. If the son of a priest lives honestly, he should be
ordained, whereas if the son of a knight leads an evil

life, he should not be, for do not the sacraments regener-
ate a man "in the uterus of the church?"[59] Using an illustration from the Noyon epistola, he declared that the
sins of the fathers are not to be visited upon the sons,
and reminds his correspondent that Christ himself was de-
scended from the sinner Tamar.[60] Finally, Theobald
claims, as had Serlo, that the church should proclaim the
efficacy of baptism and not the celibacy law, to which he
adds that his policies are based on the liberating power of
grace rather than the bondage of the law.[61] With these
statements, the two Norman churchmen have added to the
claims of married priests a new theological dimension, an
element which had taken second place to the political in
some of the literature.

But despite Theobald's and Serlo's hostility towards
monks, the fact remains that a segment of the defenders of
clerical marriage was monastic. The motivation of this
group was political, as can be seen in the polemics ham-
mered out in 1111 by the monks of Lorsch. The poem Carmen
Laureshamense, written in celebration of Henry V's return
to Germany, is mainly a quarrel of imperialist monks of the
old school with their brethren who follow the new, Gregorian ways.[62] Basing part of their attack on the way the
Gregorians stir up the people against married priests, they

criticize the Roman party for forcing celibacy on honest, unwilling clerics. The monks argue that God himself has established marriage from the creation of the world, so that the human race will increase, and has declared the marital union to be indissoluble. No special argument is made for priestly marriage; the strength of the _Carmen_'s position is that it assumes that priests come under the general biblical sanction of marriage.

II.

The   Demand   for   Toleration   of   Clerical   Marriage

From the early 1070's two factors served to polarize the struggle over marriage: Gregory's unrelenting attack on married clergy and the heightened tensions between papacy and empire. The issues of celibacy and of control of ultimate political power in Europe became intertwined and in some cases confused; the wives and children of priests were made pawns in the struggle for political hegemony. Up to this time all the writers defending marriage had believed it was the traditional right of clergy, and had insisted on _legal_ recognition. But now the polarization produced two new types of argument among the defenders of clerical marriage. Neither type approved of marriage for priests but each, for different reasons, joined forces with the married clerics. Yet the hope of legal recognition of marriage did not die among married clergy, and in fact a well-argued defense for *nuptiae* was written in Normandy as late as c. 1120. But after 1075 most of the literature argues for clerical marriage merely as a lesser evil.

The first group of polemicists might be called moderate counter-revolutionaries, law and order types, who preferred clerical marriage to the ecclesiastical revolution breaking around their heads; the second were the imperialists who put together a coalition of Gregory VII's enemies.

The most significant spokesman for the former group was the monk Sigebert of Gembloux.[63] Much read and often quoted, his *Apologia* had an immediate effect on the ecclesiastical politics of his day. Well known as an historian,[64] Sigebert focussed his attention on changing conditions in both the churches and society. When in 1074 Gregory VII had reissued the decree to the laity, Sigebert, observing that the papal party's action destroyed not only clerical marriage but also the traditional structures of local churches, was moved to speak out against it. Although he agreed with the pope that ministers of the altar

should be celibate, he feared the dissension which the enforcement of celibacy had unleashed.[65]

What Sigebert observed first of all was the confusion
among the laity over the validity of the contested sacraments. He writes with feeling of the children denied baptism, the adults deprived of confession and absolution. He
says sorrowfully that the church had been on the path of
separating superstition from religion, that traditionally
it had replaced vice by virtue, but that now the new "reforms" have replaced one vice with another.

Worse than the confusion of some laity was the hostility of others. Sigebert reports that the common people,
all too ready to heap abuses on the clergy, acted with un-
controlled fury now that they were enjoined to do so. Married priests were ridiculed in public, beaten, deprived of
their livings. While some fled, becoming destitute paupers, unable to face the people among whom they had once
lived in honor, others attempted to stand their ground and
met a worse fate, their bodies mutilated, their only vindication their fists.[66]

Sigebert's account, with its references to castration,
beatings, and impoverishment, might be suspected of exagger-
ation if we had no other reports of harsh treatment. In

England at about the same time St. Wulfstan, bishop of Worcester, showed no mercy to wedded clergy:

> The sin of incontinence he abhorred, and ap-
> proved continence in all men, especially in
> clerks in holy orders.   If he found one
> wholly given to chastity he took him to him-
> self and loved him as a son.   Wedded
> priests he brought under one edict, command-
> ing them to renounce their fleshly desires
> or their churches.   If they loved chastity,
> they might remain and be welcome: if they
> were the servants of bodily pleasures, they
> must go forth in disgrace.   Some there were
> who chose rather to go without their chur-
> ches than their women: and of these some
> wandered about till they starved: others
> sought and at last found some other provi-
> sion....   The Bishop, to avoid future scan-
> dal, would not thereafter ordain to the
> priesthood any who were not sworn to celiba-
> cy.[67]

A further example of hostile anti-clericalism was inspired

by the ex-monk Henry of Lausanne, in Le Mans in 1116, who

> began to preach against the local clergy.
> He found willing listeners.   The people of
> Le Mans were very ready to turn against
> their clergy, for these were a venal and
> loose-living lot ... and the bishops ...
> had lent their support to the counts, from
> whose overlordship the burghers were strug-
> gling to free themselves ... after a short
> course of Henry's preaching the populace
> was beating priests in the streets and rol-
> ling them in the mud.[67a]

But Sigebert's concern over the laity who attack their

priests was less than his worry that laity were taking ec-

clesiastical matters into their own hands:

> For the women workers in the weaving mills
> and the artisans in their workshops create
> by their debate nothing else than the con-
> fusing of the duties of all human society,
> the shattering of the standards for Chris-
> tian sanctity, the lowering of peoples'
> status, the dishonoring of chuch customs by
> irreligious folly, ... [and enable] the ar-
> rogant license to more shameful malice and
> dogma contrary to the Christian religion to
> be introduced.[68]

Recording even more hostile behavior in his _Chronica_ for
1074 Sigebert lamented that laity baptized their own children, used the wax from their ears (_sordido humore aur-
ium_) for chrism, trampled underfoot the wafers consecrated
by married priests, and burned the tithes set aside for the
latter.[69] Sigebert complained that many _pseudomagistri_
rose in the church, and that little heads (_capitula_) attempted to administer its affairs.

But what disturbed the historian most deeply was the
way the papal reforms abetted a growing restlessness among
the people toward both their feudal lords and feudal
church. Sigebert was shocked that

> ... new treacheries of servants against mas-
> ters [were being plotted, as well as] suspi-
> cions of masters against serfs, unfaithful
> treacheries of friends, crafty machinations
> against the power ordained by God, friend-
> ship betrayed....[70]

Again one might suspect Sigebert of undue alarm if it
were not for a similar warning from a member of the papal

party. Peter Damian also was dismayed at what he consid-

ered the arrogant assumptions of common people:

> It comes about this way in our times, that
> peasants and every kind of fool, those who
> knew almost nothing, except how to plough
> fields with ploughshares and to keep pigs
> and various kinds of livestock, now stand-
> ing at the corners and crossroads with the
> young women and their boyfriends (combubul-
> cos) do not blush to dispute sacred Scrip-
> ture: and indeed, what is shameful to say,
> they who in the night are lustful between
> women's thighs, do not fear by day to dis-
> cuss the sermons of angels, and in this way
> they decide what holy doctrine is to be.[71]

As if it were not bad enough that common laity were debat-

ing sacred doctrine, they insisted on combining sex with

theologizing. Damian could not allow even laity to involve

themselves in holy matters without insisting that they be

chaste.

It is now clear that the social unrest of which Sige-

bert and Damian wrote was the early phase of a widespread

urban revolt which rocked western Europen in the late elev-

enth and twelfth centuries. A well-documented movement of

peasants into cities occurred, causing these to grow

rapidly, especially in Flanders and north-central Italy,

precisely in Sigebert's and Damian's areas. The uprooted

rural folk formed a restless urban proletariat, cut off

as they were from their traditional village life and in

many cases suffering unemployment and poverty as well as social dislocation in their new setting. That the church was not prepared to minister to these swelling groups of city-dwellers is indicated by the accusation of the heretical reformer Tanchelm (c. 1130) that the city of Antwerp had only one parish priest, who was living in open concubinage.[72]

The new urban populations responded to these problems by joining two movements which arose simultaneously, eventually conflicting with each other but at first mutually energizing. Ascetic idealism and economic utopianism combined to form one movement, whose dynamism came from the church. The desire that property should be held in common, expressed by Damian among others,[73] grew out of monastic practice. The ideal was extended more broadly in this era when monastic reformers wanted "to convert the whole world into a hermitage."[74] The heralds of this idealistic movement, strongly supported by Gregorian legislation, stirred up much ferment among the laity around 1100, contributing to the denigration of private property, new wealth, and economic individualism, and also to the higher standards being demanded of clergy by the masses. The new vision was "the apostolic life;" if a priest did not live up to strict vows

of poverty, chastity, and service to his fellowman, his parishoners might severely judge him.[75]

On the other hand, in the movement towards corpora-
tism, a primarily secular phenomenon, the church, moved by
the Gregorian ferment, responded to the rising power of the
artisan and lesser bourgeois classes.[76] By permitting
such new customs as parish election of priests,[74] it abetted, whether wittingly or not, the movement toward community solidarity which wrested citizenship and town charters
from many a reluctant lord. Rome was seen as a symbol of
freedom because it attacked the old state churches and the
monarchies, that is, the main symbols of power which the
lower classes had begun to challenge. This image combined
in people's minds with the revolutionary new image of the
priesthood as elite crusaders; the combination gave the
Gregorians considerable standing with some of the "working
class," the artisans of village and town who treated their
clergy so harshly. It was in fact the textile weavers and
craftsmen, who in the coming century would combine with
peasants from "below" and merchants from "above" to become
the nucleus of protest groups against the power and wealth
of their overlords, whether secular or papal.[78] That
they rose against their married priests, rather than align-
ing with them in their struggle against the established pow-

ers, indicates that they identified married priests with
the old order upon whom they vented their stored-up frustra-
tions. In an earlier example of communal uprising, that of
the Milanese Pataria beginning in the 1050's and 1060's,
the papacy had backed local reform-minded priests and
working-class men and women in opposing imperial control of
city and church. The clerical leaders of the Pataria brand-
ed married priests as heretics, thereby turning the lay members against their pastors.[79]

Sigebert viewed these new happenings with alarm. Holding a conservative view of society, he did not approve of
change in any form: if workers have been dependent on
their lords, let them continue; if priests have married,
let that continue also.

In the remainder of the Apologia Sigebert criticizes
the papacy angrily. He accuses the Gregorian party of being simonists who excuse their own transgressions but who
are vindictive towards others who practice the same corruption. In order to impose chastity on some, they preach an
abominable heresy to many, and while taking up arms to free
the church they have rendered it captive. He calls their
reforms unheard-of novelties (novas falsitatum opini-
ones) and lays the blame for all these evils on the decree
instructing the laity to judge their clergy. But he is

hardest on the pope, who glorifies his own office, who claims to speak for God but who actually speaks out of his own ambition. Sigebert accuses them all of hypocrisy and of destroying the unity of the church.[80]

Sigebert quoted largely from Augustine, using his arguments on the validity of every priest's sacraments,[81] and may have borrowed from Damian's _Liber Gratissimus_ (without identifying his source) the idea that _Hoc est mysterium, quod nec bonus melius, nec malus peius facere potest_[82] and two scriptural references.[83]

Sigebert's views were in accord with those early moderates among the Gregorians such as Damian, who saw that, although universal celibacy might indeed be the apostolic goal, nevertheless to deny the validity of the sacraments of _any_ priest was to court disaster for the peace and well-being of the church. It was only the radicals such as Cardinal Humbert, Nicholas II, and Hildebrand who dared to risk havoc in order to purify the service of the altar. Sigebert saw the practical issue, and so did Clement III and the cardinals who had deserted Gregory VII after 1076. These opponents were apparently as devoted to the _ideal_ of celibacy as Gregory himself,[84] but in order to stop a revolution, they were working desperately to unite all of

Gregory's foes under their banner. They therefore enunciat-
ed a sacramental doctrine defining the sacrament as an act
of God, conferring grace no matter whether the officiant or
receiver merits it, a doctrine later known as _ex_ _opere_
operato.

Fliche, accusing Sigebert of putting words into Gregory's mouth, points out that Gregory did not actually say
that the unchaste priests' sacraments were invalid, but only forbade the laity to partake of them.[85] Fliche does
not see, as Sigebert surely did, that Gregory's threat of
excommunication against the laity and his disciplinary actions against recalcitrant bishops were in practice as radical and destructive as a change of doctrine would have
been. The distinction here is between the idealist and the
realist. Gregory took no heed of the havoc his demands
caused, whereas Sigebert, equally dedicated to the ascetic
ideal, put the welfare of the local churches first. When
the struggle is looked at in this light, one may question
the historical verdict that the Gregorian radicals were entirely right, while Sigebert and Clement III's bishops are
found only in footnotes.

The criticisms of Gregory became more sweeping in the
next broadside to be considered, the _Epistola_ of Wenric
of Trier.[86] By the time that Wenric composed his list of

accusations late in 1080, political tensions between papacy and Empire had increased. The pope had again excommunicated Henry IV and declared him deposed, and this time Gregory had backed a rival king for Germany, Rudolph of Swabia. Most of the German and Lombard bishops had responded quickly, calling for Gregory's deposition and renouncing obedience to him at the Synod of Brixen in June, 1080. The imperial side then showed that two can play the game by electing a rival pope, Clement III.[87]

In the autumn following these events Bishop Theodore of Verdun commissioned the scholasticus Wenric of Trier to draw up a list of challenges to Gregory.[88] Wenric, using as a basis for his attacks the texts from the Assembly of Worms,[89] chastises Gregory for destroying order in the church. First, the political attack on Henry IV has disturbed religious life, spreading uncertainty and contention within monasteries and dioceses. The second attack, the papal assault on the sacraments of married clergy, is, however, more damaging. Although clerical celibacy is only one Gregorian goal among several attacked by Wenric, it illustrates his main thesis that the church of Rome was unjustly attacking the traditional powers of princes over the local churches. Writing in the first person of the fear and confusion this attack raised in him, he debates whether a law

carried out through the senseless excesses of the laity
should be observed, even if it were a good law. Not only
were the clergy confounded by this law, but families were
divided by it and, what was worse, the authority of the
paterfamilias was destroyed.[90] The combined force of
these assaults on established order threatened the destruction of the priesthood, which is reviled by obscene names.
But the most damaging aspect of the church of Rome's aggressions is that they are now launched against the entire German nation.[91] Wenric's attack on Gregory is personally
venomous; the ultimate charge, here as elsewhere, is of hypocrisy, of the man who pretends to be a monk, but who in
reality takes up arms, causes blood to flow, and grows rich
by so doing.

It is worth noting that Wenric's treatise further pol-
arized the theoretical positions in the imperial-papal
struggle. By insisting on the unrestricted right of the
king to lay investiture, and claiming that a bishop's oath
to a true king was higher than his oath to a false pope,
Wenric was actually asserting that the state was omnipotent, that it had, in fact, unlimited power. It therefore
had power over the church. It follows that the monarch cannot be judged or deposed by the pope. By limiting
the pope's exercise of spiritual power, Wenric contributed

to the growing theoretical basis for a fundamental power
struggle between papacy and empire.[92]

The last of the theorists who wrote against Gregory
VII during his lifetime was Benzo of Alba. His major work,
Liber _ad_ _Heinricum_, offering little mention of the
celibacy issue, is a long plea to the German emperor to re-
vive the "Roman Empire," an ideal to which Benzo was pas-
sionately devoted. One could surmise, however, that Benzo,
staunch supporter of Henry and of Clement, would support
the married clergy and, in fact, the rapid heightening of
tensions in the 1080's brought forth two short works on
clerical marriage by him. In Book V of his _Liber_ _ad_
Heinricum, where he argues against the Patarenes whom he
fought at every chance, and in one comment on the deliberations of Brixen,[93] he criticizes the papacy for its destructive attack on priestly marriage. For his unflinching
support of the imperial cause and its anti-pope, Benzo was
driven out of his bishopric in 1077.

For further writings on clerical marriage I have
looked at the writings of other defenders of the imperial
cause but, with the exception of Guy of Ferrara, the others
do not mention the celibacy debate, absorbed as they were
in hammering out a theoretical basis for imperial power.
Neither Peter Crassus, Guy of Osnabruck, nor Cardinal Beno

discussed this issue. Guy of Ferrara's contribution is an
ambiguous one because of the way he changed sides in the
struggle. For years he had supported Gregory VII's cause;
converting finally around 1081 and receiving a bishopric
from the anti-pope, he wrote a document which gave both
sides of all the major arguments in the controversy.[94]
It is impossible to tell what Guy himself believed, for he
first defends Hildebrand, then, changing over to the views
of the imperial party, he defends clerical marriage in a
general way, saying that those who do not live by the canons should be gently taught and led, not forced to change.
For example, when defending Gregory's use of the laity to
attack married priests, Guy wrote that he himself had never
urged cruel treatment of those clergy but had always objected when the laity, for whom Gregory was not responsible,
had terrorized and murdered priests. Yet in his later work
Guy attacked Gregory himself for harshness. In sum, Guy accepted the ministry of priests who were _indigni_, arguing
that their sacraments were channels of grace.

In conclusion, the total amount of known literature
written to defend clerical marriage is not large. The two
most influential works were Ulric's and Sigebert's; both
were quoted repeatedly and one had the honor of being condemned. Throughout all of the writings compulsory celibacy

is rejected for three reasons: it is an arbitrary decree, a new invention designed to control rather than to reform men; it is enforced by men who do not themselves lead moral lives; and it forces otherwise honest men to engage in undesirable forms of sex. Both sides used emotionalism and personal attack, both quoted canons, but the party defending marriage had only ancient rulings to fall back on, whereas the papal party was able to create new law. But in the process of protesting against celibacy, married clergy and their supporters left a valuable legacy of arguments affirming the goodness of nature and of human sexuality, affirmations seldom enough found in medieval theological writings. We will turn now to a particularly subtle defense of a priest's right to marry, that of the Norman Anonymous.

CHAPTER FOUR

THE NORMAN ANONYMOUS: A MARRIED PRIEST CAUGHT IN

ANGLO-NORMAN CELIBACY ENFORCEMENT

> The word which God sows in our hearts
> teaches who should be virgins and who
> should create the fruits of marriage....
> But those who destroy this natural order,
> sin.
>
> The Norman Anonymous, c. 1100

I

The writings of the Norman Anonymous, best known for
his strong statement of theocratic kingship, also include
three tracts dealing with celibacy: J25, a defense of
priestly marriage; and J22/26, two versions of an argument
on the rights of priests' sons.[1]

Because questions of authorship and dating remain unan-
swered, the task of placing this work in the context of the
polemics of its time is complicated. There has even been
debate over its place of origin, for whereas most of the
tracts reveal a detailed knowledge of events in the archdio-

cese of Rouen, one (J29b) describes conflicts in the English church.[2] And these confusions add to the problem
that, like all historians of the Gregorian period, scholars
who have written about the Anonymous have paid scant attention to the views on clerical marriage and priests'
sons.[3] I accept the verdict commonly held today that the
author was a Norman who had knowledge of English affairs,
and go further to suggest that he was the son of a priest
who may have been married and had children himself, for he
wrote the anti-celibacy tracts in the first person, in an
impassioned style, as if from the heart.

The tracts inspired by the celibacy struggle could
have been written at any time between 1075 and 1120.[4] Because J25 is based on the earlier Norman versions of Ulric's Rescript, which appeared between 1065 and 1075, and
because the Anonymous argues for legal recognition of marriage, a position which we know was largely abandoned after
the 1080's, an early date has usually been accepted for
J25.[5] However, since the earliest date proven for the
manuscript (knowledge of the Council of Clermont) is 1096,
we must consider a later period for the Anonymous' active
life. He might have written J25 (and most of the major
tracts) in reaction to various decrees at Clermont dealing
with papal supremacy and the intrusion of papal legates in-

to local affairs, as well as with celibacy and priests'
sons.[6]

A final possibility relates to the clerogamous riots
in Rouen in 1119 against the harsher celibacy decrees of
the Council of Rheims. It has been suggested that the Anonymous was none other than Albert the Eloquent, the outspok-
en cleric summarily imprisoned by Archbishop Geoffrey for
his leadership in that rebellion.[7] If in fact the Anonymous ended his life in prison, that calamity would go far
towrad explaining the increasing fatalism of his theological views and the elegaic quality of his final tract, J31.

Turning to the tracts on priests' sons, J22/26, we
find that here the Anonymous is not arguing for official
recognition of marriage: instead he defends the
illegitimate sons of priests and their concubines; there
is no question of legal marriage. This fact indicates a
later date, after most of the writers defending clerical
marriage had ceased to demand full, legal recognition.
Since it is not likely that the terminology of J22/26 would
have been used in the 1070's, they were probably not
composed that early.

A more likely period for their composition is the
years from 1096 to c. 1110. The first clue comes from
Anselm's essay, De conceptu virginali et de

<u>originali</u> <u>peccato</u>, composed in 1101, which the Anony-
mous quoted from in J21. Since the ideas in J21 lead directly into the thought of J22, it would seem that they
were written at about the same time. Other indications for
a date after 1100 are the similarity of argument between
J22/26 and two other Norman works written after 1100 on
priests' sons, Theobald of Étampe's <u>Epistola</u> and Serlo
of Bayeux's <u>Defensio</u>.

The latest date that we have for the manuscript is
based on references to events in England beginning c. 1109.
This is the exact period of Anselm's letters to Pascal II
about priests' sons, letters which show Anselm to be far
more rigorous in interpreting the celibacy laws than the
pope himself. Since Anselm had spent much of his second
exile (1103-1107) in Normandy, the Anonymous could well
have known of Anselm's extreme interpretation and have
written against it.

All of these later dates indicate a man whose mature
career was lived out from the 1090's into the early decades
of the twelfth century. If we accept the original date of
1075 for the composition of J25 and assume that the author
was about thirty when he wrote it, then we must picture a
seventy-five year old priest rioting in Rouen in 1119. And
that stretches credulity. I propose instead a date around

1096 for J25 and not earlier than 1110 for J22/26. As for
identifying him with Albert the Eloquent's crisis in 1119,
I maintain that we cannot know exactly who the Anonymous
was. This identification awaits further work on the
sources of his thought. Meanwhile I will turn to an
investigation of the theological implications of his
writing on marriage and procreation.

Part of the material in J25 is familiar because it
comes from Ulric or his continuators.[8] The Anonymous' essay begins as they do, asking who first said that clergy
must be celibate, God or man. Since God did not will it
and scripture does not declare it, man must be the author
of this decree; other men, therefore, need not obey it.
Not only is the papacy wrong to force celibacy on priests,
but it commits a sin in preventing men from marrying. The
Anonymous follows the previous authors again in insisting
on legal marriage (matrimonium, nuptiae) and on the superiority of marriage to fornication. He quotes the Augus-
tinian claims that procreation is good and marriage is a
sacrament, and the Pauline opinion that to marry is better
than to fornicate.[9] The Anonymous uses every Biblical
reference found in the Norman Tractatus except Romans
7:3, and both quote from the Councils of Nicaea, Chalcedon,
Carthage, and Toledo.

The story of Pafnutius is not repeated, although the Anonymous could have known it from Ivo of Chartres' _Panormia_ if he wrote after 1074, as well as from Ulric and his successors. Since the Pafnutius story was condemned in 1079, the Anonymous' ommission of it is a further indication that he wrote after that date. Neither did he use his predecessors' heated debate on the validity of married priests' sacraments, nor does the argument over the opposition of law and spirit from the _Treatise on Grace_ appear in his marriage tractate, although this argument enriches other portions of the Anonymous' writings.

The Anonymous did use the arguments on free will and predestination found in the _Treatise on Grace_. Because, as Fliche has noted, he used Anselm's predestinarian terminology extensively,[10] it is possible that he, like the author of the _Treatise_, had studied under Anselm at Bec. Like Anselm he affirmed that continence is a gift of God, given to some and not to others, and that one cannot be chaste without God's gift of chastity.[11] But unlike Anselm our author does not take account of free will, of the faculty of being responsible for one's actions even though they are known in advance by God. The Anonymous declares instead that we are fore-ordained to do what we do, that indeed a priest may be preordained to be the father of

one of God's elect; God chooses whom He will to fulfill the
number of his saints, from among clergy and laity alike.
He, therefore, who would prevent God's will by enforcing
celibacy, let him beware.

Elsewhere, in two short tracts, the Anonymous went beyond the orthodox doctrine of single predestination to insist not only that the elect are preordained to salvation
but that the damned have been assigned to hell from the beginning of time. This is double predestination, a doctrine
whose extreme pessimism about human nature has brought
about the condemnation of its adherents on a number of occasions. Asking who has the right to excommunicate another, the author offers a highly political answer to a theological question, distinguishing those who are within the
"true church" from those who are damned:

> For out of the whole human race some are
> members of Christ, preelected and predes-
> tined to a life blessed by the Father, for
> whom the kingdom of God was prepared from
> the world's founding; but others are mem-
> bers of the devil, damned from eternity to
> death, who, being cursed, are thrust into
> eternal fire. If any of these, therefore,
> shall have been absolved by a bishop, not
> on account of this will he be saved, nor be
> made a member of Christ, and for such a one
> excommunication would be superfluous.... On
> the other hand, if a member of Christ ...
> shall have been excommunicated, not on
> account of this can he be damned.
> Furthermore, to excommunicate such a one

> [will bring] the danger of being excommuni-
> cated onto oneself....[12]

The Anonymous makes an assault on the authority of the established church, denying its power to offer salvation.
Not hesitating to apply these harsh distinctions to his contemporaries, the Anonymous declared that the papal party is
"the church of Satan," doomed to hell, whereas those who
live by the spirit, those presumably like the author himself, are the elect.[113]

At first reading, the Anonymous' fatalistic doctrine
can be interpreted as a passive and irresponsible position, as an excuse for indulging in sin, but it is something quite different. When the Anonymous claims that marriage is intended for some, virginity for others, and that
both are good, he is groping towards a statement of individualism. He is saying in effect that people are different,
that God has diverse plans for individuals, but he lacked a
sufficient terminology to discuss individualism. Colin
Morris has noted that

> ... the period (900-1050) was not one in
> which there was any obvious confidence in
> man or in the individual.... Before there
> could be a discovery of the individual,
> there would have to be a great increase in
> learning and an enrichment of social possi-
> bilities and fluidity.

Morris then added,

By 1050 both of these were beginning.[14]
In the Anonymous' theological struggle we see an attempt to
begin. Lacking concepts necessary to discuss individualism, he turned to the idea of God's will to explain these
differences. Indeed, it is God's predestinating will which
becomes the main causal agent in the Anonymous' theology.
He states that no one can know if a man should be celibate
except that man himself. A man knows in his heart if he
should be celibate, for God plants the seed of that knowledge in his heart; the word of God speaks in his heart.
This type of statement, based as it is on the inner awareness of the individual, is rarely found in eleventh-century
thought, not receiving full articulation until Abelard's
Ethics in the following generation.

    Elsewhere in the manuscript the Anonymous attacks the
Church of Rome for trying to guarantee the validity of the
sacraments by its laws. As if the law could perform what
only the Holy Spirit can assure! About ordination he
states that whether a man is born of the spirit is much
more important than whether he was born legitimate. Thus,
even the sacraments themselves are finally dispensable,
since if one has received the gift of the spirit, what need
has one for outer forms? Calling the author a spiritual-
ist, George Williams maintains that he mixed mystical

thought with an inexorable logic that forced him to question the new sacramental theology and celibacy rulings of
the Gregorian church.[15]

The two tracts defending the rights of priests' sons,
J22 and J26, are valuable for their subtlety of argument
and the inclusion of all of the Anonymous' major
theological ideas. For example, in order to attack what he
saw as the contemporary church's opposition of law to
spirit, he begins by asking who may be ordained. The
answer from law, that is from the Gregorian decrees, is
that only sons of legitimate unions may take orders. To
this he replies that when men choose candidates for the
priesthood by their own standards, they choose men who are
not true pastors. Furthermore, tradition is on his side:
since the apostles did not decree celibacy, it follows that
priests may marry and have sons who should be considered
legitimate.

Having asserted that the fulness of grace comes
through baptism, the author perhaps realizes the tension of
being both a sacramentalist and one who believes himself to
be under the power of the Holy Spirit, for he then contra-
dicts his affirmation of the sacraments by declaring that
while baptism is necessary for salvation, only those already elected receive its true grace.[16] Undercutting the

efficacy of the sacrament, he thereby identifies himself
with those who acknowledge the ultimate power of the
spirit.

The Anonymous emphasizes further the power of the doctrine of election by claiming that legitimate sons may be,
even after baptism, "vessels of wrath, foreknown from eter-
nity to be sons of perdition,"[17] whereas the sons of
priests may be, after baptism, "vessels of mercy, elected
before the beginning of time and predestined to life."[18]
This is the extent of the argument in J22. But the additional material of J26, its introduction and ending, con-
sists of little else besides predestinarian doctrine. In
fact, he tells us that he wrote J26 in order to emphasize
how fundamental the doctrine of election is for him.

The heart of his claims for priests' sons is that God
has foreordained certain persons to be His chosen ones, to
form His church and to sacrifice to Him, and that therefore
these persons may be born from illegitimate unions as well
as from recognized marriage -- it is not for man to know or
to judge. This doctrine of election overrules all moral
and legal arguments.

It is from this doctrine that his belief about creation is formed. Since God creates all men, he concludes
that "parents indeed are not the cause [auctores] of

their children's procreation but assistants [minis-
tri].[19]   Therefore, all procreation is good [legiti-
ma], both through nature and through God's blessing.[20]

Here the Anonymous moves beyond Augustine's view
which grudgingly accepted the necessity for human procreation. In doing so he may have been influenced by Anselm,
who had also departed from Augustine on this point.[21]
Working out these ideas in the De conceptu virginali
et de originali peccato, an essay which the Anonymous had quoted in his previous tract, J21, Anselm had pos-
tulated that the focal point of original sin is not concu-
piscence but rather a defect of will, namely envy. This
change from Augustine's view enabled Anselm to give less emphasis to the sinfulness of the senses and to an original
sexual fall from grace. Utilizing Anselm's redefinition of
original sin, the Anonymous grants that there is the sin of
Adam, originale peccatum, but it is only a general sin,
because, in fact, human nature is good: Legitima et
bona est origo humanae conditionis...."[22] Carnal birth and human sexuality are therefore also good. But
this materialist affirmation is not the ultimate good; it
is spiritual generation, springing from the union of Christ
and his spotless bride, the heavenly Jerusalem, that creates the elect. Summing up his claims for the elect the
author elaborates on I Pet. 2:9:

> You are a chosen race, not propagated from
> the unclean, corruptible seed of the flesh,
> but procreated [reborn?] from the heavenly,
> uncorruptible, seed of the high king and
> priest, and thus rightly called "a royal
> priesthood."[23]

The most surprising implication of these vigorously stated ideas, however, is the effect of the Anonymous' belief in pre-ordained vocation on his doctrine of the laity. Having said already that God's work, such as the offering of His true sacrament, is to be done by His chosen ones, not necessarily (the implication is, rarely!) by the church's priesthood, he claims that any man, even though illegitimate or lay, may belong to those chosen ones. The Anonymous carries this thought to the controversial conclusion that even a layman could administer the sacraments.[24] At this point his thought diverges sharply from the Gregorians; he would do away with all legal distinctions among Christians, whereas they worked to widen the difference between priesthood and laity.

The Anonymous is not, however, an institutional revolutionary. Rather than propose sweeping changes in ecclesiastical practice, he accepts the fact that laymen (and, increasingly, priest's sons, and the Elect in general) do not perform the church's sacraments. Given this circumstance, the true sacrament will, therefore, be the inner sacrifice made by the Christian filled with grace, and the greatest blessedness will be whatever these chosen ones do. To _receive_ the sacrament rather than to perform it, and in doing so, to receive the divine nature of Christ, becomes the greatest sacrament in the church of the Elect.[25]

The Anonymous did not stop with this limitation on the power of the priesthood. Returning to his first point, the challenge to the law, in the closing lines of J26 he dismisses canon law, [26] and joins those who, led by the spirit, do not live under the canons.[27] Nowhere in the polemical literature is there a clearer statement of an alternate concept of the church, of a desire for a church that diverges fundamentally from the Gregorian "church of Satan."

II

The extreme predestinarian belief, found in several other tracts in the manuscript,[28] is the most striking aspect in the Anonymous' thought. It must be considered not only the key to his theological formulations but also, since it placed him in direct opposition to papal doctrine, a clue to the professional and personal problems he alludes to in J3 and J31. Yet there is no trace of predestinarian thought in much of the Anonymous' writing. In particular

his other writings on the sacraments, on ordination, and on
the nature of the priesthood contradict the conclusions
reached in J22/26.[27] Since a belief in double predestination is scarcely an attitude which one might take up and
put down at will, the conflicting positions must be investi-
gated. Which position did he hold first? What made him
change?

Because the most detailed, best argued, and most forceful tracts are the predestinarian writings and the anti-
papal polemics, they may therefore indicate a mature author. The other treatises are short and simple, much like
essays written for students. It is possible that the Anonymous wrote the "school tracts" early in his career, and
that events in his life had forced him to change both his
theology and his politics by the time he wrote J25, J22/26,
and the papal polemics.

One can readily surmise how the Anonymous' life became
increasingly difficult. Two of his longest and best-argued
tracts are a defense of theocratic kingship, written possibly for Henry I.[30] They are considered to be the most extreme statement of caesaro-papism in the middle ages,[31]
and yet the author lived during a period of great struggle
between sacerdotium and regnum. Although in the Anglo-
Norman kingdom papal power made only limited inroads, the

few concessions made by the English king in the Concordat
of 1107[32] placed a limitation upon monarchy that contra-
dicted the Anonymous' vision of omnipotent royal power.
His thesis was further challenged by the growing secularization of the ideal of monarchy: the new model of government
was increasingly secular, national, and limited.[33] He
had written about a concept of monarchy which was dying at
the very time that he gave it its ultimate formulation.[34]

The papal attack on clerical marriage may have been
even more destructive to the Anonymous' basic beliefs and
personal life. He may have been forced to separate from
his wife and children, or may have suffered severe penalties for refusing to do so: loss of his benefice and sal-
ary, loss of his priestly ordination, being fined, publicly
ridiculed, imprisoned, even physically harrassed, his children disinherited and declared illegitimate -- we have seen
that these were possible hazards for a married priest after
about 1070. If the Anonymous took part in the rebellion
staged by married clergy against Archbishop Geoffrey's
forceful application of the 1119 celibacy decree, then he
experienced the shock of being set upon by the archbishop's
soldiers within the sacred confines of Rouen cathedral, of
being attacked by lay witnesses, and possibly of being
dragged off to prison. We have noted how the survivors

fled in stupefaction to their families, considering this treatment to be outrageous, unheard-of, a scandal to their calling as priests.[35] The Anonymous may have realized that the era of toleration of married clerics was indeed at an end, that the church as he and his predecessors had known it was changing in a fundamental way. Whether he chose to sacrifice his family or his career, he was faced with a wrenching decision.

From a reading of the entire manuscript this picture of the author emerges: a man given to bold thinking who, when hard-pressed, resorted to extreme intellectual solutions, but who in the end was defeated. The final essay in the Codex, J31, expresses a fatalistic resignation to the cruelties of life.[36] It also speaks of other-worldly, ascetic values far different from the positive attitude toward sexuality found in J22/26 and J25.[37] It is possible to draw a picture of a man who, finally giving in to papal pressure, became separated from his family and resigned himself to the asceticism expressed in J31. Or one can equally well imagine that he did not submit, and that the hardships of life after excommunication forced him into the fatalistic thought of what may be called the "later" tracts.

CHAPTER FIVE

THE DESTRUCTION OF CLERICAL MARRIAGE

It is difficult to understand how legislation and punishment alone, harsh and impressive as they were, could rad-
ically alter a life pattern as basic as the commitment to
marriage and parenthood, but that change occurred for numbers of parish clergy during the twelfth century. In order
to analyze this alteration, it is necessary to look at a
number of cultural and societal changes that took place in
the early part of the century.

Perhaps the most revolutionary and lasting change instituted by the Gregorians was the monasticizing of the
major clergy. Although traditional monasticism was subjected to many revisions in the century between 1050 and 1150,
two of its original ideals, obedience and chastity, not only survived but were applied to the clerical state, both
within and without the cloister, as never before. While
many of the men and women who crowded into the monastic
orders or who associated themselves with less formal celibate groups did so in order to serve others in the world,

still all took vows which had originated in other-worldly
traditions. From the conversion of secular canons into regulars to the inclusion within some orders of large numbers
of lay brethren as "monastic vassals,"[1] the movement to
"turn the world into a hermitage" proceeded at a rapid
rate. Voluntary poverty and self-renunciations such as extreme fasting and flagellation became popular symbols of
sanctity, but none carried more weight than virginity.

   At the same time, the effect on the clergy of these ascetic goals was compounded by higher standards for clerical
education and by what must be called a liturgical revolution. Well before the eleventh century the mass had developed a stress on the private devotions of the priest[2] and
on his unique role in invoking the Real Presence, so that
the eucharistic sacrament came to be seen as a miracle
wrought by God through the instrumentality of the priest
himself.[3] Now by heightening the priestly miracle of the
mass, denying the eucharistic cup to the laity, and adding
many new feast days to the liturgical calendar, reformed
monks and canons regular further exalted the priesthood,
thereby forcing secular clergy to begin to conform to their
own monastic standards. Even those who joined the new apostolic groups and remained in the lay state lived by monastic ideals. And the condition required for both the intel-

lectual and the sacramental life was celibacy, the state which above all affected the daily lives of those devoted to a religious calling.[4]

One evidence of the change produced by a more ascetic clergy can be found in the more intensely individualistic and erotic quality of devotional literature. Some of the intimacy and sensual expression which priests had formerly found in marriage may have been channeled into this new literary form; indeed, one factor in the growth of the cult of the Virgin after about 1050 may have been that Mary now represented the female principle in the lives of newly-celibate clergy. In the warmly human quality of Ailred of Rievaulx's treatise on monastic friendship and Bernard of Clairvaux's ecstatic devotions to the Virgin Mary, spiritual literature expressed a more personal ideal of love and desire.[5]

Another of Bernard's themes, the _sponsa_ _Christi_, produced a heightened form of eroticized spirituality growing out of the Bernardine celebration of the soul's mystical marriage to Christ, which was particularly influential among religious women. Taking the ancient symbol of themselves as brides of Christ, some twelfth- and thirteenth-century women and the men who wrote devotional literature for them began describing spiritual union in the passionate language of sexual intercourse between husband and wife. In the _Ancrene Riwle_ Christ is portrayed as the perfect knightly lover; in the Katharine Group poems the beauty of Christ's body is praised as one would a lover's body;[6] in Mechtild of Magdeburg's rapture Christ is the handsome young Lord who will come to dance with her[7] -- in these and many other writings, spiritual experience is sexualized. And yet, precisely because in them sexual union is symbolized, is projected into a phantasy world, the total effect of such powerful mystical experiences is further to downgrade sexuality and marriage as they are lived out in the secular world. St. Bernard's epithalamian mysticism succeeded in putting still greater distance between what he saw as the superior ascetic discipline of the monastery and the compromised carnal existence of the outside world.

Another product of the movement to enforce celibacy, well illustrated in the documents used in this study, was the expression of clerical anti-feminism. Given the long history of Christian writings hostile to women, it is perhaps not surprising that misogyny should appear as one theme in the Gregorians' attempts to discipline the church. Michael Kaufman has observed that there were

> covert links between the demands for sacer-
> dotal celibacy and the Church's misogyny,
> for one effect of the Gregorian reforms was
> the resurgence of ascetic ideals which pro-
> vided a congenial atmosphere for the
> Church's reinvigorated anti-feminism. [The
> Clergy] equated woman with insatiable sexu-
> ality, irrationality, and demonic tempta-
> tion ... the systematic defilement of women
> was intended to win the clergy back to celi-
> bacy.[8]

In sum, women were denigrated in order to make them less de-

sirable. Within an institution dominated by monastic

ideals, moreover, it was apparently not possible to toler-

ate the existence of females whose sexuality was not strict-

ly controlled by a vow of chastity. That the necessity to

control women was increasingly seen as a problem by the

church hierarchy in the late twelfth century appears clear

from the abrupt refusal by several orders to admit more

women and from the growing custom of insisting on strict

enclosure for them.[9] Unfortunately the comment of the

Premonstratensian abbot Conrad of Marchtal was not unusual:

> ... recognizing that the wickedness of wom-
> en is greater than all the other wickedness
> of the world, that there is no anger like
> that of women, and that the poison of asps
> and dragons is less dangerous to men than
> the familiarity of women, we decreed ...
> that we will on no account receive any more
> sisters ... but will avoid them like poison-
> ous animals.[10]

That women's roles were curtailed both in secular rights

and in monastic opportunities from around 1100 on has been

well documented.[11] To these handicaps may be added the

degradation to which clerical wives were subjected when

their marriages were challenged by the enforcement of celi-

bacy.   The combined force of these disadvantages ushered in

the era that has generally been agreed upon as the low

point in female status in the medieval west.

But there was a final factor which enhanced the new im-

age of the sacral priesthood, which further convinced cler-

ics to give up the idea of marriage.   The sheer power repre-

sented by the newly centralized papacy, power which every

priest could share, was a highly seductive element.   R. W.

Southern, speculating about this possibility, concludes

that

> ... the papal primacy offered to the clergy
> everywhere substantial benefits: security
> for their property, freedom from secular
> punishments, a refuge from violence, and a
> means of settling intricate disputes.   The
> status of every clerk was enhanced by the
> papal primacy, which communicated to them
> all something of the greatness of Rome.[12]

And celibacy was one of the keystones of papal power.   The

popes most absolutist about papal primacy -- Gregory VII,

Calixtus II, Alexander III, and Innocent III -- were the

popes most insistent on clerical celibacy.[13]   Many

priests may have seen the causal relation between these con-

cepts, may have acknowledged that the heights of power

which the church was approaching were not available to men
whose loyalties and resources were shared with women and
children. Thus was formed one of the most powerful and en-
during "men's clubs" that history has recorded. Since nuns
were no longer to hold positions of power in the church,
and those (men) who did hold the monopoly on spiritual power were denied any close association with women, the result
was a male clerical elite that could expect no substantial
female challenge. And yet the ecclesiastical records of
the late Middle Ages record an impressive amount of "trouble" from allegedly heretical women.[13a] Perhaps the
shut-out strategy was not a wise one.

The question remains as to why many of the laity en-
thusiastically embraced the ideal of clerical celibacy.
One clue may lie in the fact that, as a group, the laity
never were a class in themselves, as the clergy were,[14]
and never had a spirituality of their own.[15] Western
spirituality was created by monks, and even when the new
orders, especially the mendicants, tried to provide the
laity with forms of worship appropriate for persons living
in the world, the basically monastic values of the friars
themselves forced them back into a monastic mold. Not having a class image to fall back on, it is perhaps not surprising that the laity did not become articulate about

their own values or their spirituality until later in the
Middle Ages. In fact, the laity lost status in the twelfth
century, as the priesthood became more powerful.[16] In
the tenth century many clergy had thought that their marriages added to their status, but by the time that clerical
marriage was rendered null, the lay world had diminished in
importance to the point that it may no longer have seemed
worth the candle. Although urban laity formed parochial
and professional guilds and even in some areas elected
their pastors,[17] although secular governments became
everywhere markedly stronger, and despite the emergence of
a vernacular secular literature, still the clergy dominated
twelfth-century life, intellectually, politically, and spir-
itually.

A further clue resides in the evidence that, in response to these pressures from the ecclesiastical sphere,
some of the laity themselves turned to asceticism,[18]
adopting a spirituality that was in most instances anti-
sexual. In doing so they gave evidence of their dependence
on monastic ideals in formulating their own spiritual life.
In discussing the laity, Southern observes that

> the devotional literature of the twelfth
> century, with its intense interest in vir-
> ginity, helped to create in many minds a
> strong and sometimes hysterical aversion to
> the state of matrimony.[19]

In short, the monastic ideal began to penetrate not only the secular clergy but lay society as well. The church now witnessed the formation of numerous lay celibate groups vowed to apostolic poverty and service. Although in later centuries the papacy viewed such groups as subversive, in the beginning they were welcomed, and indeed they were not subversive of church order. It is not surprising that they offered their world no real alternatives to the church's goals, for, as Southern observed about Abelard and Heloise,

> ... in the end they had only one central code of conduct to fall back on -- the code of monastic Christianity.... Their age had not yet developed a plausible ethic for the secular life.[20]

Since laity with a religious calling accepted for themselves the ideals of monastic asceticism, naturally they expected the same or better from their clergy. The popular values were "apostolic poverty and chastity;" neither parish priests nor evangelists could expect any longer to escape lay censure if they did not live up to these ideals.

There was a contrasting current of twelfth-century thought which might have modified this widespread triumph of asceticism, however; for among some scholars a new humanistic and scientific concern emerged. Of the well-known components of the twelfth-century Renaissance, the one

which matters most to our discussion was the investigation
of and celebration of nature. Expressed first primarily in
the works of William of Conches and Bernard of Silvester
and exerting wide influence down to the time of Alan of
Lille, these ideas are associated with the so-called school
of Chartres[21] but are in fact the cumulative work of a
generation of thinkers.[22]

The doctrines which unite these scholars are a belief
in the importance of the workings of nature, in its integri-
ty and order, and the affirmation that theology and nature
do not contradict each other. Relying primarily on Platon-
ic and neo-Platonic thought, these Christian humanists were
led by their interest in the natural world to take seriously their developing culture, to affirm the dignity of man
as a microcosm of the universe, and in particular to produce new perceptions of the body, of all natural forms, and
of the act of generation.[23]

These results are seen in the major work of Bernard
Silvester, the epic poem The Cosmographia. Praising
the principle of fecundity and the act of procreation,
Bernard declares that the material world is potent and dy-
namic, and that worldly achievement is important. As his
translator comments, Bernard "flirts continually with mater-
ialism ... and with a sort of cosmic eroticism ..." which

he sees as perfected by reason, administered through God's
will. Like Alan of Lille, he works out this tension between matter and reason by a sacramental analogy between
cosmogony and the evolution of sacred history.[24]

Perhaps Bernard's major contribution is his attempt to
bridge the gap created long before in neo-Platonic and
Christian ascetic thought, the gap between sensual nature
and the spiritual life, between the necessity for physical
generation and the desire for autonomous rational consciousness.[25] It is of course this dualism which provides the
foundation for ascetic thought, whether of the twelfth or
of any other century. While Bernard neither transcends this
dualism nor ignores the tension which matter's (Silva's)
propensity for evil imposes on Nature's desire for order,
still he works within the confines of these classic
Christian beliefs in a new way. Maintaining a sturdy grasp
on the patriarchal, Aristotelian view of procreation, he
affirms that

> [The genital] exercise will be enjoyable
> and profitable, so long as the time, the
> manner, and the extent are suitable. Lest
> earthly life pass away, and the process of
> generation be cut off, and material exis-
> tence, dissolved, return to primordial cha-
> os, propagation was made the charge of two
> genii [masculine and feminine creativity?]
> and the act itself was assigned to twin
> brothers .... The phallus wars with Laches-
> is and carefully rejoins the vital threads

>severed by the hands of the Fates. Blood
>sent forth from the brain flows down to the
>loins, bearing the image of the shining
>sperm. Artful Nature molds and shapes the
>fluid, that in conceiving it may reproduce
>the forms of ancestors.[26]

Bernard's translator, noting that "Nature serves as a stan-

dard for interpreting the history of man's fall and redemp-

tion ... and the complex interplay of psychological forces

in all aspects of human love," concludes that here Man's

struggle to maintain right relations with the natural order

leads him to enlightenment, through contemplating the uni-

verse itself.[27]

The "Chartrians'" affirmation of man's importance en-

abled new ideas to develop in fields other than theology.

For example, the observation of diverse forms in nature co-

incided with and helped to legitimize the varieties of spir-

itual life being experimented with.[28] But perhaps more

to the point of our discussion was the way these ideas

opened up new possibilities in ethics. In taking secular

life and accomplishment seriously, theologians were forced

to work out a body of lay morality, dealing with the prob-

lems of persons living in the world. As standards of judg-

ment used by confessors were transformed by a somewhat more

psychological interpretation, the subtle distinction be-

tween counsels and precepts in Jesus' teachings were ex-

plored as they had not been before. In a work as early as
Abelard's _Ethics_ and on into the new _summae_ _confessor-_
_um_ written mainly by the mendicants, emphasis shifted from
a mechanical listing of sins and penances to the develop-
ment of norms more consonant with individual intent. The
monastic virtues of poverty, purity, and meekness were replaced by ideals secular in origin such as justice, temper-
ance, and fortitude.[29]

One may speculate about how the eleventh-century defenders of clerical marriage might have used the broader
and more sophisticated learning of the twelfth-century religious humanists. Bishop Ulric's simple argument advocat-
ing _monere_ over _cogere_ would surely have been more impressive if he could have known Bernard Silvester's concept
of spiritual growth through aspiration, or Alan of Lille's
belief in the regeneration of man, or even Andreas Capel-
lanas' dictum that without love nothing of value is accom-
plished.[30] The idea behind the plea of both the second
and third Norman Anonymous, that some are intended to be
married whereas some should be celibate, is given a solid
foundation in Anselm of Havelberg's and Honorious of
Autun's treatises on diversity, even though the latter authors did not apply their theories to celibacy. And surely
the Anonymous from Rouen would have rejoiced to read

Bernard Silvester's celebration of human fecundity and
William of Conches' assertion that all of nature is good.
But the eleventh-century spokesmen had been forced to
defend themselves without the new knowledge which would
have strengthened their arguments.

As for the future, one might have expected that the dy-
namic intellectual changes, when they came in the following
century, would have counteracted the spreading popularity
of asceticism, but they did not. An examination of one of
the twelfth-century Renaissance's most impressive fruits,
the new awareness of human experience in the study of history, may illustrate why this did not happen. Sigebert of
Gembloux, Orderic Vitalis, and John of Salisbury were examples of men who sought to know, through the events of our
existence, the conduct of God towards men. Especially did
John of Salisbury exemplify this humanistic approach by rec-
ognizing the autonomy of the forms of nature, of the mind's
methods, of the state as an objective body.[31] And yet,
when monastic historians began to search primitive historical sources for proof of the authenticity and superiority
of their way of life, they did not discover what we know
lay there, namely, the evidence for a married clergy. They
found, instead, what they were looking for, and claimed
that the apostolic church had originated as a monastic in-

stitution. Confusing "communal" with "celibate" and ignoring the apostles' involvement in the world, they created an
image of the primitive church as a monastery, an image at
odds with what we know of its preponderance of lay, married
members; the historians among the canons regular, such as
William of St. Thierry and Hugh of St. Victor, agreed with
them. Again, when the Franciscans turned to the ideal of
the primitive church, they insisted that it had been made
up of paupers and virgins.[32] Thus the asceticism that
did not begin to be dominant in Christianity until the
fourth century was read back into the first-century church
by twelfth and thirteenth-century thinkers.

Not only did this case of "special pleading" by monastic and mendicant historians occur, but others had already
attacked the proto-scientific approach to nature and history. As early as 1080 Manegold of Lautenbach had disagreed with philosophers who sought out "the natures of
things" rather than concentrating on the nature of God
which is beyond this world.[33] In this matter as in several others Manegold is following Peter Damian, who had declared that God's omnipotence overrides natural law.[34]

The fact remains that in the twelfth century ascetic
values triumphed in the church as never before. Precisely
when lay culture was beginning to shake itself out of the

rigid "survival" mold of thinking of the early Middle Ages
it was overwhelmed by a newly energized clerical class
which imposed on both itself and the laity an essentially
monastic code of values. When groups of clerics such as
the spokesmen for "natura" dissented, they, like the defenders of clerical marriage before them, were far ahead of
their time. It is ironic that the latter group must be
seen primarily as conservatives, for while they were indeed
trying to hold on to old customs and values, at the same
time they began to, were virtually forced to, formulate new
concepts about human nature. But even when these concepts
appeared as much fuller statements in the following century, they were still ahead of their time, out of step with
the broad acceptance of Christian asceticism. Life was
seen as an endless struggle between flesh and spirit, a conflict which Christian thought has not entirely resolved to
this day.

I began this chapter by suggesting that the most revolutionary and lasting legacy of the Gregorians was the monasticizing of the clergy. Along with a better-defined law
code, this change contributed to the papacy's control over
its personnel which it needed to assume the predominant
place in the European world, a role which it filled magnifi-
cently for two centuries. The papacy furthered this con-

trol by every means, and by 1215 the majority of all church appointments, at every level, had been removed from local jurisdiction and were exercised directly by Rome.[35] The radical measures for the centralization of the church instituted by the Gregorians would appear to have been justified.

I suggest that a longer view, including the church of the late Middle Ages, would produce a different evaluation. Once set aside and above the rest of society, not only by function but by life-long vows, the clergy became "a race apart."[36] And as a race apart they were set up to be not only the mentors of their society but the objects of its resentments as well. When perfection was claimed for the sacral priesthood, some were bound to fall short, and when absolute power was claimed for church authority, some were bound to challenge it; these inevitable failures contributed to the anti-clericalism and criticism of the hierarchy which plagued the church in later centuries. Since early evidence for this unrest occurs in the twelfth century,[37] it appears that lay reaction was not slow in forming against this new concept of priesthood, and the gap between clergy and laity grew rapidly in the later medieval period.

* * * * * *

In the centuries since the law of celibacy was established, two rationales for celibacy have existed side-by-side: the idea of sexual purity as essential to sacral service has not diminished, not at least until very recent years,[38] while the belief in celibate freedom as necessary for pastoral service has grown to be of equal importance.[39] The former concept, after exerting extraordinary influence for a millenium and a half, finally began to retreat in the second half of the twentieth century under pressure from more affirmative beliefs about sexuality. Vatican II not only praised the sexual act as a bond, a source of companionship, between married people, but even refrained from declaring continence to be essential to the nature of priesthood.[40] The second rationale for celibacy, while of less ancient fame, may therefore prove to be of greater durability.

One should note that over the centuries, yet another quasi-doctrinal proof for the necessity of celibacy has appeared, one that represents something of an amalgam of the original two. It is the belief that the acceptance of the vow of celibacy creates a special state, makes possible the acceptance of the charisma of priestly power. This concept is not the old belief in chastity as a gift of God, a grace freely bestowed on certain chosen ones, which, as we have seen, was an idea championed by both sides in the eleventh-century debates, by both Anselm and the Norman Anonymous. It is instead a belief in the mechanical efficacy of the celibate state instituted by the act of ordination, which creates a new state of being and of power in all ordinands.[41] Carefully implanted as a part of a seminarian's priestly formation, this belief remains only a semi-official teaching, difficult to evaluate in terms of the ongoing celibacy debates.

Two conflicting concepts of priesthood underlie all of the celibacy debates which the Roman church has endured, a conflict that can be seen as clearly in the struggles of the eleventh century as of today. The issue can be stated in this way: is being a priest defined by receiving a sacred nature, which sets one apart from secular persons; or is priesthood defined by function, by service, by one's working relationship to other Christians? In sum, is it a matter of status, of "states of life with a meaning and a value in themselves, which could be idealized and then subjected to stricter and stricter regulations,"[42] -- or is it a matter of taking a particular role within a structure dependent on many roles?

The debate today is far from academic, just as it was
in fact a fundamental issue in the Gregorian age. I do not
mean that its reality lies in pragmatic questions, such as
"can congregations support priestly families?" I refer
rather to the fact that the Christian churches of the late
twentieth century face, in the aggressive scientific secu-
larism of our age, a time of decision, a need to find some
new directions. Ours is, I believe, a crisis of two conflicting concepts of the church, no less than was the Gregorian struggle. Reflecting on the spiritual crisis caused by
huge, impersonal urban congregations, a shrinking number of
priests, and an increasingly well-educated and active
laity, Jean-Paul Audet ponders that

> ... by letting the pastoral service become
> totally sacralized, we have, by the same
> token, cut from under us most of the ordi-
> nary possibilities of adapting it to the
> changing circumstances of time, place, indi-
> viduals and societies, cultures and civili-
> zations. You cannot accept an out-and-out
> sacralization and at the same time preserve
> all your likely chances of being part of
> the living moment of history. The reason
> for this is clear: the "sacred" will al-
> ways try to assume the greatest possible im-
> mutability in order to safeguard its own
> special function .... [43]

Urging the church to reconsider its basic idea of ministry,
in order to cope with these new needs, Audet concludes that

> it would be utterly paradoxical to try to
> preserve unchanged a totally "sacralized"

> pastoral service while hoping at the same
> time to see the gospel go forwrd in step
> with the general movement of history ...
> this is therefore the main context in which
> we must see the problem of the motives for
> clerical celibacy. For it is a law that
> harmonizes extremely well with a wholly
> sacralized pastoral service; yet it is by
> no means certain that such a service is in
> the best interests of the [church
> today].[44]

In light of a need for a less asceticized and more
flexible concept of ministry, the Roman church might do well
to reconsider the model of the pre-Gregorian priesthood.
What would be lost in terms of control and of status might
be well recompensed in the areas of better meeting pastoral
needs, of a rapprochement between laity and clergy, perhaps
even of an improved status for women.[45] If the church
should opt for a "mixed ministry," one in which celibacy
was freely chosen, then the structure of the church itself
might become more open, more flexible, more free to respond
to the spiritual needs of our age. It is perhaps time to
admit that the authoritarianism of the church, that great
legacy of the Gregorians to the high Middle Ages, no longer
meets its needs -- and that the church might begin to
divest itself of authoritarianism by dispensing with one
component of its absolutist power, the monasticized
priesthood.

NOTES

INTRODUCTION

1. The subdiaconate was declared one of the major orders in 1207 by Innocent III (PL 215. 1256-57) but the Gregorians already treated it as such in respect to marriage in the eleventh century.

2. James A. Brundage, "Concubinage and Marriage in Medieval Canon Law," Journal of Medieval History, 1.1, Apr. 1975, p. 7.

3. M. Rostovtzeff, Social and Economic History of the Roman Empire, 2nd ed. rev. by E. M. Fraser (Oxford, 1957), vol. 1, ch. 11, 12.

4. A. de Roskovany, Coelibatus et breviarium. 17 vols. (Pest-neutra, 1861-1888).

5. Walter Ullmann, The Growth of Papal Government in the Middle Ages, a Study in the Ideological Relation of Clerical to Lay Power (3rd ed., London, 1970), ch. 12. J.P. Whitney, Hildebrandine Essays (Oxford, 1932) 25-34, 80-94, having stated that celibacy was one of Gregory VII's original goals, ignores it as he develops his study. Gerd Tellenbach, Church, State and Christian Society at the Time of the Investiture Contest (Stuttgart, 1935, trans. R. E. Bennett, Oxford, 1940), 41-2, 52-7, and ch. IV (89-125), considers celibacy a secondary issue in the papal agenda.

6. John E. Lynch comments that "The effective establishment of clerical celibacy in the West was one of the major accomplishments of the Gregorian reformers," in "Marriage and Celibacy of the Clergy: The Discipline of the Western Church: An Historico-Canonical Synopsis," Pts. I and II (Jurist 32, 1972, Winter 14-38, Spring 189-212). Citation from Pt. II, 189. Referred to hereafter as "Synopsis."

7. Augustin Fliche, La Réforme Grégorienne (3 vols., Louvain, 1924-37) and Histoire de L'Eglise, VIII (Paris, 1944). Cited hereafter as Réforme and Histoire. A recent interpretation of Fliche's thesis has been made by Friedrich Kempf, The Church in the Age of Feudalism (trans. A. Biggs, New York, 1969), Handbook of Church History, III, 365. Kempf shows an admirable awareness of economic, military, and social factors, and yet he too removes the issues of class and of anticlericalism from the Gregorian

197

power struggle, thereby failing to separate clearly the
political from the ascetic goals. See also Carl Mirbt,
Die   Publzistik   im   Zeitalter   Gregors   VII
(Leipzig, 1894), 239-342, 372-462; Mirbt's work was
published too early to reflect on the range of documents at
Fliche's disposal and yet he offers a more critical and
well-rounded discussion of some of the key sources.
        8.   Albert   Dresdner,   Kultur- und Sittengeschichte
der   italienischen   Geistlichkeit   im   10   und   11
Jahrhundert (Breslau, 1890). Cited hereafter as Sitten-
geschichte.
        9.   Norman F. Cantor, Church, Kingship and Lay
Investiture in England, 1089-1135 (Princeton, 1958).
        10.   Christopher Brooke, "Gregorian Reform in Action:
Clerical Marriage in England 1050-1200," and "Married Men
among the English Higher Clergy 1066-1100," Cambridge
Historical Journal 12.1, 1-21, and 12.2, 187-88, 1956.
Eugen   Rosenstock-Huessy,   The   Driving   Power   of
Western   Civilization   (Boston,   1950),   presents   a   percep-
tive interpretation of the celibacy struggle as part of his
claim that the Gregorian revolution was a turning point in
Western civilization, the event which launched the great
period of advance for the medieval West (1100-1300). He
acknowledges that a celibate clergy, absolutely obedient to
the papacy, was essential for the revolution, to serve as
troops who would fight the Empire and the lay controllers
of church rights. He accepts the Gregorian conclusion that
only   sexually   pure   priests   could   claim   the   spiritual
strength to overcome and to control the laity. This new
image of the priest, as spiritual crusader, was the creation of the Gregorians. Pierre Imbart de la Tour, Les
Paroisses   Rurales   du   IVe   au   XIe   Siècle
(Paris, 1900) and Kempf (see n.7) show how feudalism increased the need for clerics to be married, claiming that
the disruption of society from the eighth century on made
the provision of life's necessities almost totally dependent on the family unit, especially for rural clergy. Showing further how the economic aspects of feudalism might
have supported the custom of clerical families, they illustrate how this institution encouraged hereditary ownership
of churches and, therefore, an hereditary priesthood. Dresdner's study, mentioned above, spells out the connection between lay ownership of church lands and the growth of a married clergy. On this subject see also Amann and Dumas,
L'Eglise   au   pouvoir   des   laiques,   888-1057   (1940)
317-18, 476-79.
        11.   George H. Williams, The Norman Anonymous
of   1100   A.D.,   Harvard   Theological   Studies   18

(Cambridge, 1951), 146-149. Bernard Verkamp, "Cultic Purity and the Law of Celibacy," Review for Religious 30, Mar. 1971, 199-217, maintains that, from the earliest years of celibacy legislation until the pontificate of the recent John XXIII, sexual purity was the predominant rationale for compulsory continency.

12. Basic works are Herbert Grundmann, Religiöse Bewegungen im Mittelalter (Hildesheim, 1935, 2nd ed., 1961); Walter L. Wakefield and Austin P. Evans, eds., Heresies of the High Middle Ages (New York, 1969, Columbia University Press Records of Civilization #81); Jeffrey B. Russell, Dissent and Reform in the Early Middle Ages (Berkeley, 1965); see also Raffaello Morghen's article, "Problèmes sur l'origines de l'hérésie au Moyen Âge," Revue Historique 235 (1966), 1-16.

13. Arno Borst, Die Katharer (Stuttgart, 1953), 80-81. Wakefield and Evans give two examples of eleventh-century attempts to link reform movements and heresy: Landulf Senior's allegation that the Milanese reformers, the Patarenes, were allied with the heretics of Monforte, and the Bishop of Cambrai's condemnation of the reformer Ramihrd for heresy in refusing the bishop's sacrament, to which should be added Ramihrd's refusal to accept the sacrament from a married priest, Register, ed. Caspar, I. 328.

14. Wakefield and Evans, 25, 50-51.

15. Henry C. Lea, History of Sacerdotal Celibacy in the Christian Church (Philadelphia, 1867; 2nd ed. rev. 1890; 3rd ed. rev. New York, 1907; New York, 1966, without footnotes). Lea apparently did not use the earlier three-volume work of J. A. and A. Theiner, Die Einführung der erzwungenen Ehelosigkeit bei den christlichen Geistlichen und ihre Folgen (Alternburg, 1825, 1845), nor did he incorporate the new material from the Libelli in his 1907 edition.

16. For an example of nineteenth-century Catholic thought about celibacy, see G. Bickell, "Der Cölibat eine apostolische Anordnung" in Zeitschrift für katholische Theologie, II (1878), 26-64, and III (1879), 792-99, criticized at length by E. Vacandard in the articles listed below in n. 17. Bickell's viewpoint that celibacy is of apostolic origin, although rejected by most Catholic authors of this century, returned as recently as 1969 in H. Deen's Le célibat des prêtres dans les premiers siècles de l'Eglise (Paris, 1969).

17. F. X. Funk, "Cölibat und Priesterehe im Christlichen Alterthum," Kirchengeschichtliche Abhand-

lungen und Untersuchungen I, 1897, 121-155; E. Vacandard, "Les origines du célibat ecclésiastique,"
Etudes de critique et d'histoire religieuse
I, 1905 and "Célibat Ecclésiastique," DTC 2.2,
1905; Henri Leclercq, "La legislation conciliaire relative
au célibat ecclésiastique," Histoire des conciles II. 2, 1908, 1321-48; H. Böhmer, "Die Entstehung
des Zölibates," Geschichtliche Studien Albert
Hauck zum 70. Geburtstage dargebracht von
Mitarbeiter Kreise der Realenzuklopädie für
Protestantische Theologie und Kirche. (Leipzig,
1916), 6-24.
    18. See n. 10.
    19. Nancy Partner, "Henry of Huntingdon: Clerical Cel-
ibacy and the Writing of History" (Church History, Dec.
1973) gives further support to Brooke's thesis; she shows
how an important English clerical family was forced out of
orders and off its hereditary lands during the twelfth century. Marriage was not eradicated entirely, however, for
Lea reports that in 1250 Boniface, archbishop of Canterbury, was "accused of matrimony;" Lea, 242, based on Matthew Paris, Historia Anglorum III (ed. F. Madden). The
following event in Yorkshire is recorded in two sources:
that John de Boulton, rector of West Rounton, had his banns
duly called, and was married to Isabella de Aslakely in
1276 by Michael, priest of Goldsborough. Still, Lea concludes that by the mid-thirteenth century, when Cardinal
Ottoboni presided at the great council of London in 1268,
"priestly marriage may be considered to have become nearly
obsolete in England," Lea 242, Wilkins Concilia II.5.
can. 8, which mentions only concubines, not wives.
    20. Jean-Paul Audet, Structures of Christian
Priesthood: a Study of Home, Marriage, and
Celibacy in the Pastoral Service of the
Church, trans. R. Sheed (New York, 1967); Roger Gryson,
Les Origines du Célibat ecclésiastique du
premier au septième Siècle (Gembloux, 1970),
esp. p. 203.
    21. M. Boelens, Die Klerikerkehe in der Ge-
setzgebung der Kirche unter besonderer Beruck-
sichtilgung der Strafe: Eine rechtsgeschichtliche
Untersuchung von den Anfängen der Kirche
bis zum Jahre 1139 (Paderborn, 1968), and two more
recent volumes. See also Lynch (n. 6); Georg Denzler, Das
Papsttum und der Amtszölibat, vol. I: Die
Zeit bis zur Reformation (Band 5.1, Päpste und
Papsttum, Stuttgart, Anton Hiersmann, 1973); and Michel
Dortel-Claudot, "Le Prêtre et la Mariage: Evolution

de la Legislation canonique des Origines au XIIe Siècle," L'Année Canonique, 17 (1973) 319-344.

22.   Samuel Laeuchli, Power and Sexuality: the Emergence of Canon Law at the Synod of Elvira (Philadelphia, 1972). Laeuchli, by indicating the many complexities and imponderables of a psycho-sexual interpretation of historical data, suggests a way of integrating the insights of psycho-history into conciliar research.

23.   Father R. J. Bunnik produced a useful historical survey in two articles for Cross Currents in Fall 1965-Spring 1966 entitled "The Question of Married Priests." "The Origins of Clerical Celibacy in the Western Church, " by Charles A. Frazee (CH 41, March 1972), concluding with the actions of Lateran I and II, contains several errors. Two recent volumes of the Concilium Series have been devoted to the celibacy issue, Identity of the Priest (1969) and Celibacy in the Church (1972). Both contain sound historical surveys. The Concilium discussions are marked by their breadth of approach to the subject: one is aware that the priesthood is considered as only one part of the church, that the life of the laity is taken to be of equal importance and worth. Father E. Schillebeeckx's book, Celibacy (New York, trans. C. Jarrot 1968), contains a satisfactory historical section; beyond that, it is a plea for making celibacy optional in the church today. See also Philippe Delhaye, "The History of Celibacy," NCE III (1967) 372, who makes a pertinent observation about the anti-celibacy movement of the eleventh century when he remarks that the men who fought the imposition of celibacy forgot the power of the church to make new law. Although Delhaye writes a general survey of celibacy, he does not mention nuns, nor do any of the authors listed above. Apparently the term "celibacy" does not apply to female religious because they take simple, not solemn, vows. The vow of chastity prohibits them from marrying just as it forbids male religious, but as they do not officiate at the altar, and in fact are not clergy, they have not been included in celibacy legislation.

1. Roger Gryson (Origines 39-44), Boelens (Klerikerehe, 39-40), and Lynch ("Synopsis," Pt. 1, 23) make it
clear that marriage for clergy was affirmed, not merely tolerated, and that almost all scholars of the early church
have accepted this interpretation since the 1890's.
2. Conversation with Prof. Howard Kee, Boston University School of Religion. William Phipps comments:
From the third century onward it was believed that
Jesus and his apostles were celibates, even though there is
no reference to a celibate Jesus in the historical sources
of Christianity and in spite of the fact that the New
Testament states that wives traveled with the apostles....

(The Sexuality of Jesus: Theological and
Literary Perspectives, New York: Harper & Row, 1973).
3. Jean-Paul Audet, Structures of Christian
Priesthood, Ch. 5.
4. William Phipps, Was Jesus Married? (New
York, 1970). For the opposite view see Gryson, Origines,
203-04, who maintains that the Hebrew legacy of sexuality
to Christianity was a negative one.
5. Audet, op. cit., p. 7 and Ch. 5.
6. Lynch, "Synopsis," Pt. 1, 19-20, based on PG
8.1191. Clement wrote: "Of course St. Paul wholly admits
-- and how we fail to admit also -- 'that the husband of
one wife,' be he priest, bishop, deacon or layman, if he
uses marriage without reproach, 'will be saved through
bearing children.'" (I Tim. 2:15).
7. Damasus I in 375, Ad Gallos episcopos (in
Jaffé vol. I, #255) sometimes wrongly attributed to
Siricius (see Clavis patrum Latinorum, 2nd ed., ed.
E. Dekker, #1632; Gryson, Origines, 127-131). Siricius
in 385, Ad Himerium, Jaffé, #255; Siricius at a
Roman council of 386, Jaffé, #258. Innocent I in 404
ruled only that those who had married twice could not
become clerics, Jaffé, #286.
8. Audet, Origines, 86-91.
9. E. R. Dodds, Pagan and Christian in an
Age of Anxiety (Cambridge, 1965), 35-37.
10. Samuel Laeuchli, Power and Sexuality, canon
33, p. 130. The canons can best be studied in José Vives

et al., Concilios Visigóticos E Hispano-Romanos
(Barcelona, 1963), can. 33, p. 7: "Placuit in totum prohi-
bere episcopis, presbyteris et diaconibus vel omnibus clericis positis in ministerio abstinere se a conjugibus suis
et non generare filios. Quicumque vero fecerit, ab honore
clericatus exterminetur." Several scholars have argued
that this text appears to state the opposite, that is,
that it seems to forbid clerics from abstaining (see
B. Verkamp, "Cultic Purity," 200, N. 6; Boelens, Klerikerehe, 39; Audet, Structures, 13), but all agree that,
given the sense of the other Elviran canons, #33 must have
decreed that clerics not have sexual relations with their
wives. J. Rehage misinterprets the canon, therefore, when
he writes that it forbade ministers of the altar "to have
wives" (NCE III, "Canon Law of Celibacy," 366). Audet,
ibid., remarks that at that time "ministerium" meant the
service of the altar.

11. The sources are found in the Church Histories
of Socrates (Bk. I, Ch. 11; PG 67.102-02) and of Sozomen
(Bk. I, Ch. 22; PG 67.926); which are available also in
Cassiodorus, Historia ecclesiastica tripartita, in
CSEL Vol. 71, ed. Jacob and Hanslik.

12. H-L, I.1. 312-13, c. 10.

13. H-L, I.1. 1034, c. 4.

14. Verkamp, "Cultic Purity," 202.

15. ODCC, 883.

16. Ibid., 631. Based on Jerome's De perpetua
virginitate B. Mariae adversus Helvidium, PL 23.
185-206.

17. The sources for Jovinian are Jerome's Adversus
Jovinianum, Geschichte der römischen Littera-
tur, ed. M. Schanz, IV.1.474 (Munich, 1914) and Augustine's
De bono conjugali and De sancta virginitate,
Schanz, IV.2.440, and De haeresibus #82, Schanz,
IV.2.438. Augustine wrote De bono conjugali and De
sancta virginitate in answer to the claims of Jovinian,
whom he mentions specifically in cap. 22. In De haeresibus #82 he describes the heresy briefly. For Vigilantius,
Jerome's Contra Vigilantium, Schanz, IV.1.478 ff., esp.
c. 61 and c. 109.

18. Philippe Delhaye, "History of Celibacy," NCE
III. 370, 374.

19. E. Vacandard, "Célibat Ecclésiastique,"
DTC II.2, 2071; based on Synesius' Ep. 105, PG 66.1485;
my translation from Vacandard's French translation.

20. Vacandard, op. cit., 2077; based on
Apostolic Constitutions, Liber VI, c. 17; PG 1.957.

21.   R. J. Bunnik, "The Question of Married Priests,"
Pt. I, Cross Currents (Fall, 1965) 418.
22.   Jaffé #410.
23.   Charles   Munier,   Concilia   Africae   in   Corpus
Christianorum Series Latina, vol. 149 (1974) p. 13.
Other councils legislated in response to Siricius' prohibition: Turin in 398 (Concilia Galliae I.58), Toledo in
400   (Concilios   Visigóticos)   and   Milan   in   390   (Ambrose, Ep. 42, PL 16. 1124-25).   Innocent I repeated this
rule of continence in his letters to Victricius of Rouen
and Exuperius of Toulouse (Jaffé #286 and #293, 404 and
405 A.D.).
24.   Carthage in 401, c. 4.
25.   Leo I on subdiaconate, PL 54.672-73.   Jaffé
does not record this ruling.
26.   Vannes, c. 11, Concilia Galliae I.154.   See
Audet, Origines, p. 193.
27.   John E. Lynch, "Synopsis," Jurist 32 (Winter,
1972), Pt. 1, p. 30, n. 89-95, citing Gallic legislation of
the sixth century.
28.   Gerona   in   517,   Vives,   Concilios   Visigóticos, p. 40, can. 6.
29.   The Trullan synod of 692, H-L III.1.561, passed
the disciplinary decrees necessary to carry out the work of
the Fifth and Sixth General councils; hence it often is
called the Quinisext, or Fifth-Sixth, Council (ODCC, p.
1397).   A General Council is an ecumenical one, involving
both Eastern and Western chuches (ODCC, p. 993).   About the
Quinisext Francis Dvornick wrote:
> Although convoked as a General Council, the
> synod was preoccupied exclusively with dis-
> ciplinary affairs of the Eastern Church.

(The   Ecumenical   Councils.   New   York: Hawthorne   Books,
1961, p. 35.) Walter Ullmann drew a more disturbing conclusion when he recorded that "the West was not invited to partake in the deliberations" (op. cit., p. 42).   The following is the crucial legislation.   Can. 13:   "Quoniam in
Romana ecclesia pro canonis ordine traditum esse cognovi-
mus, ut diaconi vel presbyteri, qui ut ordinentur digni ex-
istimati sunt, profiteantur se non amplius suis uxoribus co-
niungendos, nos antiquum canonum apostolicae perfectionis
ordinisque servantes, hominum qui sunt in sacris coniugia
etiam ex hoc temporis momento firma et stabilia esse volu-
mus, nequaquam eorum cum uxoribus coniunctionem dissolven-
tes vel eos mutua tempore convenienti consuetudine privan-
tes. Quamobrem si quis dignus inventus fuerit qui subdiaco-

nus vel diaconus vel presbyter ordinetur, is ad talem gradum assumi nequaquam prohibeatur, si cum legitima uxore co-
habitet. Sed neque ordinationis tempore ab eo postuletur,
ut profiteatur se a legitima cum propria uxore consuetudine
abstenturum, ne ex eo a deo constitutas et sua praesentia
benedictas nuptias iniuria afficere cogamur, evangelica
voce exclamante: Quae deus coniunxit, homo ne separet, et
apostolo docente: Honorabiles nuptias et thorum immaculat-
um, et: Alligatus es uxori? noli quaerere solutionem ....
Si quis ergo praeter apostolicos canones incitatus sit ali-
quem eorum qui sunt in sacris, presbyterorum, inquimus, vel
diaconorum vel subdiaconorum coniunctione cum legitima
uxore et consuetudine privare, deponatur; similiter et si
quis presbyter vel diaconus suam uxorem pietatis praetextu
eiecerit, segregetur; et si perseveret, deponatur."
Can. 48: "Usor eius qui ad episcopalem dignitatem promo-
tus est, ex communi consensu a viro suo prius separata,
postquam hic in episcopum est consecratus, monasterium in-
grediatur procul ab episcopi habitatione extructum et episcopi providentia fruatur; sin autem digna visa fuerit, etiam ad diaconatus dignitatem provehatur." (P. P. Joannou,
Les canons des conciles oecuméniques [Pontifica
commissione per la redazione del condice di diretto canoni-
co orientale, Fonti. Fasc. IX, Rome, 1962], 140-43 and
186.)

When Pope Sergius rejected its decrees, condemning especially can. 13 allowing clerical marriage, he widened the
breach between the Eastern and Western churches. Later
when Pope Hadrian I (772-95) quoted the canons of the Sixth
Council and Pope John VIII (872-82) approved the canons
"except those opposed to the custom of the Roman Catholic
church," it was assumed by some that they also accepted the
clerical marriage provision of the Trullan deliberations,
but such was not the case. ODCC, 1378-79; NCE, 12:30;
A. A. Vasiliev, History of the Byzantine Empire,
I.224-26; Louis Brehier, Histoire de l'Eglise,
vol. 5 (Paris, 1947), 193-97.

30. Council of Tours in 567, can. 20; Concilia
Gallia, II.184.

31. Rev. 2:6 -- "Sed hoc habes, quia odisti facta Nicolaitarum, quae et ego odi ... ita habes et tu tenentes
doctrinam Nicolaitarum."

32. Audet, op. cit., 9.

33. "Mothers of the Church: Ascetic Women in the
Late Patristic Age," by R. Ruether, in Women of
Spirit, eds. Rosemary Ruether and Eleanor McLaughlin, pp.
76-79.

34. John Boswell, <u>Christianity,</u> <u>Social</u> <u>Toler-</u>
<u>ance,</u> and <u>Homosexuality:</u> <u>From</u> <u>the</u> <u>Beginning</u> <u>of</u>
<u>the</u> <u>Christian</u> <u>Era</u> <u>to</u> <u>the</u> <u>Fourteenth</u> <u>Century</u>
(Chicago, 1980), p. 200.
35. Laeuchli, <u>op. cit.,</u> p. 106-13.
36. F. Kempf in <u>The</u> <u>Church</u> <u>in</u> <u>the</u> <u>Age</u> <u>of</u>
<u>Feudalism,</u> 341 ff., gives a realistic account of the pres-
sures on a rural priest to marry.
37. Pierre Imbart de la Tour, <u>Les</u> <u>Paroisses</u> <u>Rur-</u>
<u>ales</u> <u>du</u> <u>IVe</u> <u>Siecle,</u> 138-42, 343, sees clerical
marriage as a later result of the feudalization of the
church, rather than a long-established custom which fitted
well into the new feudal patterns.
38. Dresdner, <u>Sittengeschichte,</u> 149-57 and 310.
39. Council of Agde, can. 16 (Munier, <u>Concilia</u> <u>Gal-</u>
<u>liae,</u> p. 201): "Sane si coniugati iuvenes consenserint or-
dinari, etiam uxorum voluntas ita requirenda est, ut seques-
trato mansionis cubiculo, religione praesmissa, posteaquam
pariter conversi fuerint, ordinentur." Lynch ("Synopsis,"
Pt. 1, 30, n. 87) and Bunnik ("Married Priests," pp. 430-
31) cite M. Andrieu, <u>Les</u> <u>Ordines</u> <u>Romani</u> (Louvain,
1956) IV.140-41, in reference to the blessing and special
clothing, based on Ordo Romanus XXXV.
40. Council of Tours, in 567, can. 20, <u>Concilia</u>
<u>Galliae</u> II.184: "Nam si inventus fuerit presbiter cum sua
presbiteria aut diaconus cum sua diaconissa aut subdiaconus
cum sua subdiaconissa, annum integrum excommunis habeatur
.et depositus ab omni officio clericali inter laicos...."
41. Boniface's letter, Ep. 50 (<u>MGH</u> <u>Ep.</u> <u>select.</u>
I, 82-85) trans. Ephraim Emerton, <u>The</u> <u>Letters</u> <u>of</u> <u>St.</u>
<u>Boniface,</u> p. 80.
42. Zachary's answer, Ep. 51 (<u>MGH</u> <u>Ep.</u> <u>select.</u>
I.87-88), trans. Emerton, p. 84.
43. Carloman's synod, Ep. 56 (<u>MGH</u> <u>Ep.</u> <u>select.</u>
I.101), trans. Emerton, pp. 92-93.
44. <u>MGH</u> <u>Ep.</u> <u>select.</u> I.112: "Clemens genere
Scottus est,... synodalia iura spernens proprio sensu
adfirmat se post duos filios sibi in adulterio natos sub
nomine episcopi esse posse legis christianae episcopum."
This account does not identify Clemens' bishopric, but
concludes by reporting that he was stripped of office and
placed under anathema.
45. The Synod of Châlons notation is found in <u>PL</u>
131.23, in a letter from Mantio, bishop of Châlons, to
Fulcher, archbishop of Rheims. For Pope Adrian see Delhaye, <u>NCE</u> III.374, and Bunnik, "Married Priests," 418.
46. E. Martène, <u>Veterum</u> <u>Scriptorum</u> <u>Nova</u> <u>Col-</u>
<u>lectio</u> I.1.223-24. Rainaldus and his son Raimon were ad-

vised "... talem notitiam accipere, quo neque suo, neque successorum suorum tempora aliqua contentio pro ipsis decimas passit oriri; sed omnibus diebus, prout inibi definitum fuit, stabilitum, et firmum permanere, sicuti fecit ..." (p. 224). Since the decision is granted into the time of their successors, the possibility of an hereditary claim is involved.

47. Peter Damian, PL 145.408; Amann and Dumas, 478.

48. Ratramnus, Contra Graecorum opposita, cap. 6 (PL 121.324-32).

49. Lea, pp. 118, 126, concludes thus, primarily on the basis of Rather's and Atto's complaints (see my n. 51-54). On the other hand, Dortel-Claudot argues (p. 335) that since Carolingian times many clergy, "probablement les plus nombreux," came from schools for the priesthood where they were ordained to the subdiaconate very young and therefore remained celibate. I question that assumption on several grounds. What percentage of European priests were trained in the elite Carolingian school? And, how is one to explain the many references to men who married after ordination to the subdiaconate and diaconate, and even to the priesthood, during the tenth and early eleventh centuries, if one assumes that the only married clerics were men who had married before becoming ministers of the altar? It appears that during this period the term married clergy refers to large numbers of both types.

50. B. Thorpe, Ancient Laws and Institutes of England (London, 1840) II.329, 337.

51. Rather, De contemptu canonum, PL 136.491.

53. Rather's De nuptu illicito (PL 136.567-74) deals with celibacy, particularly with priests who married priests' daughters, and who made their sons priests: "Hoc eodem modo cum omnes noverint, quia omnis, qui praeter uxorem legitimam coit, aut fornicationem aut adulterium facit; presbyter vero aut diaconus uxorem legitimam non possit habere; si filium de ipsa fornicatione, vel, quod peius est, adulterio genitum facit presbyterum, ille iterum suum, suum alter iterum ... a mulieribus valetis nullo modo, filios de vobis generatos dimitteretis saltem esse laicos, filias laicis jungeretis, ut vel in fine saltem vestro terminaretur, et nusquam in finem saeculi duraret adulterium vestrum" (PL 136.571-72). Rather was wrong to state that deacons or priests could not have legitimate wives, but he was of course correct when he said that they could not have intercourse with them. For a discussion of Rather's troubles with his married clergy, see Lea, 116-21. The prohibited periods which he was able to enforce are recorded in his Synodica, c. 15, PL 136.566.

54.   Atto, Ep. IX, <u>PL</u> 134.115-119, "Ad omnes sacerdotes diocesis Vercellensis." Atto stated further: "Praeterea quod dicere pudet, tacere autem periculum, quidam in
tantum libidini mancipantur, ut obscenas meretriculas sua
simul in domo secum habitare, una cibum sumere ac publice
degere permittant. Quarum illecebris illecti, suae domui,
cunctaeque familiae ac supellectili eas praeesse dijudicant, suumque post obitum scortum haeredem constituunt, et
quiquid de facultatibus ecclesiae, vel eleemosynis, seu un-
decunque acquirere, possunt, hujusmodi manibus distrahendum
relinquunt ... et diabolo moechandum contradant.... Et inde
saepe maximum adversus sanctam Ecclesiam oritur scandalum;
quia quos vult habere filios, cernit inimicos, et quos con-
siliarios, duros adversarios." (116-117)

55.   On the German prelates see Adam of Bremen, <u>Gesta</u>
II.61 and III.29 (<u>MGH</u> <u>SS</u> VII.328, 346). Adam recorded
that at a synod in Mainz, 1049, presided over by Henry III
and Archbishop Libentius: "Praeterea multa sancita sunt ad
ultilitatem ecclesia prae quibus nefanda sacerdotum coniugia olographa synodi manu perpetuo dampnata sunt. De mulieribus statuit eandem sentenciam, quam decessor eius.... Libentius inchoaverat, scilicet ut fierent extra synagogam et
civitatem, ne male suada pellicum vicinia castos violaret
optutus." The Augsburg decrees are cited in Mansi 18.67,
438.

56.   See my discussion of Dresdner's study, pp. 33-34.

57.   E.   Sackur,   <u>Die   Cluniacenser   in   ihrer
kirchlichen   und   allgemeingeschichtlichen   Wirksamkeit
bis   zur   mitte   des   elften   Jahrhunderts.</u>   (Halle,
1892-94) I.1-26.

58.   A.   Fliche,   <u>La   Réforme   Grégorienne</u>,
I.33; Hauck, III.345; Amann et Dumas, 478.

59.   Mansi, 18.288.

60.   Camden's <u>Britannica</u> (Frankfurt,   1616),   274.
Based   on   <u>Cartulaire   de   St.   Martin   de   Pontoise</u>,
ed.   Depoin,   469;   and   <u>Chartres   de   l'Abbaye   de
Jumièges</u>, ed. Vernier, 15-17.

61.   <u>MGH</u>,   <u>LL</u>,   sect.   IV,   <u>Constitutiones   et   Ac-
ta</u>, no. 34, pp. 70-78. See esp. p. 73 and n. 2, which
quotes Justinian's novel 123, c. 14: "Si vero post ordina-
tionem presbyter aut diaconus aut subdiaconus uxorem duxerit, expellatur a clero curial civitatis illius, in qua clericus erat, cum propiis rebus tradatur." Whether or not Benedict VIII intended to establish this harsh practice, the
synodical report does not say. On the question of clerical
serfs who would not give up their families, it is clear
that he did not intend to demote them to the lay state.

62. On Leo IX, see Peter Damian, "Contra intemperantes clericos," PL 145.411. Since legislation assigning
the status of slave or chattel to clerical wives and mistresses will appear a number of times in this history, one
must ask if the language in the various decrees and canons
means what it says. Given the fact that slavery was moral-
ly legitimate in the Roman church until 1965 and evidence
that popes owned slaves until at least the eighteenth century, it is plausible that the women and children of clerics may have been enslaved by the church (see John F. Max-
well, Slavery and the Catholic Church, [London,
1973] pp. 10, 37, 76). David B. Davis confirms that "...
for many centuries bishops, popes, churches, and monasteries continued to own slaves," (The Problem of Slavery in Western Culture [Ithaca, 1966] p. 91). I conclude that the eleventh-century references are, indeed, to
slavery rather than servanthood or serfdom.

63. Boelens, op. cit., 117, 147. Lea, op.
cit., 122, observes that for Peter Damian "obscaena mer-
etricula" may safely be translated as "wife."

64. Verkamp, "Cultic Purity," 206-07, which cites, as
additional legislation against the wives and children of
priests, canons 5 and 10 of the synod of Toledo in 653 (ed.
Vives, Concilios Visigóticos, pp. 20-21 and 24-26).

65. Segenfrid of Le Man's story is reported in Bouquet, Recueil des Historiens des Gaules et de
la France, new ed. (Paris, 1874): After years of mis-
rule, Bishop Segenfrid "... ad cumulum damnationis suae ac-
cepit mulierem, nomine Hildeburgam, in senectute, quae, in-
gresso illo ad se, concepit et peperit filios et filias.
Quibus martuis, unus superstes, nomine Albericus, remansit,
quem adultum ditavit pater rebus Ecclesiae." The chroni-
cler does not hide his satisfaction over Segenfrid's death,
observing that, as the fatal illness came on, the bishop
"... nocte insecuta dormivit cum Episcopissa." (Based on a
citation from Acta Episcoporum Cenomannensium 29.)
About the bishop of Marsico, see Damian, Ep. Lib. 4, #8,
PL 144.310. A friend had told Damian: "Albericus, in-
quit, ecclesiae meae sub nomine episcopalis incubabat officii. Hic obscenae meretriculae prolectarius adhaerebat.
Qui videlicet dum Ottonis Augusti propinquum formidaret ad-
ventum, falsum mentitus est caelibatum ... ex eadem tartar-
ei prostibuli victima filium procreavit. Qui mox ut per in-
crementa temporum grandiusculus adolevit, pater cum sibimet
in episcopali dignitate substituit."

66. Orderic Vitalis, Historiae Ecclesiasticae
V.43 (ed. A. Le Prevost, II.362-63, 367), wrote about Hugh
of Rouen: "... legis Domini violator, clara stirpe satus,

sed Christi lumine cassus. Hic XLVII annis praesulatu functus est, sed a nullo ... laudatus est. Palam memorant quod habitu, non opere monachus fuerit." Orderic on Mauger: "Hic filius Ricardi II ducis ex secunda conjuge nomine Paphia natus est, et XVIII annis ... sin apostolica benedictione et pallio, Rodonensibus dominatus est. Voluptatibus carnis mundanisque curis indecenter inhaesit, filiumque nomine Michaëlem probum militem et legitimum genuit, quem in Anglia jam senem rex Henricus honorat ac diligit."

67. Eric John, "St. Oswald and the Tenth-Century Reformation," Journal of Ecclesiastical History IX.2 (Oct., 1958), 159-69: "Unde nunc ... monasterium quod Oswaldus amplificavit et eliminatis clericorum neniis et spurcis lasciviis religiosis dei servis monachis meo consensu et favore suffultus locavit." (Royal charter, Harley MS 7513.)

68. R. R. Darlington, "Ecclesiastical Reform in the Late Old English Period," EHR 51, 1936, 385-428. The Northumbrian Priests' Law shows that it was common for a priest to have a wife or concubine (p. 405, n. 1). Ethelred's laws make clear that clerical marriage existed elsewhere in England (VI Ethelred 5.2). All the same, celibacy laws were known in Anglo-Saxon times. Oda and Wulfstan's canon of 942 says that those in holy orders who are not celibate will lose their benefices and the right to burial in consecrated ground. V Ethelred 9.1 offers favors to clergymen to leave their wives:

> But he who will turn from marriage and observe celibacy shall obtain the favor of God ... the wergeld and privileges of a thegn.... (p. 406).

1. Mansi 19.503-06 --
can. 6: "Ut episcopi nullum amplius ad subdiaconatus gradum ordinent nisi in praesentia episcopi ante altare sedis Deo promittat, nunquam se habiturum uxorem neque concubinam."

can. 8: "Ut filii presbyterorum, sive diaconorum, sive subdiaconorum, in sacerdotio, vel diaconatu, vel subdiaconatu nati, nullo modo ulterius ad clericatum suscipiantur: quia tales, et omnes alii qui de non legitimo conjugio sunt nati, semen maledictum in scripturis divinis appellantur, nec apud saeculares leges haereditari possunt, neque in testimonium suscipi. Et qui de talibus clerici nunc sunt, sacros ordines non accipiant; sed in quocumque gradu nunc sunt, in eo permaneant."

can. 19: "Ut nullus filiam suam det uxorem presbytero esse ... neque filiis eorum."

can. 20: "Ut nullus filiam presbyteri, neque diaconi, neque subdiaconi, neque uxores eorum in conjugium accipiat, quia detestibile est. Nam S. Gregorius dixit: Qui presbyteram in conjugium duxerit, anathema sit."

2. Fliche, Histoire VII, 98-101.

3. Kempf, 250-55.

4. Jungmann, The Mass of the Roman Rite, vol. I, pt. I, ch. 10-11.

5. Saltet, Les Réordinations, 180ff. For the Vallombrosan influence, see K. Woody, "Damian and the Radicals," 4-42.

6. Ronald Knox, "Finding the Law: Developments in Canon Law During the Gregorian Reform, Studi Gregoriani IX (1972) 425.

7. O. J. Blum, "The Monitor of the Popes: St. Peter Damian," Studi Gregoriani II (1947) 459-473. Blum reiterates the point made in the quotation above from Ronald Knox, namely, the connection between clerical corruption and lay interference:

... the root of the twin evils of simony and clerical marriage ... was lay investiture (469).

8.   Damian,   "Liber   Gomorrhianus,"   Opusc.   7   (PL
145.159-90).   He defined the term Nicolaitan again in De
caelibatu   sacerdotum   of   1059:   "Praeterea   non
expavescis,   o   infelix   episcope,   quia   dum   in   luxuriae
voraginem   corruis,   Nicolaitarum   haeresim   incurristi,
Nicolas quippe, unus ex his quos Petrus apostolus diacones
consecravit,   dogmatizabat   clericos   cujuslibet   ordinis
nuptialibus   foederandos   esse   conjugiis"   (PL   145.385-86).
Damian   also   used   the   term   in   Contra   intemperantes
clericos   in   his   letter   to   Bp.   Cunibert   (PL   145.414):
"Et quis est pollutus magis in anima quam ... Nicolaita?"
9.   Humbert,   in   his   "Leonis   IX   Vita"   (Pontificum
Romanorum ... Vitae,, ed. I. Watterich, Leipzig, 1862,
vol. I.128) recorded that, as is human, Leo had occasional-
ly gone astray from the command to be celibate, but that
having   been   defiled   by   pollution,   he   had   been   reborn
through "the waters of tears."
10.   Bernold,   Chronicon   (MGH   SS   V.426);   Damian,
Opusc. 18 (PL 145.411):   "In plenaria synodo Leo papa
constituit, ut quaecumque damnabiles feminae intra Romana
moenia reperirentur presbyteris prostitutae, ex tunc et
deinceps Lateranensi palatio adjudicarentur ancillae."
Also   found   in   H-L   IV.2.1007   and   n.   2   and   3.   Boelens
translates ancillae as Sklavin (p. 206).
11.   At Rheims Leo decreed:
can.   11:   "Ne   quis   incestuosae   conjunctioni   se
copularet."
can. 8:   "Ne quis monachus, vel clericus, a suo gradu
apostataret" (Mansi 19.742).   These canons have been interpreted   as   prohibiting   clerical   marriage   by   Charles   A.
Frazee, "The Origins of Clerical Celibacy in the Western
Church,"   CH   41,   no.   1,   March,   1972,   162.   Brian   Tierney,
in   The   Crisis   of   Church   and   State   1050-1300
(Englewood Cliffs, N.J., 1964) comments that "The absence
of an explicit condemnation of clerical marriage is surprising, but canons 8 and 11 have both been interpreted to im-
ply   such   a   condemnation"   (p.   31).   Leo   spoke   directly
against marriage at other times, however, whereas these canons   do   not   seem   to   treat   the   issue   of   marriage   directly.
R.   W.   Southern,   The   Making   of   the   Middle   Ages,
125-127, discusses the council of Rheims at length but does
not mention celibacy enforcement.
12.   Adam   of   Bremen,   Gesta   pontificum   Hammaburgensis,   III.   XXX: MGH   SS   VII,   346-347:   "Praeterea   multa
ibidem   sancita   sunt   ad   utilitatem   ecclesiae,   prae   quibus
symoniaca haeresis et nefanda sacerdotum coniugia olographa
synodi manu perpetuo dampnata sunt."   At the same council

Bishop Sibico of Speyer, accused of adultery, was cleared
by sacrificial ordeal. See also Tierney, Crisis, 31-32.
    13.   Bonizo of Sutri, "Liber ad Amicum" V, LDL
I.589: "... ut tam clerici quam laici abstineant se a for-
nicatorum sacerdotum et levitarum communione ...." Notes
in Jaffé I.536, ante #4215, and mentioned in Fliche,
Histoire VII.103, n. 4. Damian's reference to this action
of Leo's in Contra intemperantes clericorum, PL
145.409B lends credence to Bonizo's assertion. See also O.
J. Blum, "The Monitor of the Popes: St. Peter Damian,"
Studi Gregoriani II (1947) 468-69, and J. J. Ryan, St.
Peter Damiani, and His Canonical Sources
(Toronto, 1956) 101, n. 196. I believe that the idea was
broached in 1050, probably by Hildebrand, and that it was
he who was responsible for its enactment at the Roman synod
of 1059 and for its execution in the 1070's, once he became
pope (see n. 23 below and p. 72).
    14.   Leo's letter to the Greek abbot Nicetae, PL
143.781-2.
    15.   Lea, 154, based on Lodovico Muratori's Annali
d'Italia III.1053, Biblioteca Enciclopedica Italiana
42 (Milan, 1838) 1355-56.
    16.   Humbert, Adversus Nicetam, PL 143.983-1000,
esp. 996-1000, Cap. 25-32: "Hinc perpendentes a te tam
perverse defendi adulteria potius quam nuptias sacerdotum,
arbitramur ab inferis emersisse principem hujus haeresis
nefandum diaconum Nicolaum" (PL 143.996).
    17.   Leo and Archbishop Dabralis of Spalato: noted in
Lea, 1907 ed., 220, but I cannot find his source, "Batthy-
ani Leg. Eccles. Hung. I, 401." Stephan Kuttner, "Pope Lucius III and the bigamous archbishop of Palermo," Medieval
Studies presented to Aubrey Gwynn, S.J., eds.
J. A. Watt, J. B. Morrall, F. X. Martin (Dublin, 1961),
notes that Alexander III, c. 1170, advised a bishop of
Spalato that "bigamous persons promoted to sacred orders
must be deposed" (p. 418 and n. 35, based on Jaffé
11690). Kuttner points out that the story circulating that
there was a bigamous archbishop of Palermo whom Pope Lucius
disciplined is false, and had been confused with Alexander
III's advice to the bishop of Spalato about bigamous
clergy. Perhaps Lea identified the supposed story about
Pope Lucius with Pope Leo IX. If so, a double confusion.
    18.   The Chronicon Monasterii Casinensis report-
ed that in Stephen's brief four-month reign, he "frequenti-
bus sinodis clerum Urbis sinodis populumque convenet, maxim-
eque pro conjugiis clericorum ac sacerdotum." MGH SS
VII.693; Jaffé I, post #4375. On the Eastern custom,
Stephen ruled at a Lateran synod in 1057: "Aliter se habet

orientalium ecclesiarum traditio, aliter huius sanctae
Romanae ecclesiae. Nam eorum sacerdotes, diaconi atque
subdiaconi matrimonio copulantur; istius autem ecclesiae
vel occidentalium nullus sacerdotum a subdiacono usque ad
episcopum licentiam habet coniugium sortiendi" (Jaffé,
p. 554, post #4375).

19. Damian at Lodi: "Sed cur ego ad coacervandos canones ultra progredior, quandoquidem hos ignorare ipsi etiam
nequeunt ...? Aliquando cum me Laudensis Ecclesiae tauri
pingues armata conspiratione vallarent ... (Ps. XXI: 13),
tanquam ructum fellis in os meum evomere, dicentes 'Habemus
auctoritatem Triburiensis, si tamen ego nomen teneo, concil-
ii, quae promotis ad ecclesiasticum ordinem ineundi conju-
gii tribuat facultatem.' Quibus ego respondi: 'Concilium,
inquam, vestrum, quodcunque vultis, nomen obtineat: sed a
me non recipitur, si decretis Romanorum pontificum non concordat.' Aucupantur enim quaedam quasi canonum adulteria
sarmenta, eisque praebeant auctoritatem, ut authenticam canonum valeant vacuare virtutem" (PL 145.402). J. J. Ryan
comments in St. Peter Damiani and His Canonical
Sources, 100, that he was unable to find the "Auctoritas
Triburiensis" mentioned by Damian's opponents at Lodi. It
is possible that the Quinisext legislation of the Council
in Trullo of 692 (see Ch. I, n. 76) was being exploited by
the adversaries of clerical celibacy. It is also possible
that they were misinterpreting Burchard of Worms' Decretum
III, 75 (PL 140.689).

20. At Compostella: "Adjicimus ... a conjugio separ-
entur et poenitentiam expleant, aut ab ecclesia et consortio Christianorum expellentur. Ita disponimus de presbyteris et diaconibus conjugatis." (Mansi 19.858)

21. The evidence from Lisieux is difficult to assess
because the only record of its proceedings is the later notation by Orderic Vitalis, Historia Ecclesiastica V.9
(ed. Le Prevost, II.237-43) included in his account of the
Rouen synod of 1072. It appears from Orderic and is con-
firmed by the Norman Tractatus (see Ch. III. pp. 123-24)
that clerics of the subdiaconate and above who lived with
women were to be deprived of their benefices and that canons and archdeacons were singled out for specific punishment, namely, that they were not to have "subintroductae
mulieres" living with them. The issue of excommunication,
however, seems not to have been raised in Normandy until
the canons of Lisieux were reissued in 1072 by Archbishop
John of Rouen.

22. At Toulouse: "Placuit quoque, presbyteros, dia-
conos et reliquos clericos, qui ecclesiasticos tenuerint
honores, abstinere omnimodis ab uxoribus vel reliquis muli-

eribus. Quod si non fecerint, honore simul et officio priventur, et a propriis episcopis excommunicentur."
(Mansi 19.848)

23. Roman synod of 1059, ed. Weiland MGH, LL
IV.1.547, can. 3: "Ut nullus missam audiat presbyteri,
quem scit concubinam indubitanter habere, aut subintroduc-
tam mulierem. Unde etiam ipsa sancta synodus hoc capitulum
sub excommunicatione statuit: Quicumque sacerdotum, diaconorum, subdiaconorum, post constitutum papae Leonis de castitate clericorum, concubinam palem duxerit vel ductam non
reliquerit praecipimus et omnino contradicimus ut missam
non cantet neque evangelium vel epistolam ac missam legat,
neque in presbyterio, ad divina officia cum iis qui prae-
fatae constitutioni oboedientes fuerint maneat, neque par-
tem ab ecclesia suscipiat."

On the clergy's living habits, can. 4: "Et praecipien-
tes statuimus, ut hi praedictorum ordinum, qui, eidem prae-
decessori nostro obedientes, castitatem servaverunt, juxta
ecclesias quibus ordinati sunt, sicut oportet religiosos
clericos, simul manducent et dormiant, et quidquid eis ab
ecclesiis competit, communiter habeant."

On Hildebrand's role, see Kempf, 363. Tierney's assumption, op. cit., 43, that all of the canons promulgated at the synod of 1059 except the prohibition against
lay investiture, "were typical of earlier reform legislation," may be correct but fails to note the impact which
this Roman synod made on contemporaries. Because of the uproar which it triggered, I believe that the injunction for
a lay boycott was also original as papal legislation.

24. Jaffé #4404; Mansi 19.873.

25. LdL I.254-260, "Pseudo-Udalrici Epistola de Continentia Clericorum," ed. L. de Heinemann. Later referred
to as the Rescript of Ulric. See Fliche, Réforme
III.1-12 for the identification of Ulric.

26. Bonizo of Sutri, Liber ad amicam VI, LdL
I.594, desribes how the Patarenes led a Milanese faction to
shun the altars of married priests. See also H. E. J. Cowdrey, "The Papacy, the Patarenes, and the Church of Milan,"
TRHS, 5th ser., vol. 18 (London, 1968).

27. Damian, PL 144.359-61. The capellani of Duke
Godfrey had seized the initiative by accusing Damian of
taking money from Countess Beatrice; Damian had to defend
hmself on this charge before he could attack them for their
marriages. He did so rather unconvincingly and then wrote:
"Dogmatizitis enim sacri ministros altaris jure posse
mulieribus permisceri ... Jam vero quod impudenter as-
sertis, ministros altaris conjugio debere sociari ..."
(359, emphasis mine). Rebutting this assertion, Damian

claimed that the Council of Nicaea had ruled that only lectors or cantors could be married, and that the papal legate
at the second council of Carthage, 419 A.D., had convinced
the council to rule the same. In both cases Damian was
twisting the facts; there was no such ruling at Nicaea, and
canon 2 at Carthage stated only that ministers of the altar
must abstain from their wives (Concilia Africae,
101-02). Damian repeats this argument in PL 145.400-01.
As for the bishops, Damian's argument with them runs
throughout part I of Opusc. 18, Contra intemperantes
clericos (PL 145.387-395).
          28. Mary McLaughlin, "Survivors and Surrogates," The
History of Childhood, ed. L. DeMauze (New York,
1974), 103-05. Based on John of Lodi's Vita, PL
144.111-46.
          29. PL 145.416.
          30. In regard to his asceticism and use of erotic lan-
guage, Damian's first utterance to the effect that "hands
that perform the sacrifice must not have touched the genitals of a whore" had been made in the Liber Gomorrhianus
(PL 145.159, c. 20). He enlarged on this sentiment
twice thereafter. In De caelibatu sacerdotum (PL
145.385): "Ad impositionem manus tuae descendit Spiritus
sanctus, et tu eam adhibes genitalibus meretricum.... Porro
qui in ecclesiastica cerneris dignitate conspicuus, non te
erubescis immergere fornicibus scortatorum? Et qui praedi-
cator constitutus es castitatis, non te pudet servum esse
libidinis? ... Qui enim flamina libidinis aestuas, qua fron-
te, qua audacia sacris altaribus approquinquas? ... Praeterea non expavescis, o infelix episcope, quia dum in luxuriae
voraginem corruis, Nicolaitarum haeresim incurristi?"
          In Contra intemperantes clericos (PL 145.393):
"Manus, quae deputatae fuerant ad ordinandas in coelestis
mensae ferculo vitales epulas angelorum, tractare non metu-
unt obscenitates et spurca contagia mulierum. Si, qui inter illa terribilia sacramenta choris admiscentur angeli-
cus, mox tanquam de coelo ruentes, ad feminae foeditatis re-
labantur amplexus, et velut suis immundae coenosis vermigen-
ae luxuriae volutabris immerguntur."
          In regard to the uxorious bishops, Damian was scathing
(PL 145.379-81): "... Sanctis eorum femoribus volui ser-
as apponere. Tentavi genitalibus sacerdotum (ut ita lo-
quar) continentiae fibulas adhibere.... Hujus autem capitu-
li nudam saltem promissionem tremulis prolatum labiis diffi-
cilius extorquemus. Primo, quia fastigium castitatis attin-
gere se posse desperant; deinde quia synodali se plectendos
esse sententia propter luxuriae vitium non formidant ...
pestis haec in tantum prorupit audaciam, ut per ora populi

volitent loca scortantium nomina concubinarum, socerorum quoque vocabula ... postremo, ubi omnis dubietas tollitur, uteri tementes et puero vagientes."

31.   Damian   on   women   "who   seduced   clerics,"   PL 145.410 ff.

32.   On clerical marriage as heresy, see n. 8 above. On incest, PL 145.384-85.

33.   On the necessity for some to remain virgin, Opusc. 18 (PL 145.393): "Si per haec verba conjugalis incontinentiae passim frena laxantur, episcopis etiam, sive monachis, insuper et abbatibus libertas eadem non negetur. Et quoniam uterque sexus non diversa lege constringitur, etiam sacrae virgines ad inerenda conjugalis copulae foedera provocentur...."

On the economic motive for celibacy, PL 145.393: "Muliebris, inquiunt, sedulitatis auxilio carere non possumus, quia rei familiaris inopiam sustinemus.... [To which Damian replies] ut paupertas indigna solitudinis feminarum doceat abdicare consortium, et greges inhianter edentium prohibeat gignere parvulorum."

That non-conforming priests should leave the clergy: PL 145.887.

34.   PL 145.384.

35.   Damian to Cunibert, PL 145.414.

36.   PL 145.399-400, "Clerici cur a populo segregantur," "Nos plane, quilibet nimirum apostolicae sedis aeditui, hoc per omnes publice concionamur Ecclesias, ut nemo missas a presbytero, non evangelium a diacono, non denique epistolam a subdiacono prorsus audiat, quos misceri feminis non ignorat. See also Woody, "Damian and the Radicals," 95, n. 2.

37.   Woody, loc. cit.

38.   Tours, 1060, can. 6, Mansi 19.927: If any in major orders "mulieris cuius libet carnali detentus copula, a ministerio et beneficio altaris non cessavit sive deinceps cognoscens praelibatum apostolicae sedis interdictum, aut mulierem aut ministerium ecclesiae cum beneficio non stati deseruerit, nullam restitutionis in pristino gradu veniam sibi reservasse cognoscat." Comments on the papal legates' role at Tour and Vienne, and Damian's later mission at Chalon-sur-Saône in 1063, can be found in the article by Robert Somerville, "Cardinal Stephan of St. Grisogano: Some Remarks on Legates and Legatine Councils in the Eleventh Century," in Law, Church and Society: Essays in Honor of Stephan Kuttner, eds. Kenneth Pennington and Robert Somerville (U. of Pennsylvania Press, 1977) 157-66.

39. Damian, Opusc. 18.ii.8 (PL 145.414): "Sed nunc accedit, ut hoc insigne vocabulum novum, si praevalent, accipiat incrementum, ut qui hoc tenus dicti sunt Nicolaitae, amodo vocentur et Cadalotae (Honorius II). Sperant enim, quia si Cadalous, qui ad hoc gehennaliter aestuat, universali Ecclesiae Antichristi vice praesederit, ad eorum votum luxuriae frena laxabit."

40. Alexander II, Ep. 133, PL 146.1410; and Gratian, D LVI, c. 13, n. 48-49.

41. In 1074 Gregory VII ordered an investigation of Pibo, bishop of Toul, who, it was charged,

> had lived in open relations with a certain
> woman, by whom he had had a child, and re-
> port had it that he had joined himself to
> her by a solemn promise and by a marriage
> after the manner of laymen.

(Register II.10, ed. Caspar, pp. 140-41). Bishop Judhael of Dol was also a married man and a father (see n. 46).

42. Mansi 20.433-34. The canons of this council are lost, but the decrees on celibacy have been reconstructed from Gregory's letter to Siegfried of Mainz, Register III.4, ed. Caspar, p. 250 and n. 1. "Si qui sunt presbyteri, vel diaconi, vel subdiaconi, qui in crimine fornicationis jaceant, interdicimus elis ex Dei parte omnipotentis, et Sancti Petri authoritate ecclesiae introitum, utque dum poeniteant, et emendent. Si qui in peccato suo preseverare maluerint, nullus vestrum eorum audire praesumat officium ...." Lambert of Hersfeld, Annales for 1074, ed. Pertz, (MGH SS V) on the vow of celibacy: "Ut secundum instituta antiquorum canonum presbyteri uxores non habeant, habentes aut dimittant aut deponantur; nec quisquam omnino ad sacerdotium admittatur qui non in perpetuum continentiam vitamque coelibem profiteatur."

43. Gregory VII (Register I.30, ed. Caspar, pp. 50-51) to Gerhardt of Salzburg, Nov. 1073: "Sed est, unde fraternitatem tuam neglegentiae merito argui putamus, quod de castitate clericorum, sicut nobis relatum est, preceptis Romanae synodi, cui interfuisti, inobediens usque hodie videaris ... Inde apostolica te auctoritate ammonemus, ut clericos tuos, qui turpiter conversantur, pastorali rigore coherceas et, quod Romana ecclesia te astante de inmunditia clericorum statuit, neque gratiam neque odium alicuius considerans constanti auctoritate in ecclesia tua predicando exerceas."

Gregory's letters concerning celibacy are the following, in MGH Ep. select. II, ed. Caspar, referred to as Register, and in The "Epistolae Vagantes" of

Pope   Gregory   VII,   ed.   and   trans.   by   H.   Cowdrey
(Oxford, 1972):
   Register, Bk. I: to Gebhardt of Salzburg, #30, p. 50.
   Ep. Vagant: to Otto of Constance, #8 and 9, pp.
      18-22.
   Register, Bk. II: to Henry IV, #30, p. 163-65.
   Register, Bk. II: to Rudolph of Swabia, #45, pp.
      182-85.
   Register, Bk. II to Anno of Cologne, #67, pp 223-25.
   Register, Bk. II to Burkhard of Halberstadt, #66, pp.
      221-22.
   Register, Bk. II to Anno of Cologne, #25, pp. 156-57.
   Register, Bk. II to Dietwin of Lutich, #61, pp.
      215-16.
   Register, Bk. III to Henry IV, #3, pp. 246-47.
   Register, Bk. III to Siegfried of Mainz, #4, pp.
      248-50.
   Register, Bk. IV. to William of England re Judhael
      of Dol, pp. 322-23.
   Register, Bk. IV. to Robert the Frisian, #11, pp.
      310-311.
   Register, Bk. IV. to Adela of Flanders, #10, p.309.
   Register, Bk. IV to Josfred of Paris, #20, pp. 326-29.
   Register, Bk. V to Huzmann of Speier, #18, pp. 381-82.
   Register, Bk. IX to Hugh of Die re William of
      England, #5, pp. 579-80.

See also the agenda for the autumn synod of 1078 (Regis-
ter, p. 401).
   Ep. Vagant.: to clergy and laity of Constance, #10,
      pp. 22-26.
   Ep. Vagant.: to clergy and laity of Germany, #11,
      pp. 26-27.
   Ep. Vagant.: to Werner of Magdeburg, #7, p. 16.
   Ep. Vagant.: to the faithful of Italy and Germany,
      #32, pp. 84-87.
   Ep. Vagant.: to Hubert of Thérouanne, #41, pp.
      102-03.

   44.   In Gregory's first letter to Otto, Feb.-Mar.
1075, he notified him of the decrees of the Lenten synod:
      Nor may those who are guilty of the crime
      of fornication celebrate masses or minister
      at the altar in lesser orders ... if they
      disregard our rulings or rather those of
      the holy fathers, the people may in no wise
      receive their ministrations ... (Ep. Va-
      gantes #8, ed. Cowdrey).

Gregory's second letter, late 1075, chided Otto for his dis-
obedience:

> [We commanded that] you might drive out
> from the Lord's sanctuary the simoniac her-
> esy and the foul defilement of polluting
> lust ... [for] the whole company of the
> catholic church are either virgins or
> chaste or married.... Thus, if we know for
> a certainty that even the least of laymen
> is companying with a mistress, we rightly
> bar him from the sacraments of the altar.
> ... How then can a man be a dispenser of
> the holy sacraments, when he can on no ac-
> count be a partaker of them?
> ... Yet you loosed the reins of lust so
> that ... those who had taken concubines per-
> sisted in their crime, while those who had
> not done so yet had no fear. Oh! what
> insolence, what audacity, that a bishop
> should despise the decrees of the Apostolic
> See.... Wherefore we command you to present
> yourself to us at the approaching synod ...
> (Ep. Vagant. 20).

Gregory brought the issue to a head a few months later in
his letter to the clergy and laity of Constance. Commanding
them not to obey Otto, Gregory assured them that such lack
of reverence would not imperil their souls, because

> If [Otto] is determined to resist apostolic
> precepts, we so absolve you by St. Peter's
> authority from every yoke of subjection to
> him that ... for so long as he is a rebel
> against God and the Apostolic See you are
> bound to pay him no fealty (Ep. Vagant.
> 23-25).

For a discussion of the dating of these letters, see
Cowdrey, The "Epistolae Vagantes," pp. 160-61. That
Otto was still holding out in 1080 is clear from Gregory's
letter to William of Hirsau in May, 1080 (Register VII.
#24, p. 503).

45. Lambert of Hersfeld, Annales, ed. G. Pertz,
MGH Scriptores V.218.

46. Ibid., at Erfurt: Siegfried "sciens ... ut tan-
to tempore inolitem consuetudinem revelleret atque ad rudi-
menta nascentis aecclesiae senescentem iam mundum reformar-
et, moderatius agebat cum eis.... Ad ultimum congregata sin-
odo, pressius iam imminebat, ut relegata omni tergiversati-
one, in praesentiarum aut coniugium abiurarent aut sacri al-

taris ministerio se abdicarent.   Multas econtra illi rati-
ones asserebant.... Nonnulli etiam confusis vocibus clamita-
bant, melius sibi videri, ut in synodum regressi, ipsum
episcopum, priusquam execrabilem adversum eos sententiam
promulgaret, cathedra episcopali deturbarent, et merita morte multato, insigne monimentum ad posteros transmitterent,
ne quis deinceps successorum eius talem sacerdotali nomini
calumpniam struere temptaret." Gregory's attempt to exhort
and discipline Siegfried is recorded in Gregory's Register
II.29 and III.4 (Caspar, 161-62 and 248-50); his excommunication of Siegfried was noted in Register III.10a
(Caspar, 268-69).

     47.   Vita S. Altmanni, author unknown, PL
148.878.

     48.   Roman synod V, of 1078, can. 12, Register VI.5b
(Caspar 405-06); PL 148.802, as can. 11: "Si quis
episco-pus fornicationem presbyterorum, diaconorum, seu
subdiaconorum, vel crimen incestus in sua parochia,
precibus vel pretio interveniente, consenserit, vel
commissum sibique compertum vel auctoritate sui officii non
impugnaverit, ab officio suspendatur."

     49.   To Anno of Cologne, Reg. II.67 (Caspar, 223-
25), written to publicize the decrees against unchastity
and simony promulgated at the Lenten Synod of 1075: "Hinc
etiam ... ut ad castitatem clericorum praedicandam ...
accingaris, ut sponsae Christi, quae maculam nescit aut
rugam, candidatae et immaculatae familiae gratiosum ex-
hibeatur officium."

     50.   To William the Conqueror, about Judhael of Dol
(Ep. Vagantes, #16, p. 44): "... nuptiis publice celebratis scortum potius quam sponsam ducere non erubuit, ex
qua et filios procreavit; ... per foedae libidinis incestum
corpus suum ita in contumeliam diabolo consecraret.... Nam
adultas ex illicito matrimonio filias, praediis ecclesiae
et redditibus nomine dotis collatis atque alienatis, scelere immanissimo maritavit."

     51.   To Bishop Josfred of Paris: Reg. IV.20 (Cas-
par, 326-29): "... admonemus, ut omnibus confratribus et
coepiscopis tuis per totam Franciam ... quatenus. et illis
sacerdotibus, qui a turpitudine fornicationis cessare nolu-
erint, omne officum sacris altaribus ministrandi penitus in-
terdicant...."

     52.   To Robert the Frisian, Reg. IV.11 (Caspar,
310): "... qui vocantur sacerdotes in fornicatione positi
non erubescant contando missam tractare corpus et sanguinem
Christi non attendentes, quae insania quodve scelus est uno
eodemque tempore corpus meretricis et corpus attrectare

Christi." On his use of the term "whores," see Boelens, 147.

53. In a general way David Knowles makes the same point about the Gregorian use of terms such as fornicatio when coniugium would not be incorrect, in The Christian Centuries II: The Middle Ages (New York, 1969) p. 170.

54. Fliche, Réforme II, 216-23.

55. "Maritos ab uxoribus separat; scorta pudicis conjugibus, stupra, incestus, adulteria, casto praefert connubio; populares adversus sacerdotes, vulgus adversum episcopos concitat." Goldast, Constitutiones Imperatorum Caesarum Augustorum ac Regum S. Imperii Romano-Theutonici (Frankfurt, 1713) III.314.

56. Lambert of Hersfeld, Annales, ed. Pertz, MGH Scriptores V.220-21, Reg. III.10a (Caspar, 268-71).

57. Reg. III.3 (Caspar, 246): "Inter cetera bonarum virtutum opera ... duobus te modis ... eminentius commendasti; in altero quidem, quia symoniacis viriliter resistis, in altero vero, quia clericorum castitatem ... libenter approbas et desideras adimplere."

58. Reg. II.45 (Caspar, 184): "... ad te et ad omnes, de quorum fide et devotione confidimus, nunc convertimur rogantes vos et apostolica auctoritate ammonentes, ut, quicquid episcopi dehinc loquantur aut taceant, vos officium eorum, quos aut symoniacae promotos et ordinatos aut in crimine fornicationis iacentes cognoveritis, nullatenus recipiatis.... [Emphasis mine]

59. Reg. IV.11 (Caspar, 310-11): "... Plurimi enim eorum, qui vocantur episcopi, non solum iustitiam non defendunt, sed etiam, ne clarescat, multis modis occultare nituntur. Tales vero non episcopos, sed Christi habeto inimicos. Et sicut illi non curant apostolicae sedi oboedire, ita vos nullam eis oboedientiam exhibete...."

60. The desertion in 1084 of thirteen cardinals, all important to Gregory's administration, was a severe blow to the pope's battle against the empire. Among the defectors were Peter the chancellor, Theodinus the archdeacon, Peter the oblationarius with all his staff save one, Pappo, head of the College of Regionarii and all his staff, Cincius, the pope's boyhood friend and head of the Judices with all his subordinates, John, head of the School of Cantors and all his staff, and the Prior of the Scriniarii. (Noted by J. P. Whitney, Hildebrandine Essays, 92, based on Meyer von Knonau, Jahrbucher des Deutschen Reiches unter Heinrich IV und V [Leipzig, 1898-1909] III.525, n. 7.)

61. LdL II.60-88.

62.   Bernold, *Chronicon*, ed. Pertz, MGH SS
V.436: "In hoc synodo papa ... scriptum quod dicitur sancti Oudalrici ad papam Nicolaum de nuptiis presbyterorum, et
capitulum Pafnutu de eadem re, immo omnia sacris canonibus
adversa, damnavit." Bernold's is the only known reference
to this condemnation.

63.   Fliche, *Histoire* VIII. 134-36, based on the
texts from Worms (MGH Leges, Const. I.106-113) and
letters of Henry IV (*ibid.* 108, 113, 144). Fliche,
Réforme II.281, on the three letters issued by the
imperialists at Worms: "Les trois textes qui viennent
d'être analysés constituent une résponse aux
Dictatus Papae."

64.   Wenric of Trier, LdL I.286-88, lists the grievances concerning celibacy enforcement at Brixen.

65.   *Ibid.* See my discussion of this passage of Wenric's treatise in Ch. Three.

66.   Lea, 195. Based on Honorius III's *Vita Gregorii VII*, 15. One must note that Honorius' biography was
written over a hundred years after the event by a pope also
dedicated to eradicating clerical unchastity.

67.   *Liber ad Gebehardum*, ed. K. Franke, Ldl
I.308-430. See especially chapters 16-24, 67-68, 76-78.
Manegold based several of his passages on Bernold's *Apologeticus*: Mangeold's c. 22, 71, 72 were extrapolated from
Bernold's c. 11-13, 16-19. Manegold on deposing the king:
"Ad vero, si ille (rex) non regnum gubernare, sed regni oc-
casione tyrannidem exercere, iusticiam destruere, pacem con-
fundere, fidem deserere exarserit, adiuratus iuramenti necessitate absolutus existit, liberumque est populo illum de-
ponere, alterum elevare, quem constat alterutre obligatio-
nis rationem prius deseruisse.... Super quo igitur scelere
postquam hunc Romana sinodus iusta, ut supra probatum est,
ratione deposuit, regia dignitate privavit, nulla regie po-
tentatis reverentia a christiano populo fuit exhibenda.
Pertinuit igitur ad apostolici officium populum de his se-
curum reddere, quem de exhibitis sacramentis vidit sollici-
tum estuare." (392) Fliche claims that this is "ou les
droits du peuple sont pour la première fois pris en
sérieuse consideration" (*Histoire* VIII.196). For a
more critical view of Manegold, see Carlyle, *A History
of Medieval Political Theory in the West*
(Edinburgh, 1916) vol. III.163-167, and Mirbt, 233.

68.   *Ibid.*, c. 22, "Ut incontinentes penitus dampnen-
tur": After quoting many sources -- Nicaea, popes Silvester, Leo I, and Innocent I, and Augustine's *De bono
coniugali*, Ambrose's *de officiis* and especially Jerome's *Contra Jovinianum*, he concluded: "Si igitur Inno-

cencius papa presbyteros, qui in presbytero filios genuisse
asserebantur, discussos sive convictos a sacerdotali officio arceri precepit, eius successor Gregorius parum pecca-
vit, dum non eos, qui filios generasse quadem adhuc ambigui-
tate infamantur, sed in stupris et fornicacionibus publice
et inverecunde noscuntur iacere, a sacris ministeriis alien-
avit.... Videsne igitur, quam sapienter noster apostolicus,
immo quam clementer, fornicariis ministris et presbyteris
ministrandi accessum interdixit, quos concors et consona omnis sanctorum auctoritas patrum vel ad acriorem redigendos
vel perpetuo anathemate dampanados vel penitus a clero iudi-
cavit disturbandos?" (349, 353)

     69.   Manegold uses one of Damian's coarsest arguments
to prove the necessity for cultic purity. Having described
how the priests of the Old Testament were contaminated after sacrificing animals, Damian asked: "Et quis est pollutus magis in anima quam ... Nicolaita? ... Alter vero, dum
carnem suam per obscenitatem fornicationis polluit, conse-
quenter in anima omnia fedae contaminationis inquinamenta
transfundit; et hic ergo pollutus in anima nicholominus dicitur, atque idea quidquid tangit attaminat, quia, dum in illius petulantiae voraginem labitur et animam simul et corpus purulento caenosae libidinis squalore fedat." (Manegold, 422; Damian, PL 145.414) His source for the treatment of priests' sons is the ninth council of Toledo held
in 655: "proles autem alienata pollutione non solum parentum hereditatem nunquam accipient, sed etiam in servitute
eius ecclesiae, de cuius sacerdotis vel ministri ignominia
nati sunt, iure perenni permanebunt." (Manegold, 355; Toledo, can. X, Concilios Visigóticos, ed. Vives, et
al., pp. 24-26.)

     70.   Ibid., pp. 353-55, 419-20: In "De dampnatione
infelicium muliercularum sacris ministris prostitutarum"
and "Cur populis Symoniacorum et Nicolaitarum officia pro-
hibeantur," Manegold uses a long quotation from Damian's tirade against women who consort with priests; an excerpt
will suffice to illustrate it: "Venite itaque, audite me,
scorta, prostibula, volutabra porcorum pinguium, cubilia
spirituum immundorum, nymphae, syrenes, lamiae, dianae, et
si quid adhuc portenti, si quid prodigii reperitur, quod
nomini vestro competer iudicetur. Vos enim estis demonum
victimae, ad eterne mortis incendium destinatae...." (353;
Damian, PL 145.410). See my trans. and discussion, pp.
60-62.

     71.   Gregory I: "Si enim quasi peccatum ariolandi est
repugnare et quasi scelus idolatriae nolle acquiescere,
sola obedienta est, que fidei meritum possidet. Qua sine
quisque infidelis esse convincitur, etiam si fidelis esse

videatur.   (In moralium libro, 35.14, c. 28; PL
76.765) In Manegold's time the term "infideles" carried
the double connotation of being unfaithful to one's feudal
lord as well as to Christ, in the sense of having no faith,
whereas the haeretici are those who hold to the wrong
faith (du Cange, IV.354 and 154-55).   For Damian, see Ep.
ad Cunibertum, PL 145.398 ff.
    72. Manegold, pp. 421-30.   For Bernold, see his "Apo-
logeticus," 17-19, LdL II.80-84, esp 83.
    73. "Liber de vita christiana," ed. E. Perels, Texte
zur Geschichte des romischen und kanonischen
Rechts im Mittelalter herausgegeben von der
preussischen Academie der Wissenschaft, I (Berlin,
1930). See especially III.28-29.   For the events at Piacenza, see Paul Fournier, "Bonizo de Sutri, Urbain II et la
comtesse Mathilde d'après le Liber de Vita Christiana de Bonizo," Bibliothèque de l'Ecole des
Chartres, vol. 76 (1915) 263-98, esp 274-75.
    74. "Liber de vita christiana," I.43.   Council of Pia-
cenza, ed. Weiland, MGH Consts. IV.1.562, can. 3 and 9.
Fliche, Histoire VIII.267.   Kempf, 389, on Urban's legislation at Piacenza: "It is obvious that the decrees, which
were open to varying theological interpretations and were
lacking in consistency, left the dogmatic problem un-
solved."
    75. Gebhardt: Ep. ad Heremannum, ed. K.
Franke, LdL I.271-79.   Bernard: probably the author of
Liber canonum contra Heinricum IV, ed. Thaner,
LdL I.471-516.   Bernold: Apologeticus, LdL I.94-101.
Anselm of Lucca: Liber contra Guibertum, ed. E.
Bernheim, LdL I.517-28.
    76. Urban II, Jaffé #5471; Ep. 70, PL 151.356.
    77. Anselm, Ep. 391, Opera Omnia V (ed. Schmitt)
336-37; Henry of Huntingdon, Historia Anglorum, Bk.
VII; Eadmer, Historia Novorum 172, 175, 457, 459.
    78. On Aldebert, see Ivo's letter to him, Ep. 277 (PL
162-279):   "Dicunt enim quidam de majoribus Cenomannensis
ecclesiae, qui anteactam vitam tuam se nosse testantur,
quod ultra modum laxaveris frena pudicitiae, in tantum ut
post acceptum archidiaconatum accubante lateribus tuis
plebe muliercularum, multam genueris plebem puerorum et
puellarum.   Tu nost.; qui ... post sacrum ordinem lapsus
non solum non debet ad majorem gradum conscendere, sed nec
in eo in quo lapsus est ordine ministrare."
    79. Melfi, 1089, c. 12 (Mansi 20.724) "Quod si ab
episcopo commoniti non se correxerint, principibus licentiam indulgemus, ut eorum feminas mancipent servituri.   Si

vero episcopi consenserint eorum pravitibus, ipsi officii interdictione mulctentur."

80.   Paulus   Bernried,   Vita Gregorgii VII,   81, 107 (ed. J. Greving); also PL 148.71-72, 108. Orderic II.64.

81.   Lea claims, without documentation (p. 264), while discussing Pope Calixtus' actions of 1119, that in 1090 Urban promulgated the first decree delcaring void the marriages of men in the subdiaconate and above:

> [Calixtus' decree] was a bold innovation. With the exception of a decretal of Urban II in 1090, to which little attention seems to have been paid, we have seen that previous to Calixtus, the sacrament of marriage (for clerics) ... was respected and its binding force was admitted.... Calixtus now ... declared the sacrament of marriage to be less potent than the religious vow. [Emphasis mine]

The only reference I can find for clerical marriage in Urban's decrees near that date concerns a synod in Szaboles, Hungary, in 1092, where it was ruled that a woman who becomes the second wife of a priest must be separated from him but can remarry, because her "marriage" to him was not valid (Mansi 20.759-60). However, the tenor of that and other canons was the opposite of what Lea claimed. Urban appears to have been offering legitimacy to the Hungarian clergy, to be condoning "one legitimate marriage" for a priest (can. 3). Boelens (Die Klerikerehe, 154) believes that these Hungarian decrees do not declare clerical marriage invalid; he observes, however, that Urban's ruling at Melfi on the subdiaconate was a step towards declaring clerical marriage null. Paschal II's decree of Troyes in 1107 forbidding unchaste clergy to enter a church or to associate with laity also furthered this intention, although the former prohibition had already been made by Gregory VII and the latter by Victor II at Toulouse (1056). But Boelens concludes that none of this legislation declared nullity (Boelens 157.164-66).

82.   Melfi, can. 14 (Mansi 20: 724): "Presbyterorum filios a sacri altaris ministeriis removendos decernimus, nisi aut in coenobiis aut in canoniciis religiose probati fuerint conversati."

83.   Mansi 20.803, based on Bernold's Chronicon, 1095.   Weiland, MGH Constitutiones IV.1.560-63, does not include this canon among the sixteen which he lists from Piacenza. F. J. Gossman, Pope Urban II and Canon Law (Washington, D. C., 1960), p. 3, comments that

the acts of Piacenza, since they are found only in Bernold's résumé and in one later reconstruction, are difficult to work with.

84. Robert Somerville, The Councils of Urban II, I.144, can. 10-12. Mansi 20.817 (here can. 10 is numbered 9): "Ut nullus sacerdos, aut diaconus, aut subdiaconus, sed et nullus qui canonicam habet, fornicationis sibi copulam adjungat. Quod si quis federit a canonica omnino arceatur." The Clermont decree was reissued at Rouen, Tours, Nimes, and Poitiers (Boelens, 155). On cathedral canons, see T. P. McLaughlin, "The Prohibition of Marriage against Canons in the early Twelfth Century," MS 3 (1941), 94-100.

85. Orderic, in II.64, claimed this action stemmed directly from Leo IX's reform synod of 1049. See my Chapter Two, n. 20-22, for the church-wide celibacy legislation of 1055-56, and Chapter Three, pp. 117-18 for my discussion of Lisieux.

86. Orderic II.162 and n.1.

87. Ibid., 64, n.1; and 8 and n.1. Mansi XX.33ff.

88. On Robert and Bernard, see Gaufridus Grossus, Vita Bernardi Tironiensi, PL 172.397-99, c. 6, 49-54. Robert and Bernard were incensed that "... pro consuetudine tunc temporis per totam Northmanniam hoc erat, ut presbyteri publice uxores ducerent, nuptias celebrarent, filios ac filias procrearent, quibus haereditario jure post obitum suum ecclesias relinquerent; filias suas nuptui tradentes multoties, si alia deesset possessio, ecclesiam dabant in dotem. Dum autem uxores acciperunt, antequam sibi eas conjungerent in praesentia parentum jurabant, quod nunquam eas desererent ...." Bernard preached against these deadly customs in assemblies of priests, when "... Quadam die dum in Constantiis populo publice praedicaret, quidam archidiaconus uxorem habens et filios, cum magno presbyterorum atque clericorum comitatu advenit et cur ipse, qui monachus ac mundo mortuus erat, viventibus praedicaret requisivit. Bernardus respondit.... Haec, et alia hujusmodi viro Dei prosequente, atque populo secum acclamante, nutu Dei praedictus archidiaconus ferocitatem atque arrogantiam animi sui aliquantisper deposuit, et presbyteros atque uxores eorum ab ejus laesione compesciut." See also Ernst Werner's discussion of Robert's career, in Pauperes Christi (Leipzig, 1956) 53-58.

89. R. R. Darlington, "Ecclesiastical Reform in the late Old English Period," EHR 51 (1936) 385-428.

90. Vita Wulfstani of William of Malmesbury, Camden 3rd Series, 40, 53, ed. R. R. Darlington. Discussed by Darlington, "Ecclesiastical Reform in the late Old English

Period," 407. For Lanfranc's decree, see Wilkins, Concilia I.367, and his Ep. 21 (PL 150.526) which illustrated
his insistence that married clergy not be promoted.
    91. Orderic, Pt. II (ed. Chibnall) 38-39.
    92. Brooke, "Clerical Marriage," 56 and n. 29, 59 and
n. 52.
    93. Orderic, Pt. II.V (PL 20.556) can. 3: "... Si
vero paroecianorum vel dominorum aliquis eum accusavit,
habeat accusatus inducias, ut cum episcopo possit loqui:
et si purgare se voluerit in eadem paroecia cui servit,
praesentibus parochianis pluribus ante ministros episcopi
et coram judicio se purgabit." William assures the bishops
that he has encroached on their rights only temporarily, because they have themselves failed to act. Can. 5: "Presbyteri ab episcopis vel ab eorum ministris praeter iustos red-
ditus episcopi, vi vel minis dare nihil cogantur. Propter
eorum feminas nulla pecuniae emendatio exigatur."
    94. Gregory VII, writing to William the Conqueror in
1076 concerning Judhael, complained of Judhael's simony and
continued: "Qui etiam nec hoc scelere contentus iniquitate
super iniquitatem apposuit et, quasi simoniacum esse parum
et pro nihilo deputaret, nicolaita quoque fieri festinavit.
Nam in ipso tam perniciose adepto episcopatu nuptiis publice celebratis scortum potius quam sponsam ducere non erubuit, ex qua et filios procreavit; ut qui iam spiritum suum
animarum corruptori per simoniaca commercia prostituerat,
per foedae libidinis incestum corpus suum ita in contumeliam diabolo consecraret.... Nam tamen hoc usque conatus malitiae substitit, sed etiam atrocissimum facinus turpissi-
mumque flagitium horrendo etiam sacrilegio cumulavit, Nam
adultas ex illicito matrimonio filias, praediis ecclesiae
et redditibus nomine dotis collatis atque alienatis, scelere immanissimo maritavit." Epistolae Vagantes, #16
(ed. Cowdrey) p. 44. On Willam's refusal to reform the
scandal at Dol, see Gregory's letter to him of 1077, Register IV. 17 (ed. Caspar) 322-23; J-L #5027. On the other
Breton irregularities, see Lea, 312, based on Roujoux's
Histoire de Bretagne II.98-99.
    95. David R. Bates in his "Character and Careeer of
Odo, Bishop of Bayeux (1049-1097)" Speculum 50 (Jan.
1975) 1-18, assesses the contribution of this worldly
prelate and the bishopric he ruled for half a century:
        ... no other bishopric [than Bayeux] pro-
        duced so many men of distinction, and even
        if it produced no one with the intellectual
        power of the Norman Anonymous, its contribu-
        tions to the practical government of con-

quered England and of its bishoprics and
monasteries was fundamental and unrivalled.
Bates, p. 4, concludes that Odo had only one wife, one son,
and no concubines, despite Orderic's accusation that he was
a womanizer.

96. Brooke, "Clerical Marriage," 57 and n. 36, n. 38,
n. 39.

97. Orderic, Pt. II (ed. Chibnall) 57-58, reports
that Guitmond had been strongly critical of William the Conqueror's drive for power and of the greed of his churchmen.
When the latter retaliated by objecting to Guitmond's appointment,

> They found nothing, however, to object to,
> in a man of his worth, but that he was the
> son of a priest. Upon this, Guitmond ...
> petitioned to travel abroad.

98. W. Camden, _Britannia_ (Frankfurt, 1616). Referring to the monastery of St. Peter and St. Paul: "Comes
Rogerus ... cui plures possessiones concessit, et una cum
illis Ecclesiam S. Gregorii, eo scilicet tenore ut cum Canonici, qui in ea Praebendas habebant, morte deficerent,
Praebendae in dominium monachorum devenirent. Unde controversia orta est non parua: Canonicorum enim filii litem
monachis intenderunt, ut in paternis Praebendis succeder-
unt. Eo enim tempore canonici, et Sacerdotes in Anglia
caelibem vitam non egerunt, et inoleverat usus ut beneficia
ecclesiastica cognationis iure haereditario descenderent.
Sed haec controversia sub Henrico primo composita, cum in
beneficiis Ecclesiasticis haeredem non debere succedere et
leges de Sacerdotum coelibatu sub id tempus rogatae sunt."

99. Wilkins I.382; Mansi, 20.1151, can. 5: "Ut presbyter, quandiu illicitam conversationem mulieris habuerit,
non sit legalis, nec missam celebret; nec si celebraverit
ejus missa audiatur." Can. 6: "Ut nullus ad subdiacona-
tum, ut supra, ordinetur sine professione castitatis."
Can. 7: "Ut filii presbyterorum non sint haeredes Ecclesiarum patrum suorum." See also Anselm's Ep. 257, written in
1103 (ed. Schmitt, IV.169-70).

100. Henry of Huntingdon, _Historia Anglorum_ (ed.
T. Arnold) Rolls Series #74 (1879) VII.234. Discussed by
Nancy Partner in "Henry of Huntingdon: Clerical Celibacy
and the Writing of History," _Church History_ XLII.4
(Dec. 1973) 467-75.

101. Mansi 20.1229; Wilkins I.387-88.

102. Anselm on monks, _Opera Omnia_ IV.165 (ed.
Schmitt) Ep. 254: "Quoniam autem ipsi malunt dimittere
quidquid pertinet ad presbyteri officium quam feminas: si
aliqui inveniuntur casti, faciant pro illis. Si autem

nullus aut paucissimi tales inveniuntur, iubete ut interim
monachi missas dicant populo, ubi ipsi fuerint, et faciant
corpus domini, quod per clericos portetur aegrotis."
Anselm on priests' property and wives (Wilkins I.388, can.
10): "Omnia vero mobilia lapsorum posthac presbyterorum,
diaconorum, subdiaconorum, et canonicorum tradentur
episcopis, et concubinae cum rebus suis, velut adulterae."
Wives came under further attack at the London Council of
1127, when it was ruled that the woman of a cleric who,
having been separated, returned to him, would be tracked
down by the bishop's ministers and handed over either to
ecclesiastical discipline or episcopal servitude (Wilkins
I.410-11).

   103.   Anselm, Ep. 374, Opera Omnia V (ed. Schmitt)
318, on married priests in Canterbury who kept both wives
and benefices: "Scripsit mihi archidiaconus noster Willel-
mus quia nonnulli presbyteri, qui sub ejus sunt custodia,
iterum repetentes prohibitas feminas in immunditiam, a qua
salubri consilio et jussione abstracti fuerunt, se revolver-
unt. Quod cum idem archidiaconus vellet corrigere, omnino
ejus monitionem et susceptibilem jussionem nefanda super-
bia contempserunt. Qui ... superbos et inobedientes gladio
excommunicationis percussit. Quam excommunicationem besti-
ali insania contemnentes, ministerium sanctam polluere,
quantum in ipsis est, non formidant. Quapropter ego An-
selmus ... confirmo eandem excommunicationem...."

   104.   Pascal II, Ep. 74; Anselm, Ep. 223, Opera
Omnia IV (ed. Schmitt) 127. Can. 6 of the Council of 1108
made clear Anselm's sense of urgency by allowing married
priests only eight days to separate from their wives, before being excommunicated (Wilkins I.88). Anselm also discussed the enforcement of celibacy in Ep. 257 (Schmitt
IV.169-70).

   105.   Ep. 365 from an anonymous writer to the exiled
Anselm, Opera Omnia (ed. Schmitt) V.308-09: "De
clericis quid dicam, que circiter omnes revoli sunt ad
iniquitatem pristinam?"

   106.   Anselm, Ep. 391, Opera Omnia V.365. (See
also Epp. 391-94, Vol. V.336-39, and Eadmer, Historia
Novorum IV, PL 159.484.) Henry appears to have resumed
the collection of cullagium after Anselm's death (Henry
of Huntingdon, Historia Anglorum, 250-51).

   107.   Wilkins I.378-80; Anselm, Opera Omnia
IV.127, Ep. 223.

   108.   Ivo, Ep. 70, to Galterius of Meldenses, PL
162.90: "... ex litteris domnae Adelae audivi turpissimam
famam de monasterio Sanctae Farae, quod jam non locus sanc-
timonialium, sed mulerium daemonialium prostibulum dicendum

est, corpora sua ad turpes usus omni generi hominum prosti-
tuentium." Ep. 200, to Daimbert of Sens, PL 162.206-07:
"in Ecclesia Senonensi ... grave scandalum emersisse cogno-
vimus, partim propter cantorem ipsius Ecclesiae, qui contra
sacramenta quae fecit, indebitam sibi sedem temeraria ambi-
tione occupavit, partim propter quemdam de praelatis Ecclesiae, qui publice sibi duo scorta copulavit et tertiam pelli-
cem cui matrimoniales tabulas faciat jam sibi praeparavit."
See also Ivo's letter concerning the married Bp. Aldebert,
noted in my Chapter Two, n. 73.

    109.   Orderic Bk. XII, c. 25 (ed. Chibnall) vol.
VI.290-95. Orderic found Archbishop Geoffrey to be a man
"guilty of many indiscretions ... severe in his aspect and
manner, harsh in his censures ... and indiscreet..." (p.
292). Considering that Orderic was a monk, his report on
the riot is surprisingly sympathetic to the married clergy.

    110.   Wilkins, Concilia I.408, 410, 411.

    111.   Henry of Huntingdon, Historia Anglorum, 245-
47. Translated and discussed by N. Partner, op. cit.,
472. The Winchester Chronicon reported the event in
the same way, but not the Anglo-Saxon Chronicle (Partner, Ibid.) nor Gilbert Foliot (Ep. 194, noticed by
Brooke, "Clerical Marriage," 70, n. 62).

    112.   Henry of Huntingdon, Historia Anglorum,
250-51.

    113.   Brooke, "Clerical Marriage," 53 and n. 18, n.
19.

    114.   Ibid., 59-60 and n. 53. For Roger of Salis-
bury, see C. L. Kingsford's article in DNB 17.103-06.

    115.   Hauck, Kirchengeschichte Deutschlands,
III.904-11.

    116.   Mansi, 21.236, can. 5: "Presbyteris, diaconibus
et subdiaconibus, concubinarum et uxorum contubernia prorsus interdicimus. Si qui autem huiusmodi reperti fuerint,
ecclesiasticis officiis priventur et beneficiis .... Sane
si neque sic immunditiam suam correxerint, communione care-
ant christiana."

    117.   When many priests, having lost office and commun-
icant status, still refused to give up their marriages, Manasses ordered Duke Robert of Flanders to seize the wives.
At this provocation the Flemish clergy rebelled and the
archbishop was forced to back down. Lambert of Arras wrote
that Manasses had instructed Duke Robert that "... conjuges
eorum, nisi ob hujusmodi consortio declinarent, vobis cae-
terisque principibus vestris capiendas post factam excommunicationem exponentes (Ep. 60, PL 162.670). Manasses is
here carrying out one of Urban II's decrees from Melfi (see
n. 79).

118.   Lateran I, can. 21, COD p. 194: "Presbyteris, diaconibus, subdiaconibus et monachis concubinas habere seu matrimonia contrahere penitus interdicimus, contracta quoque matrimonia ab huiusmodi personis disiungi et personas ad poenitentiam debere redige ...." Noting that canons 18-22 are wanting in one manuscript, the editors do not grant them full status as canons of Lateran I (p. 188). There appears to be no question, however, about can. 7, which forbids ministers of the altar to live with wives or concubines (p. 191).

119.   About the importance of this decree Michel Dortel-Claudot wrote:

Même si cela n'est pas clairement dit sur le moment, le canon 7 de Latran I, complété par des dispositions analogues d'Alexandre III et Innocent III, aboutit à cette règle pratique: ne peut être ordonné prêtre qu'un homme libre de toute attache avec une femme, c'est-à-dire veuf ou célibataire. C'est la Loi du célibat, proprement dite, et sous sa forme actuelle.

"Le Prêtre et le mariage," 343.

120.   Boelens, Die Klerikerehe, 167.

121.   Ibid., 168.

122.   Council of the Palatine, can. 5, Mansi 21.387.

123.   Council of Clermont, can. 4 (Mansi 21.438) and council of Rheims, can. 4 (Mansi 21.458). Robert Somerville in "The Council of Pisa, 1135: A Reexamination of the Evidence of the Canons," Speculum 45 (1970) 98-114, points out that much of the same legislation on clerical celibacy was promulgated by Innocent II at Clermont, can. 4 (1130), at Rheims, can. 4 (1131), and at Pisa, can. 4 (1135), and cautions that we do not have the canons from Piacenza (1132) nor from the synod which may have been held in Liège (1131) pp. 110-11. I will observe below the implications of the additional wording in the Pisan canon.

124.   Somerville, "The Council of Pisa, 1135," can. 4, p. 103; Mansi 21.489-90, can. 1: "Huiusmodi ... copulationem, quam contra ecclesiasticam regulam constat esse contractam, matrimoniam non esse sanctimus." (Emphasis mine)

125.   Mansi 21.527-28, can. 7. "Conversi professi" (lay brothers) are added to the list of celibates. Canons 16 and 21 reiterate that sons of priests cannot inherit benefices nor can they enter sacred orders unless as canons regular or monks.

126.   Raymonde Foreville comments about the celibacy
canon of Lateran II that, like those of Clermont (1095) and
Rheims (1119)
> C'est l'origine de l'empêchment canon-
> ique de mariage pour accès aux ordres sa-
> crés.... On ne saurait exagérer l'im-
> portance de cette mesure.... Certes, ce
> n'est pas a proprement parler, une concep-
> tion nouvelle.... Mais, c'est la premiere
> fois qu'une législation solonelle et
> générale entre dans cette voie dé-
> ja suivie par des synodes romains ou provin-
> ciaux.

Foreville,   _Latran_   I,   II,   III   et   _Latran_   IV
(Paris, 1965) 66.91.
127.   Gerhoh to Innocent II, LdL III.217-21: Gerhoh
wrote that one might ask, "Vere si hoc ipsum 'edere et fornicari' defenderent, si pro iusticia illud haberent et ha-
bendum suaderent, atque id pertinaciter facerent, sine du-
bio eretici essent .... Ecce non culpatur hic eroris defensio, sed ipsa factum precedens existimatio, et voluntas pec-
candi, quam idem beatus Petrus vocavit fellem amaritudinis
.... Similiter ubi culpatur illorum edere et fornicari, qui
erant in doctrina fornicatoris Nicolae, tacetur facti defensio, et agitur de solo pravitatis facto."

1. Bernold, Chronicon, MGH SS V.436. See my Chapter
Two, pp. 74-75.
2. For the identification of Ulric, and a discussion of
his arguments, see Fliche, Réforme, III.1-12. The only
flaw in Fliche's identification of Ulric as an
eleventh-century Italian bishop rather than a tenth-century
German, as had been supposed, is that Ulric does not
mention specifically the prohibition of masses. Ulric's
text is printed in LdL I.254-60, ed. L. de Heinemann,
who, not knowing the author's identity, ascribed it to a
"Pseudo-Udalricus." Mirbt discusses it, 295-98. Lea, 119,
assumed it was by Ulric of Augsburg.
3. LdL I.255-56.
4. Canon. apost. c. 6, 11, Didascalia et
constitutiones apostolorum, ed. F. X. Funk (Paderborn,
1905), 324-26. They are not printed at all in PG (Migne
ends the Apostolic Constitutions with Bk. VIII, Ch. 46,
whereas the canons are in Bk. VIII, Ch. 47). The eighty
canons were written in Syria in the fourth century; fifty
of them were published in the west. For Pafnutius, see n.
12 below and Cassiodorus, Historia Ecclesiastica
Tripartita, CSEL 71, 107-08.
5. LdL I.257. Because Ulric argues with Damian on
several points, he may be referring here to Damian's claims
about Gregory I, PL 145.402; Ulric comments only that
"Sunt vero aliqui, qui sanctum Gregorium suae sectae sum-
munt adiutorium, quorum temeritatem rideo...." The source
for Ulric's anecdote is not known; it is dismissed as a
fabella by the editors of the Vita Sancti Gregorii
Papae, Lib. I.6 (S. Gregorii Opera Omnia, ed.
ordo S. Benedicti, 230), and was denied by the author of
the Merseburg Fragment (see n. 16).
6. Jerome, In lamentationes Ieremie II.7 (PL
25.787-92).
7. Damian, Contra intemperantes clericos, Opusc.
18.1.4 (PL 145.392-94).
8. LdL I.256: "Quod specialiter ad laicos pertinere
idemmentiuntur ypocritae; qui, licet in quovis sanctissimo
ordine constituti, alienis tamen uxoribus non dubitant
abuti et, quod flendo dicimus, in supradictis saeviunt sce-

leribus....Hi nimirum non recte intellexerunt scripturam,
cuius mamillam quia durius presserunt, sanguinem pro lacte
biberunt." For the Council of Chelsea, see Spelman, Concilia I.298.

9. Augustine, Enarrationes in Psalmos 120.3;
CC 40.1787-88.

10. LdL I.256: "Qui etiam iuxta praedictum Domini
non omnes hoc consilium capere posse considerans, sed multos, eiusdem consilii assentatores, hominibus non Deo pro
falsa specie continentiae placere volentes, graviora videns
committere: patrum scilicet uxores subagitare, masculorum
aut pecudum amplexus non abhorrerre, ne morbi huius consper-
sione ad usque pestilentiam convalescente status nimirum la-
befactaretur aecclesiae.... Sed, o scelus inauditum: o
facinus toto lacrymarum fonte legendum! Si hi morte plec-
tendi sunt, qui facientibus ista consentiunt, quod dignum
illis poterit excogitari supplicium, qui cum spiritualibus
filiis haec mala extrema damnatione punienda committunt?"

11. PL 145.166.

12. John Boswell, Christianity, Social Tolerance, and Homosexuality, pp. 210-27. For the anonymous poem, see p. 217, n. 32.

13. Cassiodorus, Historia Ecclesiastica Tripartita, II.14.1-14 in CSEL vol. 71, eds. Jacob et Hanslik
(Vienna, 1952), 107-08. Because this text is referred to
by so many of the writers in this controversy, I will give
it in full here: "Synodus autem corrigere volens hominum
vitam et in ecclesiis commorantium posuit leges, quas
canones appellamus. In quorum tractatu videbatur aliquibus
introducere legem, ut episcopi et presbyteri, diaconi et
subdiaconi cum coniugibus, quas ante consecrationem
duxerant, non dormirent. Surgens autem in medio Pafnutius
confessor contradixit honorabiles confessus nuptias et
castitatem esse dicens concubitum cum propria coniuge
suasitque concilio, ne talem poneret legem, gravem asserens
esse causam, quae aut ipsis aut eorum iugalibus occasio
fornicationis existeret. Et haec quidem Pafnutius, licet
nuptiarum esset inexpertus, exposuit. Synodusque laudavit
sententiam eius et nihil ex hoc parte sancivit, sed hoc in
uniuscuiusque voluntate, non in necessitate dimisit."
Sozomen's wording, "ut episcopi ... etc ... cum coniugibus
... non dormirent" may point to the influence of the
legislation at Elvira twenty years before, and to the role
of Ossius in attempting to promote this new ruling at
Nicaea.

14. Bernold, Chronicon, MGH SS V.436.

15. Lambert of Hersfeld, Annales 1074, (MGH
SS V.217-18). See my discussion in Chapter Two, pp. 13-

14. Lambert's account uses scripture (Matthew 19:11-12 and I Corinthians 7:9) and some terminology similar to Ulric's: the papal decree, by its _violenta_ _exactione_, forced (_cogere_) men to live like angels, and _fornicationis_ ... _frena laxaret_.

16. _Fragmentum Merseburgense de caelibatu cleri_, ed. Duemmler, _LdL_ III.584-87, directly attacks Ulric's use of Pafnutius and the fish pond story about Gregory I. The author was apparently the first to point out that the _Rescript_ could not have been composed by St. Ulric of Augsburg, as the Gregorians claimed, because there was no Pope Nicholas in that tenth-century Ulric's time, to whom he could have written.

17. _LdL_ III.588-96, ed. Duemmler. On the Patarenes, p. 594; on the Lisieux canons, pp. 588-90, which are published in the _Journal des Savants_, Aug. 1901, p. 516, ed. L. Delisle. For a discussion of authorship, see Fliche, _Réforme_ III.13-14.

18. _LdL_ III.592; based on _Decretales Pseudo-Isidorianae_, ed. Hinschius, 262: "Diaconi quicumque ordinantur, si in ipsa protestati sunt et dixerunt se velle coniugio copulari, quia sic manere non possunt, hi, si postmodum uxores duxerint, in ministerio maneant, propterea quod episcopus eis licentiam dederit. Quicumque sane tacuerint et susceperint manus impositionem professi continenciam, et postea nuptiis obligati sunt, a ministerio cessare debebunt." He reminds us that the Council of Chalcedon in 451 ratified the canons of Ancyra in its first canon, that Gregory I ruled that the canons of the ecumenical councils were binding on all, and that therefore the church must respect all of Ancyra's decrees. Chalcedon, _COD._ 87, can. 1; Gregory I, _Registrum_ I.24 (ed. Ewald) Vol. I.36.

19. _LdL_ III.588-89. Augustine, _De bono coniugali_ XI.12-13, _CSEL_ 41.203-05. In regard to the conciliar texts, the author is of course referring to rulings that clerics may keep their wives; he does not deal with the fact that they forbid clerical couples to sleep together.

20. _Ibid._

21. _LdL_ III.591-92. Gangra, _Ps-Is_, ed. Hinschius, 265 (Bruns cannot be used because there the Gangra material is in Greek). Nicholas I, _Jaffé_ 2812.

22. In "Un traité inédit contre le mariage des prêtres," _Revue Bénédictine_, 35 (1923), 246-54, ed. de Bruyne, can be found another letter, of unknown provenance and authorship. Because it argues against the exact points made in the _Tractatus_, Fliche concluded that its author must have known a version of it.

23. "Eine Streitschrift für Priesterehe," ed.
Duemmler, in Sitzungsberichte der königlich-
preussichen Akademie der Wissenschaften (Berlin,
1902), I.418-44. Duemmler speculated that the author was a
German married priest; Fliche argued that he was married,
yes, but Norman, and a student of St. Anselm. See Réforme III.21-31. Referred to hereafter as "Treatise,"
   24. Opera Omnia II, c. 2-4 (ed. Schmitt) 264-68.
   25. Sitzungsberichte, 428.
   26. Ibid., 430.
   27. Ibid., 431: "Inhibito enim naturali unius mulieris coniugio, surrepit non naturalis, sed contra naturam
execrabilis sodomitica fornicatio; surrepit illicita et dam-
nabilis, non legitima, sed contra legem alienae uxoris con-
taminatio necnon etiam et merretricabilis nefanda pollutio,
quin etiam abhominabilis omnibus parentalis incestatio vel
aliarum multarum immundiciarum vel libidinum a diabolo in-
ventarum id genus, in quibus humana infirmitas periclita-
tur."
   28. Ibid. Lot's story is found in Genesis 19.
   29. For Atto, see his commentary on I Corinthians,
PL 134.148ff. For Augustine, De bono coniugali,
IV.2, Schanz, CSEL 41, which Atto uses in PL
134.288ff., especially 356.
   30. Sitzungsberichte 434.
   31. Ibid. 435-36: "Tempus vacandi orationi vel
tempus dominicarum dierum ... vel tempus sacrorum ieiunior-
um ... in quibus omnibus debent sacerdotes non solum, sed
et omnes fideles ab uxoris amplexibus abstinere et ad ecclesiam convenire ...."
   32. Ibid., 429-30.
   33. Ibid., 430: "Sunt et alii, qui nullam
informitatis humanae considerationem nec ullum
misericordiae respectum et compassionis affectum habent et
cum apostolo dicere nescientes: 'Quis infirmatur et ego
non informor' (II Cor. 11:29) dum se subditis non
conditione, qua pares, sed auctoritate, qua superiores
sunt, conferunt atque magistri videri et plus praeesse
quam prodesse cupiunt, illorum infirmitatem vi
dominationis premunt et eos sibi obedire compellunt."
(Emphasis mine.)
   34. Ibid., 437: "Quid ergo faciemus, cum fragili-
tas et humanitas labuntur? Numquid post lapsum non resurge-
mus et ad ecclesiam veniemus et peccata nostra alterutrum
non confitebimur et pro invicem, ut salvemur, orabimus?
Aut igitur non orandum semper demonstrate aut orandi tempus
et tempus non orandi, et tempus amplexandi et tempus non amplexandi nobis distinguite aut qualis sit oratio, cui va-

care debeamus aut quibus haec exceptio et indulgentia da-
tur, nobis intimate."
     35.   Dionysus   the   Areopagite,   Ep.   ad   Pynitum
Gnasiorum, PG 120.386-87.
     36.   LdL   III.573-78,   ed.   Böhmer,   contains   the
letters from both Cambrai and Noyon. See Mirbt, 302-04.
The impetus may well have come from the campaign of Hugh of
Die launched against clerical marriage and the ordination
of priests' sons at the synod of Poitiers the previous
year.
     37.   Augustine,   De   bono   coniugali,   16.18   CSEL
41.210-12;   Isidore,   In   Genesim   31.66   (PL   40.386).
The material indicating a knowledge of Dionysus the Areopagite's letter is as follows:
     From the Cambrai epistle -- "Gravia onera nobis impon-
ere satagunt" and "episcopus noster ... ad imponendum praedictum onus cervici nostrae multus ac vehemens nuper incubuit ..." (LdL III.575-76).
     From the "Treatise on Grace," quoting Dionysus' letter
to Pynitus, bishop of Gnasius (Gnatia?) -- He admonishes
Pynitus "ne gravia onera discipulorum cervicibus imponat
neve fratribus necessitatem compulsae castitatis indicet
..." (Sitzungsberichte 438).
     38. Sitzungsberichte 575: "Quicquid autem in tali-
bus agitur, a quibusdam adinventum dicitur atque suggestum
qui totius catholicae religionis, eucaristiae videlic atque
baptismi, confessionis et penitentiae, quae pro nihilo du-
cunt, destruere machinantur sacramentum.... Qui (The Patarenes) etiam ideo abhominari dicuntur coniugium, quia inrev-
erenter et impie operantur quod abhominabile est et nefari-
um. "
     39.   Ibid., 575-76: "Pastores autem nostri, tamquam
Romanae auctoritati appareant obedientes, his et talibus
aurem libenter accommodant; gravia onera nobis imponere satagunt ... consuetudinibus nostria contraire non desi-
nunt.... Quorum astipulationi episcopus noster consentiens
nos intolerabilitier aggressus, ad imponendum praedictum onus cervici nostrae multus ac vehemens nuper incubuit, quia
et clericos coniugatos chorum intrare et ministrare et eorum filios ad sacros ordines provehi inibuit."
     40.   "Siquidem contra illud quod filios clericorum a
sacris ordinibus repellendos esse moliuntur, in expositione
generationis Iesu Christi scriptam invenitur: '(Dominus)
noster Iesus Christus non solum ab alienigenis, sed etiam
de adulterinis voluit nasci commixtionibus, nobid magnam
fiduciuam praestans, ut qualicumque modo nascamur, tantum
et illius vestigia imitemur, ab illius corpore non separe-
mur, cuius per fidem membra effecti sumus.'"   (LdL

III.576-77.) Although the quotation within the passage has not been identified, a similar reference can be found in Hugh Metellus' epistola to Garbodus, previously attributed to Augustine. (LdL III.714).

41. The six letters, "Bernaldi presbiteri adversus quendam Alboinum presbiterum," are found in LdL II.7-26. Bernold's "Apologeticus," which I discussed in Chapter Two, is found in LdL II.60-88; see especially c. XI ff. See also Mirbt, 284-98.

42. Bernold wrote that "Dicis igitur in epistola tua Sozomeni capitulum iccirco tibi autenticum videri, quia certo loco et tempore a probatis personis sit recitatum, scriptum atque translatum; sed falleris in has consequentia."

43. Wido of Osnabruck's Liber de controversia inter Hildebrandum et Heinricum imperatorem (LdL I.466) quotes Cassidorus' report on the election of Ambrose by Valentinian in the Historia tripartita.

44. Jaffé I.147, #1112; MGH Ep. select. I.67.

45. LdL II.16: "... et uti Pafnutius ante consecrationem legitime ductis uxoribus, similiter occasionem fornicationis abhorrens, sacerdotes non commisceri contradixit: sic etiam mihi homunculo, veluti cum tam sanctis viris in id consentienti, nimis ac nimis temerrari nostri temporis prohibitio, non ex omni parte beata videri potuit."

46. Ibid., 17.

47. Ibid., 12: "Ut quid pudibunda patris Noe denudare non pavescis, cum certum sit te de modo tu ipse peccatum in alio vis damnare peccatum?"

48. Ibid., 14 and n. 7.

49. Ibid., 21-22: "Anathema etiam, quod subiungis, maxime convenit sectatoribus Sozomeni, et ut compendiosius dicam, Sozomenistis, qui non dico approbant, immo causa et caput sunt, ut seculares incitentur contra sacerdotes. Ipsi enim sua nefandissima persuasione simpliciores presbyteros ad contemnendos canones adeo confortant, ut rectores ecclesiarum necessario Gregorianas sententias ad seculares proferant."

50. Mansi, 20.437: "... ipsum (Gaufriedus) de concilio rapiunt, trahunt, impingunt, colaphizant, conspuunt, multisque contumeliis affectum, ad domum regis perducunt." This account is also found in Acta Sanctorum, I.754-57.

51. Lambert of Hersfeld, Annales, MGH SS V.163, 218; Mansi 20.445.

52. Gregory VII, Registrum IV, 20, ed. Caspar. Wakefield and Evans, Heresies of the High Middle Ages, 95-96.

53. The "Defensio" is found in LdL III.580-83, ed.
H. Böhmer and E. Duemmler. Böhmer does not identify the
author, beyond conjecturing that it may have been Serlo of
Bayeux who likely wrote it after the Council of Clermont in
1095. Mirbt calls it "Querela in gratiam nothorum," as it
was labeled in Bouquet's edition (See Mirbt, 68 and 301-03
and Bouquet XI.444-46). R. Foreville, "L'Ecole de Caen au
XIe siècle et les origines normandes de l'Université
d'Oxford," Etudes mediévales offertes a M. le
dôyen A. Fliche (Montpellier, 1952), IV.98, n. 59,
assumes it was written by Serlo, and I accept her
identification.

54. LdL III.580:
Fonte sacro lotum vel mundat gratia totum,
Vel non est sacri mundatio plena lavacri.
Hec qui tractatis, prolatores novitatis,
Dum nova iura datis, lavacri ius evacuatis.
Legislatores, hominum perpendite mores,
Atque modum vite, quod et equum, sit.
　　　　stabilite!
Quisque sui portet peccati pondus oportet,
Nec sit dampnatur patris pro crimine natus.

55. Ibid., 581:
Nunc homines vite turpis, mechi, sodomite,
Et qui furta patrant, in nos obprobria
　　　latrant
Vel bene moratos, et dispiciunt male natos:
Lex premit ista bonos et sublevat ad mala
　　　pronos.
Cur homo dedecorat quem rex supremus
　　　honorat?

Ergo censure talis quo regula iure
Sorte sua privat male natum, si bene vivat?
Quod si perduras nec ius attendere curas,
Qui nova iura paras et leges ponis amaras,
Et sic nos mordes, prius illas destrue
　　　sordes,
Que gravius ledunt et plus a lege recedunt!
Quid pena vitas urgere gravi sodomitas?
Hec species morbi, qua mors gravis imminet
　　　orbi,
Si bene res isset, prius exstirpanda
　　　fuisset.

56. Trans. John Boswell, Christianity, Social
Tolerance, and Homosexuality, pp. 398-400. (Bos-

well's text omitted lines 5-6, which he has kindly supplied
to me by correspondence.) From a previously unpublished
thirteenth-century manuscript in Munich, Bayerische Staats-
bibliothek, clm.17212, fols. 26v-27v. Because of the similarity between lines 3-10 and Serlo's bitter complaints
about the sodomites' hypocrisy and legalism, and lines 14-
19 and his affirmation of procreation, I suggest a borrow-
ing between the two poems.

57. Ibid., 581-82.
58. Theobald's letter to Roscelin is in LdL
III.603-07, ed. H. Böhmer; the letter to Philippe can be
found in PL 163.765. Böhmer speculated that this
Roscelin might be Anselm's well-known opponent, but
rejected that idea. See also Raymonde Foreville (as cited
in n. 53 above), pp. 90-99.
59. LdL III.605: "Sic ergo cuiuscunque generis sit
ille novus homo, in utero generatur ecclesiae, generatus
corporis Christi indubitanter aggregatur...."
60. Ibid.: "Ideoque Deus nasci voluit de progenie
peccatricis, ut discerent homines peccata parentum non obes-
se sibi. Unde in genealogia Christis nulla sanctarum nomi-
natur, sed Thamar et aliae tres, quas divina pagina repre-
hendit, apponuntur, ut qui pro peccatoribus veniebat, de
peccatricibus nasci dignaretur...."
61. Ibid., 606: "Quia nimirum quemlibet sacro fonte renatum vel plenarie divina mundat gratia, vel sacri mundatio lavacri non est sufficiens nec plenaria, quod contra-
dicit fides catholica. Non enim sunt ex leges iudicandi,
quorum Deus ipse est pater, et quos peperit Christi gratia,
omnium regeneratorum piissima mater, nec debemus illis de-
lictum patris sive thorum matrix improperare, sed, potius
morum perfectionem diligenter attendere quoniam patris sive
matris perpetratum crimen non potest filiis 'paradisi clau-
dere limen'...."
62. See MGH SS 21.430-33 (ed. K. Pertz) for the
"Carmen Laureshamense." Discussed in Wattenbach, Deutschlands Geschichtsquellen II.39 and n. 1, and 378; and in
Mirbt, 80 and 304-05. Referring to the reform-minded monks
of Hirsau, the clergy of Lorsch wrote:

> ...
> Hoc autem temere presumunt scisma docere:
> Quod neque vir nuptus, casta quoque coniuge
>   functus,
> Et nec legitimo mulier sociata marito,
> Umquam salventur, nisi primum dissocientur,
> Et quae possidedant disiuncti cuncta
>   relinquant ...
> Spernunt in tantum rectores ecclesiarium

Tam   gravis   in   clerum   turget   contemptus
    eorum,
Ut   nolint   missas   audire   per   hunc
    celebratas,
Nil divinorum querentes officiorum"
          (p. 431).

63. _LdL_ II.436-48, ed. E. Sackur, Sackur, and later Fliche, argued for date of composition shortly after
the papal attack of 1074. Fliche, _Réforme_, III, maintained that the struggles ceased to center on nicolaitism
after 1076, that they then turned into the contest for supremacy between papacy and empire, and that Sigebert would
most likely have written the "Apologia" in the heat of the
celibacy battle, that is to say, c. 1075.

64. Sigebert's _Chronicon_ and _De viris illustri-
bus_ (MGH SS 6.300-74) are excellent examples of the
historical genre at the turn of the eleventh century.
NCE 13.204.

65. _Marbodi Episcopi Redonensis Opuscula Ali-
quot_, ed. Böhmer, _LdL_ 691-94. Marbod, another prominent cleric who wrote a bit later (c. 1100) that the sacraments of unchaste priests must not be shunned, was known
for his homosexual love poems (see Boswell, pp. 248-49,
370-71). In his case, a homosexual orientation seems not
to have turned him against married clergy, as was the case
in Serlo's allegations (see above, pp. 140-42).

66. _LdL_ II.438.

67. William of Malmesbury, _Vita Wulfstani_, ed. R.
R. Darlington, Camden 3rd series (London, 1928), 53; trans.
J. Peile, _The Life of St. Wulfstan_ (Oxford,
1934), 81.

67a. Norman Cohn, _The Pursuit of the Millen-
ium_ (New York, 1972), 39. Based on _Actus pontificum
Cenomannis_ (ed. Busson), 407-15.

68. _LdL_ II.438: "Quid enim aliud etiam muliercularum textrina et opificum officinae iam ubique personant,
quam totius humanae societatis iura confusa, christianae
sanctitatis statuta convulsa, popularis status subitam
immutationem, ecclesiastici decoris impiam delirationem ...
fidem neglegi, et impudentiori malitiae licentia inperia et
christianae religioni contraria dogmata induci...."

69. MGH SS. VI.363.

70. _LdL_ II.438: "... novas in dominos perfidias
servorum, omnimodas in servos suspiciones dominorum, infi-
dissimas sodalium proditiones, dolosas in ordinatam a Deo
potestatem machinationes, amicitiam ledi...."

71.   Damian, <u>PL</u> 144.337:   "Hoc itaque modo fit in diebus nostris, fit rustici et insipientes quique, qui nil pe-
ne noverunt, nisi vomeribus arva proscindere, porcos ac di-
versorum pecorum captabula custodire, nunc in compitis ac
triviis ante mulierculas et combubulos suos non erubescant
de Scripturarum sanctarum sententiis disputare: imo, quod
turpe est dicere, in tota nocte subant inter femora mulierum, die non verentur tractare de sermonibus angelorum, et
hoc modo sanctorum dijudicant verba doctorum."

72.   Norman   Cohn,   <u>Pursuit   of   the   Millenium</u>,
35-36.

73.   Damian,   <u>PL</u>   145.490,   <u>Contra   clericos   regu-</u>
<u>lares proprietarios.</u>

74.   Damian, referring to Romuald, founder of the Cam-
aldolesans,   in   <u>Vita   beati   Romualdi</u>   37,   ed.   Giovanni
Tobacco   in   <u>Instituto   storica   Italiano   per   il   Med-</u>
<u>io   evo</u>   94   (1957)   78.   Quoted   from John   H.   Mundy,   <u>Eur-</u>
<u>ope   in   the   High   Middle   Ages,   1150-1309</u>   (New
York, 1973), 293-94.

75.   Norman   Cohn,   <u>Pursuit   of   the   Millenium,</u>
156-57.

76.   Ernst   Werner,   <u>Pauperes   Christi: Studien</u>
<u>zu   sozialreligiosen   Bewegungen   im   Zeitalter   des</u>
<u>Reformpapsttums</u> (Leipzig, 1956), 155-64.

77.   Dietrich   Kurze,   <u>Pfarrerwahlen   im   Mittelal-</u>
<u>ter: ein   beitrag   zur   Geschichte   der   Gemeinde</u>
<u>und   des   Niederkirchenwesens</u>   (Köln-Graz,   1966),
474-76.

78.   John   H.   Mundy,   <u>Europe   in   the   High   Mid-</u>
<u>dle Ages</u>, 239-42.

79.   Werner, <u>ibid.</u>

80.   <u>LdL</u> II.443-44, 447.

81.   Augustine,   <u>Tractatus   in   Evangelium   Johan-</u>
<u>nis</u> V:8,   11,   13,   15,   18,   19;   <u>CC</u> 36.44-52.   This materi-
al   from   Augustine   was   not   used   by   Damian   in   the   <u>Liber</u>
<u>Gratissimus.</u>

82.   Sigebert, 441; Damian, <u>LdL</u> I.30.

83.   Philippians 1:18 (Sigebert, 440; Damian, 34), and
John 11:51 (Sigebert, 440; Damian, 29).

84.   The relevant document for Clement's views is in
<u>LdL</u> I.626.   See also Mirbt, 301.

85.   Fliche, <u>Réforme</u> III.46 and n. 1.

86.   <u>Wenrici   scolastici   Treverensis,   epistola</u>
<u>sub   Theoderici   episcopi   Virdunensis   nomine   com-</u>
<u>posita, LdL</u>   I.280-99,   ed.   K.   Francke.   See   Mirbt,   299
and   24-25;   Fliche,   <u>Réforme</u>   III.144-69;   Tellenbach,   115
and   159-60.   Also   see   Martène's   <u>Thesaurus</u>   <u>I</u>,   230ff.,

which prints the same material from an "unknown author."
Lea, 191-92, follows Martène.
    87. MGH Const. I.117-20.
    88. To defend the ordinations of married and simoniac-
al priests, he borrowed from Flodoard's Historia ecclesiae remensis (MGH SS XIII.471); and from Auxilius'
treatise on the contested ordinations of Pope Formosus,
De ordinationibus a Formoso papa factis (PL
129.1072).
    89. The texts from Worms, MGH Const I.106-13.
    90. LdL I.287-88.
    91. Ibid., 286.
    92. LdL I.289: "Non est novum, regiam dignitatem
indignari in eos, quos vident in se sacrilega temeritate in-
surgere; non est novum, homines seculares seculariter sa-
pere et agere. Novum est autem et omnibus retro seculis inauditum, pontifices regna gentium tam facile velle divi-
dere, nomen regum, inter ipsa mundi initia repertum, a Deo
postea stabilitum, repentina factione elidere, cristos Domini quotiens libuerit plebeia sorte sicut villicos mutare,
regno patrum suorum decedere iussos, nisi confestim adqui-
everint, anathemate damnare." Wenric denies the validity
of unjust excommunications and of papal absolutions of sub-
jects from their oath to a ruler (291).
    93. From Benzo's work on the Patarenes, Liber ad
Heinricum V.1, MGH SS, XI:
        Sed Prandelli Asinander, asinus hereticus,
        Congregavit Paterinos ex viis et sepibus,
        Et replevit totam urticis et vepribus.
        Qui dicebant: "Non est templum, non est
            sacerdotium";
        Nuptiarum improbabant stabile negotium
        Sacrafitium ridegant, sedentes in ocium.
                                    (648)
    94. Guy of Ferrara, "De scismate Hildebrandi," LdL
I.529-67, ed. R. Wilmans, discusses celibacy on pp. 543-44
and 558-60.

NOTES to CHAPTER FOUR
THE NORMAN ANONYMOUS: A MARRIED PRIEST CAUGHT IN
ANGLO-NORMAN CELIBACY ENFORCEMENT

1.   Die   Texte   des   Normannischen   Anonymus,
ed. Karl Pellens (Wiesbaden, 1966), referred to hereafter
as "Pellens." J25 is found on pp. 204-09, J22 is on pp.
116-25, and fragments of J26 are on pp. 209-12. Pellens
claims that his edition is complete, but it lacks thirty-
seven pages from the only manuscript copy known, Codex 415,
Corpus Christi College, Cambridge. Because Pellens decided
not to print similar (although not identical) passages from
J22/26, most of one of the tracts on priests' sons, J26, is
among the missing material (ms. 252-262). For this reason
Pellens' work is an unsatisfactory reference for my discussion. For the omitted pages, one must turn to the earlier
publication of part of the Anonymous, Heinrich Böhmer's
work in LdL III.649-55.
2.   For speculation on the identity of the Norman
Anonymous see Heinrich Böhmer, Kirche und Staat in
England und in der Normandie (Leipzig, 1899) 261-
65, who thought the author was Archbishop Gerard of York;
Norman Cantor, Church, Kingship and Lay Investiture, 174-97, who agreed with Böhmer; Harold Scherrinsky,
Untersuchungen zum sogennanten Anonymus von
York (Würzburg, 1940), 114ff., who located the author in
Rouen; George H. Williams, The Norman Anonymous of
1100 A.D. (Cambridge, Mass., 1951), 88-127, who nomi-
nated the archbishop of Rouen, William Bona Anima, as author; Kennerly M. Woody, "Marginalia on the Norman Anonymous," Harvard Theological Review 66:2, April 1973,
273-88, who believed it may have been Albert the Eloquent,
priest in the archdiocese of Rouen, who in 1119 was imprisoned for resisting the archbishop's celibacy decree, and
Karl Pellens who in the edition above, pp. xxix and xxxii
and in Das Kirchendenken des Normannischen Anonymus (Wiesbaden, 1973), 22-25 and 27-31, proposed that the
author was a royal tutor at the Norman court. I can find
no conclusive evidence identifying the author. Perhaps the
wisest advice comes from Ruth Nineham, who declared that
the author may never be identified but that what is needed
now is a careful study of his theology ("K. Pellen's Edi-

tion of the Tracts of the Norman Anonymous," <u>Transactions of the Cambridge Bibliographical Society</u>, IV.4, 1967, p. 304).

3. For example, Pellens' long work on the Anonymous' thought, <u>Kirchendenken</u>, devotes only eight pages (207-14) to the tracts on procreation and marriage and is therefore another of many works which focus on the ecclesio-political aspects with scant attention to the theological.

4. The earliest date we have proof for in the manuscript is 1096 (knowledge of the events of Urban II's council at Clermont, Nov.-Dec. 1095, is found in J2, pp. 10-15); another verified date is 1101, when Anselm's <u>De conceptu virginali et de originali peccato</u> was written (quoted in J21, p. 111). Böhmer (<u>LdL</u> III.645) suggested a date as early as 1075, reasoning that the tract might have been a response to the Rouen celibacy decree and riot of 1074. The latest date which has been speculated is after 1119, when another riot against celibacy enforcement broke out in Rouen (Woody, "Marginalia," 287-88). As for the speculation that he was the son of a priest, George Williams has proposed that the Anonymous was William Bona Anima, son of Radbod, bishop of Seez (<u>The Norman Anonymous</u>). I venture the possibility that he was married and/or a father, because of the personal style of J22/26 and J25.

5. J25, the only tract in Codex 415 which was reproduced elsewhere before the <u>LdL</u> appeared in 1897, was first translated and published by Bishop Joseph Hall in 1634, as part of "The Honour of the Married Clergie Maintained" (London, 1634), I.786ff., and can also be found in his <u>Works</u>, ed. P. Wynter (Oxford, 1863), VIII.619-30. It received further publication when in 1690 Edward Brown republished the <u>Fasciculus Rerum Expetendarum</u> of Artius Gratius (Cologne, 1535) adding several "English" tracts to the collection of works primarily by continental reformers such as Hus and Hutten; one of these was J25.

6. In J3 the Anonymous complained about Urban II's ruling that placed Rouen under Vienne, that is, that made the Archbishop of Lyon/Vienne a metropolitan over the archbishop of Rouen. In a number of tracts he argued against the superiority of the bishop of Rome over other bishops, and against papal excommunications. The archbishop of Rouen at the time of the council of Clermont, William Bona Anima, was suspended immediately after the council for refusal to submit to Vienne.

7. Kennerly M. Woody, "Marginalia," 288.

8. For a discussion of J25, see Fliche, <u>Réforme</u>, III.34-38.

9. Augustine, "Liber super Genesi ad Litteram," IX,
c. 7, PL 34.397; and "Contra Faustum," XXII, c. 27, PL
42.418. Quoted in Pellens, 206.
10. Examples of the Anonymous' wording which Fliche
claims is not only predestinarian but also Anselmian, Réforme III.35-38. The context in which the Anonymous
writes, moreover, stressing as it does the preelection of
some to hell as well as of some to heaven, gives, as Fliche
observes, "les théories de St. Anselme ... sur ce point
une curieuse déformation," (p. 36), a heavier predestinarian stress; "Voluit enim Deus ab aeterno et ante seculum
omnes homines creare in seculo, certo quidem ordine, quo
precogitavit et predestinavit eos se creaturum.... Quae-
cunque ... predestinationem mentis predisponentem ac preor-
ginantem omnia necessario secuntur ... (p. 207). Si ergo
voluit Deus et predestinavit alios futuros virgines, alios
nuptiarum fructum facientes ... (p. 208)."
11. "Qui(a) autem virgines esse debeant, et qui nuptiarum fructum facientes, docet eos verbum, quod Deus seminat
in cordibus illorum.... In quorum vero cordibus seminat
verbum virginitatis, ipsi virginitatem servare desiderant;
in quibus vero verbum nuptiarum seminat, ipsi facere nuptiarum fructum appetunt." Pellens, p. 209.
12. Pellens, 203: "Nam omnium hominum alii sunt mem--
bra Christi, preelecti et predestinati ad vitam benedicti a
Patre et quibus regnum Dei paratum est a constitutione mundi; alii membra diaboli, ab aeterno dampnati in mortem et
maledicti ituri in ignem aeternum. Horum igitur, si quemlibet episcopus absolverit, non propter hoc salvus erit, nec
membrum Christi poterit fieri, talemque excommunicare super-
fluum esse videtur.... Quodcontra, si membrum Christi ...
excommunica verit, non propter hoc poterit dampnari. Eoque
talem excommunicare excommunicanti periculosum est atque
dampnabile."
13. The papacy as the church of Satan: "Ex eo autem,
quod Romana est, non talis est, sed paucos, electos et Dei
filios habet, multos reprobos et diaboli filios.... Quod
quidem ecclesiam Sathane possumus appellare, non Christi"
(J30, p. 230). Judging from what the Anonymous wrote elsewhere, by "living by the spirit" he meant to live by the
power of grace, rather than by canon law. He frequently
contrasted law with spirit.
14. Colin Morris, The Discovery of the Individual 1050-1200 (London, SPCK, 1972), 36.
15. Williams, Norman Anonymous, 149-55.
16. "... illi qui electi sunt in Christo ... cum
baptizantur, aqua simul et Spiritu sancto baptizantur"
(Pellens, 98).

17. Romans 9:22; Pellens, 118.
18. Romans 9:23; Pellens, 118.
19. Pellens, 117, 211.
20. Pellens, 211.
21. George H. Williams, Anselm: Communion and
Atonement (St. Louis, 1960), 74-75.
22. Pellens, 211.
23. Pellens, 212: "Vos genus ... electum, non de im-
mundo et corruptibili carnis semine propagatum, sed de cel-
esti et incorruptibili semine summi regis et sacerdotis pro-
creatum, et ideo recte vocatur regale sacerdotum."
24. J22/26: "Sacerdos, qui hanc immolat, est omnis,
qui exibet membra sua hostiam viventem.... Cuius etiam
imago est ille, qui in lapideo templo immolat.... In hoc
templo sancta fides cordis est altare, cuius typus est altare lapideum, quod in illo est." (Pellens, 121)
            J26:   "... omnes electi sacerdotes esse
monstrantur, qui sacrificium laudis Deo immolant....
(Pellens,. 212)
            J22/26: "Si ergo sanctos et perfectos vult eos
esse vult etiam, ut nulla eis desit sanctitas, nulla perfectionis gratia, sed omnem habeant gratiam administrandi etiam sancta et divina tractandi misteria...." (Pellens,122)
I interpret "omnis" to include laity because of the context. The Anonymous' thought, ever filled with contradic-
tions and unusual juxtapositions, is never more apparently
ambiguous than in his use of the term "sacramentum." He begins by meaning the concrete performance of baptism or the
mass, but before he is finished, he claims that "receiving
the spirit" supercedes even being baptized, and that a con-
trite heart may be a truer oblation than the offering of
the eucharist. On the ambiguous nature of his thought, see
G. H. Williams, The Norman Anonymous, 167-74.
25. "Illud quoque mirandum est, quod is, qui habet potestatem manducandi et bibendi corpus et sanguinem Christi,
non debeat habere potentatem pronunciandi verba, quibus con-
ficitur corpus et sanguis Christi cum multo salubrius sit
atque beatius manducare et bibere, si tamen digne fiat,
quam verba illa pronuntiare. Ad hoc enim pronuntiantur, ut
corpus et sanguis Christi conficiatur -- ad hoc vero confici-
itur, ut illud manducemus et bibamus -- ad hoc manducamus
et bibimus, ut in Christo maneamus et Christum manentem in
nobis habeamus, participes facti non tantum gratiae, sed
etiam divinae ipsius naturae. Quod et (electus) sacerdotio
sanctius atque beatius esse videtur...." (Pellens, 123)
26. Gal. 5:18; Pellens 212: "The law of the canons
prohibits that such should be ordained. But the Apostle

says, 'If you are led by the Spirit, you are not under the law.'"

27.   The seeds of this radical position may lie in Sigebert of Gembloux's refusal to acknowledge the canons he disagreed with (LdL II.448).   The Anonymous, however, in a manner typical of his thought, carries this refusal to the extreme.

28.   J14 "On baptism" (Pellens, 94-98), J24d (Pellens, 202-04) "On the power of binding and loosing," and J30 (Pellens, 230-31) "There are two churches, one of Satan, the other of Christ," present predestinarian views similar to J22/26 and J25.   The last two, short tracts which appear to have been added after the major portions of the quires were filled, may have been composed later in the author's life.   Several other tracts use predestinarian terminology without being dominated by that doctrine: J24 "On consecration" (Pellens, 129-80, esp. 165 and 196-200), J24c "On the laity as the true Christians" (Pellens, 200-201), J31 "On charity," J28 "Against the Pope," J13a "On apostolic election" (Pellens, 92-93).

29.   See especially J8 "On being a true pastor," J16 and 17 "On priestly ordination," and J18 "On priestly conse-cration."

30.   J24 "On consecration" (Pellens, 129-80 and 196-200; see LdL III.662-79) and J28 "Against the Pope" (Pellens, 214-15).   On their possible connection with Henry I, see Williams, Norman Anonymous, 92-93.

31.   Ernst Kantorowicz, The King's Two Bodies, a study in medieval political theology (Prince-ton, 1957), 42-81, esp. 49.

32.   Cantor, Church, Kingship and Lay Investi-ture, 268-73.

33.   Fritz Kern, Kingship and Law in the Middle Ages, trans. S. B. Chrimes (Oxford, 1939), 119.

34.   Kantorowicz, 80-81.

35.   Orderic, Ecclesiastical History (ed. and trans. Chibnall) VI.290-95.

36.   J31 "On charity among the communion of the saints" (Pellens, 180-95).   "Si ergo discipulus Christi es, si non es de mundo, sed ipse elegit te de mundo, propterea odit te mundus et tu illum debes habere odio.   Noli querere in illum manentem civitatem, de quo tu non es, noli in illo amare animam tuam, sed odio habeto" (189).

37.   Ibid.   "Ideo, vero caritas patris non est in vobis, quia diligitis concupiscentiam carnis et concupiscen-tiam oculorum et superbiam vitae, quae non est ex patre, sed ex mundo est" (189).   But to the "imittatores Christi" he said: "Tu vero mundo crucifigeris tunc ... et cum car-

nem tuam sicut imitator Christi crucifigis cum vitiis et
concupiscentiis, et cum temet ipsum abnegas et tollis cru-
cem tuam et venis post ipsum, quem spiritu ambulans sequer-
is" (191; cp. Mt. 16:24).

NOTES to CHAPTER FIVE
THE DESTRUCTION OF CLERICAL MARRIAGE

1. R. W. Southern, Western Society and the Church in the Middle Ages (Penguin Books, 1970), 258. Hereafter cited as Western Society.

2. J. A. Jungmann, The Mass of the Roman Rite, trans. F. Brunner, Vol. I. 92-127.

3. R. W. Southern, "Lanfranc of Bec and Berengar of Tours," in Studies in Medieval History presented to F. M. Powicke (Oxford, 1948), 36ff.

4. John H. Mundy, Europe in the High Middle Ages, 292, 285.

5. Ailred of Rievaulx, "De spirituali amicitia," PL 195.659-702; Bernard, Sermones in Cantica Canticorum, PL 183.785-1198. Bernard's adoration of the Virgin led him to disagree with Anselm's verdict that the Virgin was conceived and born in sin; Bernard conceded that she was conceived in sin but insisted that she was sanctified before birth (Ep. 174, PL 182.332-36).

6. John Bugge, Virginitas, Ch. IV.

7. Mechthild of Magdeburg, The Flowing Light of the Godhead, trans. Lucy Menzies (London, 1953), 21-23.

8. Michael W. Kaufman, "The Conception of Woman in the Middle Ages and the Renaissance," Soundings: an Interdisciplinary Journal, LVI.2 (Summer, 1973), 143.

9. Southern, Western Society, 310-18.

10. Annales Premonstratenses, ed. E. L. Hugo, ii.147. Discussed by Southern, Western Society, 314.

11. JoAnn McNamara and Suzanne Wemple, "Sanctity and Power: the Dual Pursuit of Medieval Women," in Becoming Visible: Women in European History, eds. Renate Bridenthal and Claudia Koonz (Boston, 1977), 90-118; Brenda Bolton, "Mulieres Sanctae," Studies in Church History 10 (1973), 77-99.

12. Southern, Western Society, 127.

13. Lea's observation in Sacerdotal Celibacy, 279.

13a. A. Barstow, "Marguerite Porete," unpublished paper read at the American Academy of Religion, Dallas, Texas, Nov. 7, 1980.

14. M. D. Chenu, Nature, Man and Society in the Twelfth Century; Essays on New Theologi-

cal Perspectives in the Latin West, eds. and
trans. Jerome Taylor and Lester K. Little (Chicago, 1968),
227. Hereafter cited as Nature, Man and Society.
The same point is made by Southern, Western Society,
38-39.
    15. Thomas Gannon and George Traub, The Desert
and the City: an Interpretation of the History of Christian Spirituality (Toronto, 1969),
134-35.
    16. Southern, Western Society, 36-39.
    17. Dietrich Kurze, Pfarrerwahlen im Mittelal-
ter: ein Beitrag zur Geschichte der Gemeinde
und des Niederkirchenwesens, esp. 474-76.
    18. Brooke, "Clerical Marriage," 61, claims that by
1150 asceticism had become popular, both as a practice for
the laity and as an expectation held up to their pastors.
    19. Southern, Western Society, 311-12.
    20. Southern, Medieval Humanism and Other
Essays (New York, 1970), 95.
    21. R. L. Poole's "The Masters of the Schools at Par-
is and Chartres in John of Salisbury's Time," EHR #35
(1920) 321-42, established these thinkers as a school at
Chartres, and J. M. Parent in La doctrine de la
Creation dans l'école de Chartres began the
systematic study of their writings. The fame of the
"school" continued to rise until 1970, when R. W. Southern
assembled considerable evidence that it had never existed
as such and that these thinkers had actually taught at Paris ("Humanism and the School of Chartres," Medieval Humanism, 61-85). This question does not matter to my study,
especially since the author I am primarily interested in,
Bernard Silvester, taught at Tours.
    22. Chenu, Nature, Man and Society, 20.
    23. Ibid., 5.
    24. Winthrop Wetherbee, The Cosmographia of
Bernardus Silvestris (New York, 1973), 30-31 and 56-57.
    25. Ibid., 44-45.
    26. Ibid., 126 and n. 108.
    27. Ibid., 19. See also D. Economou, The God-
dess Natura in Medieval Literature (Cambridge,
Mass., 1972), 60ff., and Brian Stock, Myth and Science in the Twelfth Century: A Study of
Bernard Silvester (Princeton, 1972).
    28. See, for example, Anselm of Havelberg's Dialog-
us (PL 188.1141ff.) and his Liber de diversis ordinibus (PL 213.814ff.) and Honorius of Autun's Eluci-
darium i, 11 (PL 172.1116); noted and discussed by
Chenu, Nature, Man and Society, 217-18 and 26.

29.   Chenu, Nature, Man and Society, 229.
About this twelfth-century affirmation of secular experience, Chenu concluded not that it secularized theology or
spirituality, but rather that theology incorporated and in
a sense spiritualized part of lay experience. I assume
that both processes were taking place, and I have chosen to
investigate the extent to which the former occurred and to
speculate about what its influence might have been.
30.   Wetherbee, The Cosmographia, 52, 58-59.
31.   Chenu, Nature, Man and Society, 173-75
and 196-97.
32.   Ibid., 204-06 and 239; Wetherbee, The Cosmographia, 7.
33.   Manegold, Liber contra Wolfelmum 22, MGH
Quellen zur Geistesgeschichte des Mittelalters 8,
ed. W. Hartmann (Weimar, 1972), 93-98.
34.   Damian, De divina omnipotentia 3 (PL
145.600-01); cf. Manegold, op. cit. 74-76; both are
noted in Wetherbee, The Cosmographia, 7 and n. 22-23.
35.   Southern, Western Society, 161-62.
36.   The phrase is Christopher Brooke's: "Gregorian
Reform in Action," 70.
37.   Southern, Western Society, 300-01.
38.   Bernard Verkamp, "Cultic Purity and the Law of
Celibacy," maintains that, from the earliest years of celibacy legislation until the pontificate of the recent John
XXIII, cultic purity was the predominant rationale for compulsory continence.
39.   This argument for celibacy remains the corner-
stone of the church's continuing insistence on compulsory
celibacy; see the "Decree on the Ministry and Life of
Priests," par. 16, The Documents of Vatican II,
eds. W. M. Abbott and J. Gallagher (London, 1966), 565-66.
When Protestantism chose optional celibacy, creating again
a mixed ministry, it faced the sexual issue in part, allowing that marriage existed for more than procreation, but
was never able to create an affirmative doctrine of sexuality, nor did it even begin to deal with the meaning of marriage for the life of the clergy. See Anne Barstow, "The
First Generation of Anglican Priests' Wives," in Women
in New Worlds, Vol. II, eds. Hilah Thomas and Rosemary Skinner (Nashville, 1982).
40.   As I write this in 1981, pondering the most
recent papal pronouncements on sexuality, both clerical and
lay, I question whether the brief, twenty-year period of
"pro-sex" thinking in the Roman Church is not already at an
end.

41.   Schillebeeckx, _Celibacy_, 62-77, especially 68-69.

42.   Audet, _Structures_, viii.

43.   _Ibid._, 108.

44.   _Ibid._ For a longer discussion of the effects of a celibate priesthood on the church, see my forthcoming book on the subject from Crossroad Publishers.

BIBLIOGRAPHY

A. Texts

Adam of Bremen. Gesta pontificum Hammaburgensis III. (ed. J. Lappenberg) MGH SS VII.267-389.

Alboin. See Bernold of Constance, "Epistolae."

Anonymous. "Eine Streitschrift für Priesterehe" (ed. Dümmler), Sitzungsberichte der königlich-preussichen Akademie der Wissenschaften I (Berlin, 1902) 418-44 (called "A Treatise on Grace").

Anonymous. Tractatus pro clericorum conubio (ed. Dümmler) LdL III.588-96.

Anselm. Opera Omnia (ed. F. Schmitt). 7 vols. Edinburgh: Thomas Nelson, 1946.

Bernard Silvester. Cosmographia (trans. Winthrop Wetherbee). New York: Columbia University Press, 1973.

Bernold of Constance. Chronicon. MGH SS V.400-467.

_____. Apologeticus, XI-XIII. LdL II.70-75.

_____. Epistolae: "Bernaldi presbiteri adversus quandam Alboinum presbiterum," LdL II.7-26.

Boniface. MGH. Epistolae Selectae. Vol. I: S. Bonifatii et Lullii Epistolae (ed. M. Tangl). Berlin, 1916.

Bonizo of Sutri. Liber ad amicum V-VI. LdL I.

_____. Liber de vita christiana (ed. E. Perels). Texte zur Geschichte des romischen und Kanonischen Rechts im Mittelalter herausgegeben von der preussichen Akademie der Wissenschaft I. Berlin, 1930.

Brown, Edward. _Appendix ad Fasciculum rerum expetendarum_
    et fugiendarum. Tomus Secundus. Ab Arthuino Grat-
    io, editum Coloniae, A. D. 1535. London: Richard
    Chiswell: 1690; Tuscon, Arizona: Audax Press,
    1967.

Cambrai and Noyon, the clerks of. _Epistolae_, ed.
    Böhmer. _LdL_ III.573-78.

Cassiodorus. _Historia Ecclesiastica Tripartita._ _CSEL_
    vol. 71, eds. Jacob, Hanslik. Vienna, 1952.

Gratius, Ortuin. _Fasciculus Rerum Expetendarum ac fugien-_
    darum. Cologne, 1535.

Gregory VII. _Das Register Gregors VII_, ed. Erich Caspar.
    MGH Epistolae Selectae II. Berlin, 1920.

_____. _The "Epistolae Vagantes" of Pope Gregory_
    VII, ed. and trans. H. E. J.Cowdrey. Oxford,
    1972.

Guy of Ferrara. _De scismate Hildebrandi_, ed. R. Wilmans.
    LdL I.529-67.

Hall, Joseph. _Works_, vol. VIII, ed. Philip Wynter. Ox-
    ford: Oxford University Press, 1863.

_____. "The Honour of the Married Clergie Main-
    tained," I. London, 1634.

Henry of Huntingdon. _Historia Anglorum_, ed. T. Arnold.
    Chronicles and memorials of Great Britain and Ire-
    land during the middle ages, #74. London, 1879.

Humbert of Silva Candida. _Adversus Nicetam_. _PL_
    143.983-1000.

Lambert of Hersfeld. _Annales_, ed. G. Pertz. _MGH Scrip-_
    tores rerum Germanicarum II. Hannover, 1843.

Lorch, monks of. "Carmen Laureshamense," ed. K. Pertz.
    MGH SS 21.430-33.

Manegold of Lautenbach. _Liber ad Gebehardum_, ed. K.
    Franke. _LdL_ I.308-430.

_____. Liber contra Wolfelmum. MGH Quellen zur Geistesgeschichte des Mittelalters 8, ed. W. Hartmann. Weimar, 1972.

Mechtild of Magdeburg. The Flowing Light of the Godhead, trans. L. Menzies. London, 1953.

Norman Anonymous. Die Texte des Normannischen Anonymus, ed. Karl Pellens. Wiesbaden: Franz Steiner Verlag, 1966.

Orderic Vitalis. Historiae ecclesiasticae, ed. Le Prevost. Paris, 1838-55. Ecclesiastical History, ed. and trans. Chibnall. Oxford, 1969- .

Paul of Bernried. Vita Gregorii VII Papae. Pontificum Romanorum vitae I (ed. J. Watterich) 474-546. Leipzig, 1862, 1966.

Pseudo-Isidore. Decretales pseudo-Isidorianae et capitula Angilramni, ed. Hinschius. London, 1863.

Serlo of Bayeux. "Defensio," eds. H. Böhmer, E. Dümmler. LdL III.580-583.

Sigebert of Gembloux. Apologia, ed. E. Sackur. LdL II.436-48.

Theobald of Étampes. Epistola ad Roscelinum, ed. H. Böhmer. LdL III. 603-607.

Ulric of Imola. "Pseudo Udalrici epistola de continentia clericorum," ed. L. de Heinemann. LdL I.254-60.

Wenric of Trier. "Epistola sub Theoderici episcopi Virdunensis nomine composita," ed. K. Franke. LdL I.280-99.

William of Malmesbury. Vita Wulfstani, ed. R. R. Darlington. London: Royal Historical Society, 1928.

B. References

Amann, Émile et Dumas, Auguste. L'Église au Pouvoir des
Laïques: 888-1057   (Vol.   VII   of   Histoire   de
l'Église). Paris: Bloud et Gay, 1940.

Audet, Jean-Paul. Structures of Christian Priesthood: a
study of Home, Marriage, and Celibacy in the Service of the Church, trans. R. Sheed. New York:
Sheed and Ward, 1967.

Baer, Wolfram. "Kritische Anmerkungen zum sogenannten Anonymus von York." Festiva Lanx: Studien zum mittel-
alterlichen geistesleben. München, 1966.

Baldwin, James W. Masters, Princes, and Merchants: the
Social Views of Peter the Chanter and His Circle.
Princeton: Princeton University Press, 1970.

Barstow, Anne L. "The First Generation of Anglican Clergy
Wives," in Women in New Worlds, Vol. II, eds. Hilah Thomas and Rosemary Skinner. Nashville: Abing-
don Press, 1982.

Bassett, William and Huizing, Peter (eds.) Celibacy in
the Church. New York: Herder and Herder, 1972.

Bates, David R. "The Character and Career of Odo, Bishop
of Bayeux (1049-1097)." Speculum 50 (1975) 1-20.

Benson, Robert L. The Bishop-Elect: a Study in Medieval
Ecclesiastical Office. Princeton: Princeton University Press, 1968.

Blum, O. J. "The Monitor of the Popes: St. Peter Damian,"
Studi Gregoriani II (1947) 459-73.

Boelens, Martin. Die Klerikerkehe in der Gesetzgebung der
Kirche   unter   besonderer   Berücksichtigung   der
Strafe ... von den Anfängen der Kirche bis zum
Jahre 1139. Paderborn, 1968.

Böhmer, Heirich. "Die Entstehung des Zölibates," Ge-schlichtliche Studien Albert Hauck zum 70 Geburts-tage dargebracht von Mitarbeiterkreise der realenzyklopädie für protestantische theologie und Kirche. Leipzig, 1916.

_____. Kirche und Staat in England und in der Normandie. Leipzig: Theodor Weicher, 1899.

Bolton, Brenda. "Mulieres Sanctae." Studies in Church History 10 (1973) 77-97.

Borst, Arno. Die Katharer. Stuttgart, 1953.

Boswell, John. Christianity, Social Tolerance, and Homo-sexuality. Chicago: University of Chicago Press, 1980.

Bouquet, Martin. Recueil des Historiens des Gaules et de la France. New ed. (Paris, 1874) vol. X.

Brackmann, Albert. "Die Uraschen der geistigen und politi-schen Wandlung Europas im 11 and 12 Jahrhunderts," Historische Zeitschrift 149 (1934) 229-39.

Brett, Martin. The English Church under Henry I. Lon-don: Oxford University Press, 1975.

Brooke, C. N. L. "Gregorian Reform in Action: clerical marriage in England, 1050-1200," CHJ, 12:1 (1956).

_____. "Married Men among the English higher cler-gy, 1066-1200," CHJ, 12:2 (1956).

_____. Medieval Church and Society: collected Es-says. London: Sidgwick & Jackson, 1971.

Brundage, James A. "Concubinage and Marriage in Medieval Canon Law," Journal of Medieval History, I.1 (April, 1975).

Bruns, Hermann. Canones Apostolorum et conciliorum veter-um selecti Berlin, 1839; Turin, 1959.

Bugge, John. <u>Virginitas: the History of a Medieval</u>
        <u>Ideal</u>. The Hague: Nijhoff, 1975.

Bunnik, R. J. "The Question of Married Priests," <u>Cross</u>
        <u>Currents,</u> vol. XV (Fall 1965) 407-31.

Camden, William. <u>Britannica</u>. Frankfurt, 1616.
Cantor, Norman. <u>Church, Kingship and Lay Investiture in</u>
        <u>England, 1089-1135</u>. Princeton: Princeton Univer-
        sity Press, 1958.

Carlyle, R. W. and A. J. <u>A History of Medieval Political</u>
        <u>Theory in the West</u>. Vols. III, IV. Edinburgh,
        1916.

Chenu, M-D. <u>Nature, Man and Society in the Twelfth Cen-</u>
        <u>tury: Essays on New Theological Perspectives in</u>
        <u>the Latin West</u>, eds. and trans. Jerome Taylor and
        Lester K. Little. Chicago: University of Chicago
        Press, 1968.

Cohn, Norman. <u>The Pursuit of the Millenium: Revolution-</u>
        <u>ary Messianism in Medieval and Reformation Europe</u>
        <u>and its Bearing on Modern Totalitarian Movements</u>.
        3rd edn. New York: Oxford University Press, 1972.

Darlington, R. R. "Ecclesiastical Reform in the Late Old
        English Period," <u>EHR</u> 51 (1936) 385-428.

Davis, David Brion. <u>The Problem of Slavery in Western Cul-</u>
        <u>ture</u>. Ithaca: Cornell University Press, 1966.

de laBrosse, O. "Bulletin de théologie: Célibat sacer-
        dotal." <u>Révue des Sciences philosophiques et</u>
        <u>théologiques</u> 55 (January, 1971) 137-50.

de Lapparant, Pierre. "Un précurseur de la Réforme Ang-
        laise: l'Anonyme d'York," <u>Archives d'histoire et</u>
        <u>de la littérature du Moyen Age</u> 15.149-67. Paris,
        1946.

de la Tour, Pierre Imbart. <u>Les Paroisses Rurales du IVe</u>
        <u>au XIe Siècle</u>. Paris, 1900.

Dempf, Alois. <u>Sacrum Imperium</u>. Munich, 1929; Darmstadt,
        1954.

Denzler,Georg. Das Papsttum und der Amtszölibat. Vol.
    I: Die Zeit bis zur Reformation. Stuttgart:
    Anton Hiersemann, 1973.

deWulf, Maurice. "Le Panthéisme Chartrain," Beitrage Zur
    Geschichte der Philosophie und Theologie des Mittel-
    alters. Supplement III, Vol. I.282-88. Münster,
    1935.

Documents of Vatican II, eds. W. M. Abbott and J. Gallag-
    her. London, 1966.

Dodds, E. R. Pagan and Christian in an Age of Anxiety:
    Some Aspects of Religious Experience from Marcus
    Aurelius to Constantine. Cambridge: Cambridge
    University Press, 1965.

Doprtel-Claudot, Michel. "Le prêtre et le mariage:
    évolution de la législation canonique des
    origines au XIIe siècle," L'Année Canonique 17
    (1973) 319-44.

Dresdner, Albert. Kultur- und Sittengeschichte der
    italienischen Geistlichkeit im 10. und 11.
    Jahrhundert. Breslau: Verlag von Wilhelm
    Koebner, 1890.

Economou, George D. The Goddess Natura in Medieval Litera-
    ture. Cambridge: Harvard University Press, 1972.

Fliche, Augustin. La Réforme Grégorienne. 3 vols.
    Louvain, 1924-37.

_____. La Réforme Grégorienne et la Reconquete
    Chrètienne (Vol. 8 of Histoire de l'Eglise).
    Paris: Bloud et Gay, 1944.

Foreville, Raymonde. "L'Ecole de Caen au XIe siècle et
    les origines normandes de l'Université d'Oxford,"
    Études médievales offertes a M. le doyen A.
    Fliche. IV.90-99 (Montpellier, 1952).

_____. Latran I, II, III et Latran IV. (His-
    toire des Conciles Oecuméniques 6). Paris, 1965.

Fournier, Paul. "Bonizo de Sutri, Urban II et la Comtesse Mathilde d'après le Liber de Vita Christiana de Bonizo," Bibliothèque de l'École des Chartes, vol. 76 (1915) 263-98.

Frazee, Charles A. "The Origins of Clerical Celibacy in the Western Church," CH 41.2 (June, 1972) 149-167.

Funk, Franz Xavier. "Cölibat und Priesterehe in Christlichen Altertum," Kirchengeschichtliche Abhandlungen und Untersuchungen,I.121-55. Paderborn, 1897.

Gannon, Thomas M. and George W. Traub. The Desert and the City: An Interpretation of the History of Christian Spirituality. Toronto: Macmillan Co., 1969.

Goldast, Melchior. Collectio Constitutionum imperialium. Frankfurt, 1713.

Gonsette, J. Pierre Damien et la Culture Profane. Louvain: Publications Universitaires, 1956.

Gossman, Francis J. Pope Urban II and Canon Law. (Canon Law Studies # 403). Washington, D. C.: Catholic University of America Press, 1960.

Grundmann, Herbert. Religiöse Bewegungen im Mittelalter Untersuchungen über die geschichtlichen Zusammenhänge zwischen der Ketzerei, den Bettelorden und der religiösen Frauenbewegung im 12. and 13. Jahrhundert und über die geschichtlichen Grundlagen der deutschen Mystik. 2nd ed. Hildesheim, 1961.

Gryson, Roger. Les Origines du Célibat ecclésiastique du premier au septième siècle. Gembloux: Editions Duculot, 1970.

Hefele, Karl J. von. Histoire des conciles (French trans. Henri Leclerq). Paris, 1907-38.

John, Eric. "St. Oswald and the Tenth-Century Reformation," Journal of Ecclesiastical History IX.2 (October, 1958) 159-69.

Jombart, E. "Célibat des clercs," Dictionnaire de Droit Canonique. III.132-56.

Joyce, George H. Christian Marriage: an Historical and Doctrinal Study. 2nd edn. London: Sheed and Ward, 1948.

Jungmann, J. A. The Mass of the Roman Rite, trans. F. Brunner. New York: Benziger, 1951.

Kantorowicz, Ernst H. The King's Two Bodies: a Study in Medieval Political Theology. Princeton: Princeton University Press, 1957.

Kaufman, Michael W. "The Conception of Woman in the Middle Ages and the Renaissance," Soundings: an Interdisciplinary Journal LVI.2 (Summer, 1973) 139-63.

Kempf, Friedrich. The Church in the Age of Feudalism, trans. A. Biggs. (Handbook of Church History, vol. III.) New York, 1969.

Kern, Fritz. Kingship and Law in the Middle Ages, trans. S. B. Chrimes. Oxford, 1939.

Knowles, David and Obolensky, Dimitri. The Christian Centuries: the Middle Ages. "The Christian Centuries" series, vol. 2. New York: McGraw Hill, 1969.

Knox, Ronald. "Finding the Law: Developments in Canon Law during the Gregorian Reform," Studi Gregoriani IX (1972) 419-66.

Kurze, Dietrich. Pfarrerwahlen im Mittelalter: ein Beitrag zur Geschichte der Gemeinde und des Niederkirchenwesens. (Forschungen zur kirchlichen Rechtsgeschichte und zum Kirschenrecht, Bd. 6.) Köln-Graz, 1966.

Kuttner, Stefan. "Pope Lucius III and the Bigamous Archbishop of Palermo," Medieval Studies in Honor of Aubrey Gwynn, eds. John Watt, et. al., 409-53. Dublin: privately printed by Colm O'Lochlainn, 1960.

Laeuchli, Samuel. Power and Sexuality: the Emergence of Canon Law at the Synod of Elvira. Philadelphia: Temple University Press, 1972.

Lea, Henry C. History of Sacerdotal Celibacy in the Chris-
     tian Church. Philadelphia, 1867. Third edn.,
     rev.: London, 1907. Edition without notes: Uni-
     versity Books, 1966.

Leclercq, Henri. "La législation conciliare relative au
     célibat ecclésiastique," Histoire des Conciles
     II.2 (1908) 1321-48.

Liotta, Filippo. La Continenza Dei Chierici nel Pensiero
     Canonistica Classico, du Graziano a Gregorio IX.
     Milan, 1971.

Lynch, John E. "Marriage and celibacy of the clergy: the
     discipline of the western church: an historico-
     canonical synopsis," Jurist 32 (Winter and
     Spring, 1972) 14-38, 189-212.

Mansi,G. D. Sacrorum conciliorum ... collectio.
     Florence, 1759.

Martène, Edmond. Veterum Scriptorum Nova Collectio.
     Paris, 1700.

McDonald, A. J. Berengar and the Reform of Sacramental
     Doctrine. London, 1930.

_____. Lanfranc. London, 1944.

McKeon, Peter R. "The Lateran Council of 1112, the 'Her-
     esy' of Lay Investiture, and the Excommunication of
     Henry V," Medievalia et Humanistica XVII, 1966.

_____. "Gregory VII and the Primacy of Archbishop
     Gebuin of Lyons," Church History 38.1 (March,
     1969) 3-8.

McLaughlin, Mary. "Survivors and Surrogates: Children and
     Parents from the Ninth to the Thirteenth Centur-
     ies," The History of Childhood, ed. Lloyd DeMauze
     (New York: Psychohistory Press, 1974) 101-182.

McLaughlin, T. P. "The Prohibition of Marriage against Can-
     ons in the early Twelfth Century," Mediaeval Stud-
     ies 3 (1941) 94-100.

McNamarra, Jo Ann, and Wemple, Suzanne. "Sanctity and Pow-
     er: the Dual Pursuit of Medieval Women," Becoming
     Visible: Women in European History, eds. Renate
     Bridenthal and Claudia Koonz, 90-118. Boston:
     Houghton Mifflin, 1977.

McNulty, Patricia. St. Peter Damian, selected writings on
     the spiritual life, trans. with an introd. Lon-
     don: Faber and Faber, 1959.

Mirbt, D. Carl. Die Publizistik im Zeitalter Gregors
     VII. Leipzig: Hinrichs'sche Buchandlung, 1894.

Moorman, John R. H. Chuch Life in England in the Thir-
     teenth Century. Cambridge: Cambridge University
     Press, 1945.

Morghen, Raffaello. "Problemes sur l'origines de l'héré-
     sie au Moyen Âge," Révue Historique 235 (1966)
     1-16.

Morris, Colin. The Discovery of the Individual, 1050-
     1200. New York: Harper Torchbooks, 1973.

Morrison, Karl F. Tradition and Authority in the Western
     Church, 300-1140. Princeton: Princeton University
     Press, 1969.

Mozley, J. B. Presdestination: a Treatise on the Augus-
     tinian Doctrine. Third Edition. London: John
     Murray, 1883.

Mundy, John H. Europe in the High Middle Ages, 1150-
     1309. New York: Basic Books, 1973.

Nineham, Ruth. "K. Pellens' Edition of the Tracts of the
     Norman Anonymous," Transactions, Cambridge Biblio-
     graphical Society, IV.4 (1965) 302-09.

_____. "The So-Called Anonymous of York," Journal
     of Ecclesiastical History 14 (1963) 31-45.

Oxford Dictionary of the Christian Church, 2nd edn., ed.
     Frank Cross. London, 1974.

Parent, J. M. La Doctrine de la Création dans l'école de Chartres. Publications de l'Institut d'Études Médiévales d'Ottawa, VIII. Ottawa, 1938.

Partner, Nancy. "Henry of Huntingdon: Clerical Celibacy and the Writing of History," CH 41.4 (December 1973) 467-75.

Pellens, Karl. "The Tracts of the Norman Anonymous: c. c. c. c. 415," Transactions, Cambridge Bibliographical Society, 4 (1965).

_____. "Unitas Ecclesiae im sogennanten Liber de unitate ecclesiae conservanda," Festschrift Hans Foerster, Freiburger Geschichtsblätter 52 (1963-64).

_____. Das Kirchendenken des Normannischen Anonymus. Wiesbaden, 1973.

Phipps, William. The Sexuality of Jesus: Theological and Literary Perspectives. New York: Harper & Row, 1973.

_____. Was Jesus Married? The Distortion of Sexuality in Christianity. New York: Harper & Row, 1970.

Poole, R. L. "The Masters of the Schools at Paris and Chartres in John of Salisbury's Time," EHR 35 (1920) 321-42.

Rosenstock-Huessy, Eugen. The Driving Power of Western Civilization. Boston: Beacon Press, 1950.

Rostovtzeff, M. Social and Economic History of the Roman Empire, 2nd edn, rev. by E. M. Fraser. Oxford, 1957.

Ruether, Rosemary R. New Woman, New Earth: Human Liberation in a Theological Perspective. New York: Seabury Press, 1975.

Russell, Jeffrey B. Dissent and Reform in the Early Middle Ages. Berkeley: University of California Press, 1965.

Ryan, J. J. <u>St. Peter Damiani and His Canonical Sources</u>
Toronto: Pontifical Institute, 1956.

Sackur, Ernst. <u>Die Cluniacenser in ihrer kirchlichen und
allgemeingeschichtlichen Wirksamkeit bis zur mitte
des elften Jahrhunderts.</u> Halle: Niemeyer, 1892.

Salter, Louis. <u>Les Réordinations.</u> 2nd edn. Paris: Lib-
rarie Victor Lecoffre, 1907.

Schanz, Martin. <u>Geschichte der römischen litteratur bis
zum gesetzgebungswerk des kaisers Justinian.</u>
Munich, 1935-66.

Scherrinksy, Harold. <u>Untersuchungen zum sogennanten Anonymus von York.</u> Würzburg, 1940.

Schillebeeckx, Edward. <u>Celibacy,</u> trans. C. Jarrot. New
York: Sheed and Ward, 1968.

Somerville, Robert. "Cardinal Stephan of St. Grisogono:
Some Remarks on Legates and Legatine Councils in
the Eleventh Century," <u>Law, Church, and Society:
Essays in Honor of Stephan Kuttner,</u> eds. Kenneth
Pennington and Robert Somerville (University of
Pennsylvania Press, 1977) 157-66.

_____. "The Council of Pisa, 1135: A Re-Examina-
tion of the Evidence for the Canons." <u>Speculum</u>
45 (1970) 98-114.

_____. <u>The Councils of Urban II.</u> Vol. I, De-
creta Claromontensia. Amsterdam: A. M. Hakkert,
1972.

Southern, R. W. <u>The Making of the Middle Ages.</u> New
Haven: Yale University Press, 1952.

_____. <u>Medieval Humanism and Other Studies.</u> New
York: Harper & Row, 1970.

_____. <u>St. Anselm and his Biographer: A Study of
Monastic Life and Thought 1059-c.1130.</u> Cambridge:
Cambridge University Press, 1963.

_____. Western Society and the Church in the Mid-
dle Ages. Pelican History of the Church, vol. II.
Harmondsworth: Penguin Books, 1970.

Southern, R. W. and Scmitt, F. S. Memorials of St. Anselm. London: The British Academy, 1969.

Stock, Brian. Myth and Science in the Twelfth Century.
Princeton, 1972.

Tellenbach, Gerd. Church, State and Christian Society at
the Time of the Investiture Contest, trans. R. E.
Bennett. Oxford: Clarendon Press, 1940.

Theiner, J. A. and A. Die Einführung der erzwungenen Ehelosigkeit bei den christlichen Geistlichen und ihre
Folgen. Altenburg, 1825, 1845.

Thorpe, Benjamin. Ancient Laws and Institutes of England. London, 1840.

Tierney, Brian. The Crisis of Church and State, 1050-
1300. Sources of Civilization in the West, R. L.
Wolff, general editor. Englewood Cliffs:
Prentice-Hall, 1964.

Ullmann, Walter. Growth of Papal Government in the Middle
Ages, a Study in the Ideological Relation of Clerical to Lay Power. London: Methuen, 1955; 2nd
edn., 1962; 3rd edn., 1970.

_____. A History of Political Thought: the Mid-
dle Ages. New York: Penguin, 1965.

_____. Principles of Government and Politics in
the Middle Ages. London: Methuen & Co., 1961.

_____. Review of Karl Pellens' Die Texte des Nor-
mannischen Anonymus. Historische Zeitschrift
206 (1968) 696-703.

Vacandard, E. "Célibat Ecclésiastique," DTC II,
2068-87. Paris, 1905.

Vasiliev, A. A. History of the Byzantine Empire. Madi-
son: University of Wisconsin Press, 1958.

Verkamp, Bernard. "Cultic Purity and the Law of Celibacy,"
     Review for Religious 30 (March, 1971) 199-217.

Wakefield, Walter and Evans, Austin, eds. Heresies of the
     High Middle Ages. New York: Columbia Univversity
     Press, 1969.

Wattenbach, Wilhelm. Deutschlands Geschichtsquellen im
     Mittelalter. Berlin, 1873.

Wemple, Suzanne F. Atto of Vercelli: Church, State and
     Society in Tenth-Century Italy. Rome: Edizioni
     di Storia e Letteratura, 1979.

Werner, Ernst. Pauperes Christi: Studien zu sozial-
     religiösen Bewegungen im Zeitalter des Reformpapst-
     tums. Leipzig: Koehler & Amelang, 1956.

Whitney, J. P. Hildebrandine Essays. Oxford: Clarendon
     Press, 1932.

Wilkins, David. Concilia Magnae Britannae et Hiberniae.
     London, 1737; Brussels, 1964.

Williams, George H. Anselm: Communion and Atonement.
     St. Louis: Concordia Publishing House, 1960.

_____. "The Bearing of Christology Upon the Rela-
     tionship between Church and State as Illustrated by
     the 'York' Tractates." Union Theological Seminary
     dissertation, 1946.

_____. "The Golden Priesthood and the Leaden
     State," Harvard Theological Review 50 (1957)
     37-64.

_____. The Norman Anonymous of 1100 A. D., Har-
     vard Theological Studies 181. Cambridge, Mass.,
     1951.

Woody, Kennerly M. "Damiani and the Radicals." Columbia
     University dissertation, 1966.

_____. "Marginalia on the Norman Anonymous," Har-
     vard Theological Review, 66.2 (April, 1973)
     273-88.

TEXTS AND STUDIES IN RELIGION

FOR A COMPLETE LIST OF TITLES AND PRICES PLEASE WRITE:

The Edwin Mellen Press
P.O. Box 450
Lewiston, New York 14092